A Theory of Contemporary Rhetoric

A Theory of Contemporary Rhetoric

Richard Andrews

Routledge
Taylor & Francis Group
NEW YORK AND LONDON

First published in paperback 2024

First published 2014
by Routledge
605 Third Avenue, New York, NY 10158

and by Routledge
4 Park Square, Milton Park, Abingdon, Oxon OX14 4RN

Routledge is an imprint of the Taylor & Francis Group, an informa business

Library of Congress Cataloging-in-Publication Data

A theory of contemporary rhetoric / edited by Richard Andrews.
pages cm
1. Rhetoric. I. Andrews, Richard, 1953 April 1– editor of compilation.
P301.T48 2014
808—dc23
2013025572

ISBN: 978-0-415-50355-6 (hbk)
ISBN: 978-0-415-50354-9 (pbk)
ISBN: 978-0-203-12902-9 (ebk)

DOI: 10.4324/9780203129029

Typeset in Sabon
by Apex CoVantage, LLC

Contents

List of Tables

Acknowledgments

No book on the communication arts can be the work of a single author, and I wish to acknowledge the voices and influences that have helped me to forge the present book. These include my Linguistics tutor at Oxford, Avril Bruton, whose weekly one-to-one sessions gave me an insight into the discipline that was so different, and yet so closely related to the literary studies that took up the rest of my week; Gunther Kress, whose generosity in recognizing the closeness of rhetoric to his own project of the exploration of multimodality and social semiotics has been a lasting inspiration; Paul Prior, whose work on rethinking rhetoric has been a great influence; and Brian Street, Viv Ellis, Wayne Sawyer, Terry Locke, Terry Eagleton, Lilie Chouliaraki, Myrrh Domingo, Sally Mitchell, Mark Reid, Peter Medway, Michael Simons, and Jude Fransman have all contributed in their different ways. I am grateful to Clifford Siskin and Leslie Santee Siskin of New York University for their generosity in involving me in The Re:Enlightenment Project; to David Kirkland of New York University for a public lecture at the Institute of Education London in May 2012 and conversations at the Institute of Contemporary Arts about rhythms of justice in hip hop and everyday textual practices; to Stephen Boyd Davis and Martina Margetts at the Royal College of Art, London, for organizing the symposium "Representing Research Knowledge" in February 2012; and to my fellow presenters: Mine Dogantan-Dack, Anna-Marjatta Milsom, and Michael Hohl.

Colleagues at the Institute of Education continue to provide a climate for learning and intellectual exploration: Carey Jewitt and Andrew Burn in the fields of new technologies and media in relation to rhetoric; colleagues in English and Drama, including John Yandell, Anton Franks (now The University of Nottingham), Gillian Anderson, Anne Turvey, Morlette Lindsay, and Theo Bryer; those in English as a second and world language: John O'Regan, Siân Preece, Amos Paran, Catherine Wallace, John Gray, and Lin Pan; support at senior levels especially from Chris Husbands, Michael Reiss, and Mary Stiasny; colleagues at the Centre for Holocaust Education (Stuart Foster, Kay Andrews, Paul Sammons, et al.); the Centre for Research and Evaluation in Muslim Education (Farid Panjwani, Idris Mears, Farah Ahmed, Ibrahim Lawson, Arshad Ali, et al.); the International Centre for Intercultural Studies (Jagdish Gundara, Jack Peffers, and Bob Ferguson); heads of department in Sue Rogers, Jacek Brant, Ann Phoenix, Marjorie Smith, and David Gough; and the Centre for Research and Development in Catholic Education (Gerard Grace, et al.); as well as colleagues at the Institute of Ismaili Studies, especially Fayyaz Vellani, for illuminating conversations about the relationship of discourse to faith, civilization, and culture. I wish to thank particularly Julia Douetil for commissioning the sonnets on reading that appear in chapter 9. Colleagues at New York University's Steinhardt School have been an inspiration, too: Mary Brabeck, Jim Fraser, Gordon Pradl, and Joe Salvatore. I would also like to thank Manjit Benning, Sarah Smith, Rachel Shaw, and Eve Wade who, through their diligence, hard work, and unerring support, have enabled me to work on this book during my tenure as Dean.

I am grateful to Tony Burgess, Jane Miller, Wayne Sawyer, and the editors of the journal *Changing English* for permission to reproduce and rework "Moffett and Rhetoric" in chapter 3 from volume 17:3, 251–60 (September 2010); and to Geoff Barton, Geoff Dean, and Gary Snapper for permission to revise a short contribution to a special issue of English-*Drama*Media on the future of English (June 2011), issue 20, p. 17.

An earlier version of chapter 8 on multilingualism and rhetoric was given as a paper at the 4th Institute of Education-Beijing Normal University conference on education in Beijing, October 2012. It appeared in the conference papers: *Papers on Equity and Quality in Education,* Vol. 3, 419–35. I wish to acknowledge Yan Fei, Pan Zimeng, and Jin Tinghe, as well as the doctoral students named in the chapter, for allowing me to use their work.

Part of the chapter on framing was written in Cannes in 2012 at the summer home of Nicky Stanley, in Théoule-sur-Mer. Thanks go to her generosity for giving Dodi and me a few inspirational days there as a break from London. Chapters 5 and 10 were written in the Adirondack Mountains of upstate New York. My debt to Dodi Beardshaw, David Andrews, Zoë Briggs, and Grace Andrews remains huge.

Parts of chapters 6 and 13 appeared in the inaugural lecture series published by IOE Press. I am grateful to Jim Collins and IOE Press for permission to reprint extracts from that lecture.

Chapters 11 and 12 owe much to colleagues in the Centre for Multimodal Research at the Institute of Education: Gunther Kress, Carey Jewitt, Andrew Burn, Caroline Pelletier, Di Mavers, Jeff Bezemer, Myrrh Domingo, and Sophia Diamantopoulou; and also to a seminar held at the Institute in December 2011, led by Caroline Haythornthwaite. In particular, I wish to acknowledge the generous input of Mary Hamilton, Lesley Gourlay, Rose Luckin, Mary Lea, Robin Goodfellow, David Barton, and Chris Jones for helping me move to a notion of textual practices as a way forward for thinking about literacy/literacies. I have also had engaging discussions with Marianne Lagrange at Sage, London, on transformations in the world of publishing and am grateful to her for her generosity and support.

The book draws on a number of research projects:

Arts Council/Photographers' Gallery/Artec grant for photography and digital arts in the curriculum, 1994–7

Arts Council grant to establish fellowship in "Framing Visual and Verbal Experience," 1995

Arts Council grant for visual literacy research, May 1997

Arts Council/Institute for International Visual Arts grant, July 1997

Economic and Social Research Council, Research Seminars competition: Dialogue and Communities of Enquiry in Elearning in Higher Education: June 2004 [award reference: RES-451–26–0314]

Economic and Social Research Council, Research Seminars competition: New forms of doctorate—the influence of multimodality and e-learning on the nature and format of doctoral theses in Education and the social sciences. July 2008 [award reference: RES-451–26–0629]

I wish to thank Linda Bathgate, Naomi Silverman, Kayley Hoffman, and Julia Sammaritano at Routledge New York for their willingness to support this theoretical excursion; to Katie Carney for her excellent project management work; and to Routledge for publishing its precursors: *Argumentation in Higher Education* (2009) and *Reframing Literacy* (2010). Thanks must also go to the publisher for the reissue of *Rebirth of Rhetoric: Essays in Language, Culture and Education* in 2011.

Preface

For the purposes of this book, I have defined rhetoric as the *arts of discourse.*

Most of the time we are unconscious of rhetoric. The arts of how to construct speech, writing, painting, sculpture, architecture, and other forms of cultural expression are real, but they are a means to an end: communication. Even the design of a building, or of a bridge, is intended to allow for human traffic and communication. These designs have, as their prime mover, the social: the need for people to communicate with each other, sometimes for its own sake and at other times to make things happen.

The unconsciousness of rhetoric is evident. We talk to each other over breakfast. The social event or *schema* is time-limited, habitual, ritualistic. If we wish to widen the boundaries of rhetoric, we could say that the very layout of the breakfast table is rhetorical. More usually, we would confine rhetoric to the discourses that happen over breakfast: plans for the day, how one felt on getting up, some silences. The exchanges (if there is more than one person) are part of the rhetorical dynamic. If a single person is sitting alone, the rhetorical exchanges may still take place in thought, or even in uttered speech. But there is unlikely to be any conscious shaping of the utterances for particular effect.

Even in more public contexts, the rhetorical design of communication can be unconscious, especially if the genres of social interaction are well established. A student attends a class in a school, college, or university. The timetable is set, defining when the class begins and ends as well as the space in which the class is to take place. Other students make their way to this classroom or lecture hall, and where they sit partly determines the kind of social interaction that is to take place. The teacher, lecturer, or professor engages the students; different kinds of interaction may take place (or not); the students leave the space, hopefully wiser than when they entered it. They may have spoken to the teacher and/or fellow students and perhaps taken notes. Many do not question the nature of the interaction, politically or rhetorically.

Rhetoric is, however, present in these occasions and in most other human social interactions, from the personal to the public. It is behind the design of who is talking with whom about what, and how. Rhetoric does not often ask the additional question: why? It sees that as part of philosophy. Rather, it operates in the everyday world, in all its communicative manifestations, to provide a framework for designing, making, and understanding discourse. It follows that once rhetoric is recognized and defined, it can be learnt and/or taught, thus enhancing the power of rhetoric to *improve* the quality of communication.

In some cultures, and in some uses, the term *rhetoric* has negative associations. It is associated with sophistication, political cant, hypocrisy, and a masking of the truth in persuasive language. It has acquired this reputation through a narrowing of the definition of rhetoric to "the art of persuasion." In turn, resistance to persuasion has taken the form of a distrust of persuasive language and, thus, of the narrowly conceived notion of rhetoric.

The current book takes a more generous view of rhetoric, seeing it as the art behind choices in communication of all kinds. Choosing to write a short story to capture a particular moment or issue is a rhetorical choice; the genre of the short story (in all its forms) helps to determine the writing and its reception by an audience. The writer has the choice as to whether to meet the conventional demands of the genre, or whether to experiment. In a chance encounter on a street, someone walking along has the choice as to whether to say a brief hello to a passerby that he or she half-recognizes, whether to engage in a fuller conversation, or whether to say nothing at all. The gaze between the two walkers is also rhetorical.

It is not just in speech and writing that rhetoric operates. There is a range of modes—the image, the moving image, sound, gesture, movement—in addition to the verbal arts, and these can be (and usually are) used in combination. Such multimodality is now recognized as prevalent in society. At the same time, there is proliferation in a range of media that carry the coded messages of the modes: books, television screens, computer screens, mobile devices, tablets, live speech in the air. This book addresses the range of modes and media as part of its attempt to compose a theory of contemporary rhetoric.

Why do we need a new theory of rhetoric? Part of the answer is that the vestigial classical rhetorics are now no longer fit for purpose. They were designed for public fora and the art of persuasion and have been adapted as guidance in the art of academic and political writing. Their value cannot easily be applied to a wider set of social needs, especially when we move from the public to the personal domains. Second, we need to be able to make sense of (and provide a rationale for) the range of discourses that take place in the contemporary world, in a range of modes, media forms, and languages. Third, the very nature of multimodality, now well established as a way of understanding the resources and affordances available to communication, requires another dimension of theory in order to situate it in political and social contexts and to complement its grounding in social semiotics.

Rhetoric is not just about the analysis of communicative acts in their social and political contexts. It is also about making and designing from a wide range of possible resources. More specifically, it is about making and designing a message with certain materials in a particular context for a particular audience. Part of the challenge of rhetoric is choosing the right forms for the communicative needs of the particular situation, being open to dialogue and dialectical exchange, and ensuring that communication takes place efficiently, elegantly, and purposefully.

Finally, rhetoric thrives in democracies. Indeed, it helps to make democracies work by framing arguments and difficulties and helping us to understand and, if possible, resolve them. These are not democracies that are peddled for commercial gain as empire-building enterprises, but democracies that connect individual lives and aspirations to public networks and institutions; democracies that accept that differences exist and that aim to tolerate and resolve them through argumentation; democracies in which freedom of expression is respected but also where the content of that expression can be challenged.

It is in the spirit of freedom of speech—but also freedom in a wider range of modes of expression—that the present book has been conceived and composed. Freedom implies responsibility for the quality and ethics of communication. Rhetoric provides a background theory for communication of all kinds, with application in a number of fields. This book may not cover all the possibilities, but it may provide a basis for future discussion and development in the arts of discourse and communication.

1

Introduction

Prelude 1

Berlin

A city of memorials, a crossroads in time.
So much memory, it is impossible
to live in the present. You either re-live the past
or stare blankly into the future.

Blood, spirit, intellect are separate.
Obsession with the body.
Over-reliance on the rational.
A soul-less interest in the material.
Only in the Tiergarten,
away from the regimented suburbs and
the epic gateways, the Potsdamerplatz
and the Reichstag, are the pleasures

of bike tracks that intersect through the trees,
the distant sound of chamber music,
birds in the trees, and the promise of coffee
and conversation at the very centre of Europe.

Prelude 2

I am sitting in a café on a street in Berlin.

First, the words. Every car is named—VW, Audi, Renault—and all have number plates that carry as many letters as numbers: country of origin within Europe, the European stars, regional identification. Shop signs are in German and English. With a mix of words, telephone numbers, and invitations to go beyond for more information: Twitter, Facebook connections. There are banners announcing new shops and cafés about to open. On lampposts, there are road signs and political advertising (there must be an election soon). People pass by with clothes and bags that carry brand names. In the café, people are reading menus, books (novels, guides) newspapers, and magazines.

In speech, there are groups of two, three, and four in the café. Some people, on their own, are talking into cell phones. There is more than one language: a mix of languages sometimes. Some of the people walking by are on cell phones, too.

Sounds: voices, laughter, car horns, ringtones, the sound of tires on cobbles and on tarmac, the noise of the café kitchen, the rustle of papers.

Beyond words are clothes, car designs, road design, buildings, and scaffolding indicating that a building is being restored.

And then, beyond these designed and made forms are beings themselves: the human form in all its variety, dogs, birds hovering in the trees, the blue sky and clouds passing at a high level after a storm the previous day.

All these notes I am making with a biro on a waiter's notepad headed "Rossler. Ihr Getranke-Specialiist. Ihr Partner in Berlin und Brandenburg." Then I transpose them into type on a Macbook Air in my hotel room, via a conventional (at least for the twentieth century and first part of the twenty-first) QWERTY keyboard. I am conscious, every now and then, of Christopher Isherwood's "I am a Camera," of *Goodbye to Berlin,* of the layered pre-history of voices and history and literature that precedes me and that informs my own perceptions and communications. The time dimension is hardly touched on, otherwise.

This is the rhetoric of the street. It hardly begins to account for the interlinked rhetoric of communication in an ordinary street in Berlin. I have hardly engaged with the people or the street, except to order a cup of tea, drink it, pay the bill, and leave. But even the bill is a record of a simple and also complex social interaction.

Rhetoric is ever present in these moments in a number of ways. It preserves the balance of human communication, reflects the schemata, *is* the schemata (in a speech act theory sense), enables the world to move on in a small way, and combines highly rational behavior with bodily needs (eating) and pleasures (drinking Darjeeling tea). Even the type of tea brings another part of the world, its production and economy, into the frame.

The frames are invisible, though we could trace their parameters. The occasion described above is that of the "stop for tea" or refreshment. As it's specifically tea on this occasion, the ritual of the infusion, then the milk, then the infusion again (unusual for a Briton). The German/English encounter is managed adequately with minimal linguistic resources. Tea and coffee houses punctuate the streets of the city. There are enough people to fill the pavement tables of this particular café on a Tuesday afternoon in September. There are economics behind that: economics of time, resource, attention, choice, and intention.

There is multimodality here, but also more than multimodality. Multimodality is ubiquitous: sound, printed words, spoken words, images, moving image, moving objects, gesture, the physics of the situation. There is also a range of media at play. The contact of the natural and physical worlds is a perpetual interplay. Symbols attach themselves to things or operate free of attachment, though always physically grounded.

Booth (2004) defines rhetoric as "*the entire range of resources that human beings share for producing effects on one another;* effects ethical, practical, emotional and intellectual [parentheses omitted]. It is the entire range of our use of 'signs' for communicating, effectively or sloppily, ethically or immorally." (xi) However, part of the problem with this definition is its emphasis on "resources" and "producing effects on one another." The view is materialistic and rhetor-centered and runs close to the edge of the definitions of rhetoric that invite pejorative readings. Such cornering of rhetoric is not Booth's intention, but the definition allows such a reading. My own emphasis is on the arts of discourse, thus giving the listener or reader or viewer—the receiver of the message—as much power as the rhetor (speaker, writer, producer). Rhetoric inhabits the space between communicators. And although Booth attempts to refine definitions of actors in rhetoric via a number of specific terms—listening rhetoric, rhetrickery, rheterology, rhetorologist—it is only the distinction between *rhetor* and *rhetorician* that I think is helpful: the rhetor being the communicator, the rhetorician being the student of rhetoric. The other terms are modish and serve to make the field less unified, more subject to superficial critique, and more like a quasi-science. Rhetorically speaking, they serve to weaken the defenses of the theory in their very attempt to stake out new ground.

The Limitations of Words

Rhetoric, throughout its history, has been associated with words. Words, whether spoken or written, listened to or read, have been central to its development. They still are. The affordances of words are several: in speech, in most cases, they are a naturally occurring feature of human communication; they can be combined in countless combinations to make and communicate meaning; they are relatively economical in terms of production (unlike, say, film or still images); and, albeit that words differ from language to language, and even from dialect to dialect, they can be translated. Even with the "turn to the visual," they have survived.

Judt (2010), in an essay on words, extols their virtues as a self-confessed, articulate lover of the mode. Regarding articulacy, he talks of it as being typically regarded as "an aggressive talent" (149) but notes, too, that rhetorical flexibility "allows for a certain feigned closeness—conveying proximity while maintaining distance" (149–50). The essay notes that words may deceive, especially where form transcends content, and that "sheer rhetorical facility, whatever its appeal, need not denote originality and depth" but that "*inarticulacy* surely suggests a shortcoming of thought" (150). The core of the argument that good rhetoric revealed clear thought and expression is contained in the following:

> For many centuries in the Western tradition, how well you expressed a position corresponded closely to the credibility of your argument. Rhetorical styles might vary from the spartan to the baroque, but style itself was never a matter of indifference. And 'style' was not just a well-turned sentence: poor expression belied poor thought. Confused words suggested confused ideas at best, dissimulation at worst. (151)

The relationship between language and thought moves the debate to the philosophical domain and asks the following question: what exactly is the relationship between thought and communication? This and related questions of what we might term the *ontology* or *proto-genesis* of rhetoric are not dealt with here, as they are more than adequately addressed in Vickers's *In Defence of Rhetoric* (1989) where he explores the Platonic-Aristotelian axis and the continuing paradigm war between philosophy and rhetoric (ideas and the expression of ideas). It is not the case that such debates need not concern us here; rather, that our attention is focused more pragmatically on the choreography of everyday, professional, and academic discourse. The position of the present book is that the thesis and antithesis of the philosophy-rhetoric debate is a tired dialectic and that the synthesis of the two positions allows us to focus more sharply on not only the inextricable nature of communication and thought, but on contemporary practices and the generation of new theory that will shed light on the patterns of these communicative practices.

Judt (2010) suffered from a variant of motor neuron disorder: one that deprived him of speech in his last years. But the relationship between clear communication and the articulation of thought continued to be a preoccupation. In reference to the debate between philosophy and rhetoric, his dependence on language was countered by a loss of control of words, and yet "they still form with impeccable discipline and unreduced range in the silence of my thoughts . . . Communication, performance, assertion: these are now my *weakest* assets. Translating being into thought, thought into words, and words into communication will soon be beyond me and I shall be confined to *the rhetorical landscape of my inner reflections*" (153–4). This latter phrase has my italics (the others are Judt's). As testimony from an active mind in the grip of a loss of oral articulacy, it is a telling tribute to the power of rhetoric to map the nature and direction of thought—as if the outside, public channels and patterns of communication had lent shape to the formulation of thought. Stronger justification comes from the final paragraph of the essay: "No longer free to exercise it myself, I appreciate more than ever how vital communication is to the republic: not just the means by which we live together but part of what living together means. The wealth of words in which I was raised were [*sic*] a public space in their own right" (154).

It is partly Judt's inspiration that has led me to write this book in words only, eschewing the chance to produce a multimodal text. It is a decision that has consequences, some of them in limiting the scope of the book itself. But in other ways, it has forced me to try to articulate a theory of contemporary rhetoric and to translate what I have wanted to "say" in other modes into words.

The social and political *raison d'être* of rhetoric with regard to the maintenance of the republic for the public ("the arts of social and political discourse") is reinforced by Judt's inspirational account. His emphasis on words is pre-multimodal, but the principles he outlines would apply to the multimodal as well as to the modes and sub-modes of verbal language: clarity of expression, sharp distinctions between words, and a belief in rhetoric ("from the spartan to the baroque") as a means to effect communication. As was the case for Pound, the loss of clarity and distinction in language is a loss of clarity of thought and ultimately a loss to civilized life. Such responsibility of the part of all language users emphasizes the socio-political nature of Judt's vision: a republic in which the citizens are responsible for its quality of communication as well as for its *mores*, practices, and infrastructures. Rhetoric's vision is similar: no individual exists outside the society that he or she inhabits. All have a responsibility to maintaining and developing the tools of communication that enable the society to operate. But words are not "all we have" (Judt 2010, 154). There are others resources at our disposal, and these are set out more fully in chapter 11, "Rhetoric and Multimodality."

Indeed, the limitations and affordances of words need to be set out so that we are clear, from the start, that contemporary rhetoric is more than just a science or art of verbal language. Words—verbal language, whether it is spoken or written and in any language—are abstractions from the real, material, perceived world. The nouns and verbs, adjectives and adverbs are conceptual in that they offer an *idea* of a range of possibilities in that category (green, for example, covers a multitude of actualities). They can be combined into endless permutations, with the help of "joining" words like definite and indefinite articles, prepositions, modal verbs, and conjunctions, and modulated by tense to give a sense of a position in time (in some languages). The special characteristics of verbal language can be said to be its flexibility of use (charting degrees of abstraction), its ability to link concept to concept (for example, in argumentation), its physicality (in voice), its potential for further abstraction (in written form), its potential subtlety, and its economic virtues (in normal circumstances, its relative low cost as a resource in terms of production and reception). We should also note its propensity to modulate between the relative closeness to reality (descriptive, functional, manual-like uses) on the one hand, and metaphorical uses (on a macro-scale, in terms of degrees of fictionality and distance from the real world) on the other.

Conversely, what are the limitations of verbal language? We should be cautious here, as the affordances of language can be stretched and adapted to cover what other modes can more readily achieve (for example, a painting can be described in words). But we can say that words find it more difficult to chart space; to convey close physical feeling; to replicate touch; to communicate the direct, visceral nature of the *seen,* whether in photographic or painted or sculpted form, or simply in the perceived everyday world; and to convey movement. On first consideration, it would seem that words cannot match the *senses* or combinations of sensory experience in terms of their directness. The very abstracted nature of the word removes it at one stage from the immediate experience of everyday life. This general point holds true, even though we can all provide examples of where verbal language had a direct, physical, visceral effect on a situation or state of being: a declaration of love, a decision of "guilty" or "not guilty," the communication of failure or success. We also know from speech act theory that small words ("I do" in a marriage ceremony, for example) can have long-reaching personal, legal, spiritual, financial, and public consequences. Nevertheless, we must accept that words alone do not constitute the entire communicational repertoire; thus, they should not determine the scope of rhetoric. One of the main points of the present book is that we need a new theory of rhetoric because we have come to realize that words alone do not represent the full range of communicational resource available to us to make and convey meaning.

To reinforce the point about the limitations of words, consider the following scenarios. The direction of gaze in a crowded room, especially when two sets of eyes meet, can communicate mutual interest and engagement. Hunched shoulders and a stooped physical posture in any number of sports can indicate the acceptance of defeat and the end of team effort. In a dance, the intricate positioning and repositioning of bodies in relation to each other communicate an expressive, aesthetic kind of meaning to an audience that is not expressed in words. A music composition, or the sound of wind in the trees on a winter walk in a landscape devoid of verbal language both convey the structure of feeling and perception, and the read-off of meaning, that may be partially shaped by previous verbal encounters and repositories, but in their immediate state, do not call on words for their communicational power. A final example: the construction of a city, its architecture and its layout, although partially constructed with the help of words, depends also on mathematical calculations, spatial considerations, and the sheer deployment of physical materials to "make a statement." Rhetoric, because it is the theory of the arts of discourse and communication in any mode (and, verbally, in any language), has the power not only to delineate and explore the internal workings of those separate fields and modes, but also to link them.

Reflecting on the Berlin Street

If words themselves are inadequate to the task of providing an overarching, explanatory theory for the experiences on the Berlin street, and if, too, "there is more than multimodality here," how could rhetoric describe and explain the phenomena? Further, how would a theory of contemporary rhetoric begin to make sense of the scene?

One could circumvent and short-circuit the argument by saying that a description of the scene in words defeats itself from the start. There is more to the scene than words. But we have already accepted that words in themselves—and the whole repertoire of verbal language—can perform certain functions and not others. So we need to set a more demanding challenge. If multimodality acknowledges the range and combination of modes that are deployed in the production and experience of the scene, then why cannot multimodality provide a full account of the scene? The reason is that multimodality, along with consideration of media, describes *resources* rather than operations and communicative lines. As Kress has acknowledged, multimodality does not constitute a theory (a patterned means of explaining how its constituent parts relate to each other and to the world), but rather *material for a theory.* Later in the book (chapters 11, 12) there is discussion of how social semiotics and rhetoric relate to each other in terms of providing such a theory.

In terms of media, one could say that a different mode and medium than words on a printed page might capture the completeness of the scene better than my minimal written notes in the café. To move quickly through the possibilities of soundscapes and still images (painting, photography) to fully fledged film, how would this twentieth-century medium, *film*—incorporating, as it does, moving image, sound (including speech), written words, and time/spatial characteristics—represent the actual scene? The limitations of film immediately present themselves as problems in representing the totality of the experience: first, film tends to use a limited number of cameras and thus a limited number of perspectives on the scene. It would need hundreds of cameras and the combinations of their recorded images to represent the scene in its totality. There would need to be extensive and judicious editing to frame the scene. At best, a kaleidoscopic and selective representation of the scene would be all that we could produce. There is no substitute for being in the actual scene, with smells, air quality, and ambience, even though a limited individual perspective shares the same limitations of a filmic camera position with its ability to focus, change aperture, and so forth. Second, film is subject to its own affordances and limitations—it is, by nature, a representative, selective take on a scene. Third, you need some kind of hardware viewer (the medium of smartphone, TV screen, computer screen, or cinema screen) to receive the message.

Elsewhere (Andrews 2010), I have explored the contribution of *framing* to the understanding of how communication acts are made and received. But, again, framing does not constitute a theory *per se*. It is a mezzanine-level heuristic for working out how the resources of modes, via their various media, can be made to "make sense" in a shared communicational space. Framing comes close to a theory because it draws on social and aesthetic considerations in order to define the parameters of the communicational encounter. But it remains an act (of framing) rather than an underpinning or overarching theory.

So, multimodality and framing are important constituents in helping us to make meaning and to communicate it. The third element that is needed in order to complete the repertoire of resources and heuristics is articulation. *Articulation* is a useful term in that it has two meanings: One is concerned with the clear expression of ideas, thoughts, and feelings. This aspect of the term is usually associated with words. The other is to do with the joining of parts of an entity, as in the example of an articulated truck. We can apply both meanings of the terms to a range of different modes and their combination, in order to bring the term *articulation* into line with the way we are moving: toward a comprehensive and multimodal theory of contemporary rhetoric.

Judt (2010) was particularly concerned with the sense of articulation in terms of clear expression of thought. To state clearly what is intended, without obfuscation or unnecessary decoration, hesitation, diversion, or vagueness, is an art. The articulation can be of feelings as well as thoughts and ideas, or it can be more coolly to do with the accurate and valid expression of an idea—like the design of the London underground map. This latter example makes it clear that articulation is more than just the expression of thoughts or feelings by an individual; it can also apply to sound, visual art, film-making, or design work of any kind. The idea of articulation in this sense is central to rhetoric because of rhetoric's desire to find the most appropriate form for expression of an idea or need. The underlying principle here is one of clarity and functionality, of using the modes and media of expression to provide a valid and transparent account of that which is being expressed.

But articulation can also refer to how elements of communication are joined to each other, and for what purpose, in a composition of any kind.

Examples are the joining of one piece of wood to another in a 'joint'—say, in the design and making of a chair; the linking of one idea to another in verbal argumentation; the conjunctions in a narrative; the way the frames of a comic strip or *manga* are joined (sometimes in straight sequence, sometimes with one large frame leading to smaller ones, or vice-versa); or the way different modes combine, for example, a caption with a photograph, or the score of musical composition with verbal annotations and photographs. Each *join* is a conscious compositional decision. Indeed, the joining together of parts into a new whole is at the heart of the nature of composition (as in collage, bricolage, or patchwork where joining is most obviously evident). The chapter on rhetoric and composition attempts to explore such articulation in more detail.

So far we have mentioned multimodality, framing, and articulation. There are at least three further considerations before the theory of contemporary rhetoric is complete in its outline form. These elements are outside the immediate frame of reference for composition but help to determine the framing itself. They are the time-based dimension, contextual factors, and the question of digitization.

Articulation has a part to play in the editing of a film. Conventionally, in predigital technology, each image of a film was captured on celluloid, each image was further articulated with another, and the overall articulation of the sequence, played at a particular speed, gave the impression of verisimilitude. Such time-based representation aimed to capture "real-time," at least in part, in the effort to construct a work that was either fictional or documentary. *Time,* then, is a dimension of experience that rhetoric has to accommodate in order to build a theory that is adequate to needs, not least because digital media, such as smartphones and television or computer screens, increasingly provide the means not only to read the moving image, but also to create it. From my static desk, composing text in words, the world of the moving image seems some way off; so too, to an artist composing a painting or sculpture, or to a designer working on a new object. But the dimension of time is never far away: the written text is not only composed over time, it is also read or received over time. Paintings are viewed in particular places and times. Time, if we see it from a Western perspective, is continually moving, even if we have the impression that it can stand still. Rhetoric, therefore, has to embrace the dimension of time, most ostensibly in musical compositions, in films, in TV programs, and in clips that are created for YouTube; but also as a fundamental principle of operation in the world in whichever mode and/or medium. The least that rhetoric can do is to create snapshots in time in order to create and analyze communicative phenomena; but it can do more—it can provide subcategories of analysis and consideration, such as rhythm, pace, and tempo, which in themselves help to define and create communication.

Contextual factors have been written about much in the consideration of communication in the last 30 of 40 years. They are partly a result of the significance of time and place to communication, but they are also presented as a counterpoint to the overly inward and psychological theories of communication. The social dimension of communication requires that a consideration of context takes place. Who is speaking? To whom? About what? What is the motivation, purpose, and intention? What are the social and political situations of the interlocutors? How might the communication be different if any of these factors were changed? Context is particularly important to rhetoric because consideration of rhetorical dynamics starts not with the text, but with the social and political shaping of the text and the need for communication in a particular place and time. Contexts can range from immediate contexts (the people concerned, the time, the room in which they meet, the nature of the meeting, and the formal conventions at play) to wider contexts (the current political situation, economic constraints, etc.). It is important to chart what the contextual factors are in any act of communication and to map these factors in relation to each other so that a full picture of the nature of the communication is possible. Once the factors are understood, the communication can be shaped and adjusted accordingly.

Finally, in this catalogue of the constituent elements of contemporary rhetoric, what of *digitization?* Digitization has been over-egged in one sense. Particularly from the early 1990s onwards, the rise of digitization has heralded grand claims about what it can do and how it can transform lives, societies, and politics. In many senses, such changes have happened: we can transform *information* from one mode to another, repurposing it with ease. We can store huge amounts of information in small spaces, and examine it from different perspectives and via different lenses. It has enabled electronic social networks of various kinds. Much has been written about the power and potential of digitization. In rhetorical terms, its value is that it enables us to repurpose and reshape communication; it gives us a larger repertoire of media via which to communicate; and it provides unlimited storage space. In chapter 12, full consideration is given to the relationship of rhetoric and the digital.

Toward a Theory of Contemporary Rhetoric

The record of sitting in a café on a street in Berlin is, in one sense, simple: it is the observed recording, initially on slips of paper borrowed from the waiter, of what is happening in and around the café in a given short period of time. In another sense, it is complex: the record hardly scratches the surface of what is going on in the interactions between a hundred or so people who moved through that street and around that café on that day in September 2011. Not only are there physical and spoken interactions; there are written rituals, like bills and receipts exchanged, as well as others who are recording on iPads, cell phones, or in notebooks. In addition, there is the material world of the street—buildings, cars, signs, baggage, and so on—some of which is inscribed with words, icons, logos, and images. Furthermore, there are the ambient sounds of the street: café music, the sound of radios from nearby apartments, and music percolating from headphones of passers-by.

In my initial notes, I mused that rhetoric is ever present in this scene, that the framing of the scene is virtually invisible, and that multimodality is present and ubiquitous, but insufficient to account for the wealth of communication that is taking place. The other elements of a rhetorical account—articulation, digitization, context, and the time dimension—were not considered at the time of initial recording and minimal reflection, but nevertheless play a part. Articulation is present in at least two of the senses of joining: first, in the *segues* between what we used to consider as genres or schemata (like the paying of a bill, with its own internal articulations) and the running *continuo* of experience (sitting in a café). This simple example will help to demonstrate that articulation operates to join one frame to another, one schemata to another. In this case, because the paying of a bill is part of the experience of sitting in a café, one frame is nestled within another. The line between the *continuo* of everyday experience, and the framed genre, is transgressable, fuzzy, and permeable. Articulation helps us to see the nature of those joins. Digitization is evident in a number of ways, many invisible to the eye. Had I been writing and sketching on an iPad, it would have been more evident. Even so, the instantiation of sound as mentioned previously; the wireless device via which the bill is paid at the table; the electronic navigating systems of cars that pass—all these and more are driven digitally, and transform information for particular purposes digitally. Context and time—in effect the immediate framing of space and the 30 minutes or so of sitting in the café—require some discussion. The context is not "framed" tightly, though the café itself is (even though it spills out on to the street). The café is situated on a street, and views each way are extensive: one way to a major road junction, the other way into a denser part of the city. The context is, if we take the widest aperture possible, limitless—we have to provide framings of some kind in order to be able to make sense of the place and the experience. We can term that framing *orientation*. We can also move between foregrounded activity and phenomena—the tea cup, the table—and much further distant contextual elements, like Berlin, Germany, Europe. Moving between the foregrounded phenomena and those at more distance is a process of positioning, of multiple framing, and articulation. Time is a less tangible, more elusive factor. Again, in one sense, it looks simple: I sat at the table on September 14, 2011, between 3:30 pm and 4:00 pm. If I had done the same thing half an hour later, or a day later, would the experience have been different? Actually, I did go back the next day to test exactly that (and because it was an excellent café). Much was the same. I do not think that the account I wrote on the first day would have been very much different from that on the second day. There were different people (even the waiters), different cars; but the same buildings, same street, same signs, same city. The weather was slightly different, and, of course, if I came back in a different season, or in a different year, there might be more significant and noticeable changes: the café might no longer be there, I would be older or younger, and so on. The rhetoric of the scene would have changed.

We can thus say about the case of the Berlin café experience in relation to rhetoric that it helps us to define a spectrum of possibilities with regard to a theory of contemporary communication. At one end of the spectrum, we can use rhetoric to account for micro- and mezzo-social encounters, like the paying of a bill or a brief conversation with a stranger. There are formalities to observe with the bill: the customer requests the bill, orally or by gesture. The waiter calculates it and brings it to the table. There may be a pause. In due course, the customer pays the bill in one of a range of different ways, and either personally to the waiter, in his or her absence, or at a central till. The transaction is completed with a greeting, with thanks, or simply in silence. This example is close to a social schema, and the rhetoric of the situation is largely prescribed. In a brief conversation with a stranger, there are fewer *rules*. One person initiates it by finding common ground for talk; the other reciprocates fully or not; the parameters of the conversation will be set by mutual agreement. There is a range of such speech, written and multimodal genres from the personal to the wider public sphere.

At the other end of the spectrum is the total experience of the period in the café in the Berlin street. By *total* experience, I mean not only the total perceived and necessarily selective experience of one person and their observations, but the totality of the communicational networked scene in that place and at that time. The scene frames a multitude of social and communicational encounters, all framed, more widely, by the economic and political contexts that allow people to spend time in a café on a Wednesday afternoon in a European city. Within the chosen frame of the scene on the street, the communication could be charted. An exhaustive record of every conversation, every sign, every written transaction, every photograph, every physical movement—all in relation to the fixed phenomena of buildings and the moving objects of cars, bicycles, and so on—could be attempted and would be interesting. It would lend itself to multimodal discourse analysis. Behind that possibility are the instruments and dimensions of rhetoric (multimodality, articulation, framing, digitization, context, time) that allow a somewhat broader analysis in terms of how the political interfaces with the social and communicational. The broadness does not mean that the tools of analysis and creation are more abstract; rather, that they can be deployed at macro-, mezzo-, and micro-levels according to the purposes of the analysis. They are tools of process rather than of product. Their scaffolding is light: it can be constructed and taken down quickly.

Social network theory needs only be deployed if the relations in any field of analysis (any framed social encounter) are such that they affect the communication—because rhetoric's focus is on the communicational dimension. But social network theory meshes well with a rhetorical perspective. Its vocabulary of *nodes* and *ties* has application in considerations of where the clustering takes place in any social network, and where the strong and weak ties of communication are (and what the nature of communication along those connections is). In relation to the previous discussion, what were termed macro-, mezzo-, and micro-levels of communicational encounter can be mapped on to notions of whole networks—in this case, a section of a street in Berlin—or more limited perspectives, like the personal network of connections observed by the person in the café. If the limitations of scope of network analysis—and of the wider rhetorical picture—are bounded by the extent of data that can be collected, then analytics could help process a wider set of data that has been possible previously, and so the wider rhetorical perspective can be taken. The advantage of positioning rhetoric in relation to social network theory and analysis is principally that both can look at loosely bounded and hybrid social encounters as well as more conventional social patterns (*genres* as social action). While network analysis is more interested in the extent to which the structure and composition of ties affects social norms, rhetoric focuses on the agency of the actor/rhetor and his or her audiences, and the socio-political determinants of their communication. Rhetoric is both productive and analytical. There is more room for individual and group *agency* in rhetoric, as well as a longer tradition of adapting rhetoric to contemporary circumstances.

In order to explore the potential of rhetoric to account for the contemporary world, the book moves next to a historical account of why rhetoric is relevant, and how it comes to be in its present state. Chapter 2 explores this dimension in depth, arguing that classical rhetoric has had too strong a hold on twentieth-century discourses and that we need to fashion a new theory that is fit for purpose. The third chapter looks at rhetoric in relation to English studies, one of its traditional partners in epistemological boundary-making. In particular, the break-up of the field of English studies into first and second language learning, literary studies, film and media studies, and so on, is seen in the light of the potential unifying theory of rhetoric—which also has the advantage of not being associated with only one language. Consideration of the lasting influence of the work of Moffett (1968) forms a large part of this chapter. Chapter 4 addresses the practical issue of the nature of composition in a theory of contemporary rhetoric, linking the putting together of ideas in the verbal arts to that in the visual, aural, and spatial arts. The centrality of composition to a theory of rhetoric is reaffirmed, but not without a separation of the concepts of rhetoric and composition as currently conceived in many writing courses in higher education institutions. Chapter 5 concentrates on the political dimension of rhetoric and, specifically, on issues of power that influence and inform communication. Notions of critical literacy and critical discourse theory are addressed, and the suggestion is made that "critical" is an epithet that has outrun its usefulness (the same is argued in relation to "literacy")—and that discourse and rhetoric are clearer, more useful, and more technically precise terms. This chapter looks outward to media representation of politics itself to show how rhetoric operates in the public sphere.

The relationship between rhetoric and argumentation is discussed in chapter 6. As argumentation is often foregrounded in rhetorical theory, the chapter asks why this is and what part argument and rhetoric play in contemporary democracies. This chapter is followed by one on framing—already discussed initially—which is seen to have a crucial part to play in the creation of meaning as well as the definition of what is made, what is studied, and what is analyzed. The case for rhetoric's contribution to pedagogic theory is made here and again in chapter 13. Chapter 8 focuses on multilingual rhetoric, acknowledging that rhetoric does not confine itself to a single language but can be applied to any language. The interest is largely on world languages (English, Mandarin, Spanish, Arabic), but languages spoken by fewer people are also considered. Language policy and globalization are issues that are addressed here, with an account of how rhetoric can unify the field of inquiry and practice. The next two chapters address the fictional and literary dimension of rhetoric: first, in looking at form as a rhetorical device in relation to poetics; and second, in exploring the relationship between rhetoric and theatre.

The last part of the book is devoted to some of the key aspects of rhetoric that have been mentioned previously: multimodality and digitization. Chapter 11 addresses multimodality as a set of resources that are available for communication and specifically looks at the case for backgrounding multimodality with social semiotic theory. Similarities and differences between social semiotic theory and rhetoric are discussed. Chapter 12 looks at the impact of the digital revolution on rhetoric, in particular at the transformative power of the digital to recast one form of information into another. These chapters are followed by two final chapters: one on rhetoric and education, which draws out the pedagogical implications of rhetoric; and one on the future of rhetoric, which casts a critical look at the nature of contemporary rhetoric and whether it can provide a sufficiently comprehensive theory of communication to be of real use to other disciplines and in practical, everyday situations. This final chapter, then, discusses rhetoric as one of a small number of key disciplines or meta-disciplines that, while not returning to the medieval *trivium* of grammar, logic, and rhetoric, might provide a toolkit for making sense of contemporary communication as part of a wider field of knowledge production and use.

2 Why Rhetoric?

Etymology and History

The Oxford English Dictionary (OED) is a good place to start in an exploration of the etymology of rhetoric—which will, in turn, reveal aspects of the meaning of the term and its uses over the centuries. First, *rhetoric* is defined as "the art of using language so as to persuade or influence others; the body of rules to be observed by a speaker or writer in order that he [sic] may express himself with eloquence." Immediately we can see that the traditional definition is inadequate to contemporary needs. *Language,* if associated with words only, is too narrow a term to compass the range of rhetoric in a multimodal world; *persuasion* and *influence* may be Aristotelian formulations of the function of rhetoric, but these intentions are only part of a wider, more generous conception of the art, which includes other functions of communication, such as informing, clarifying, and delighting (and a range of others). The *body of rules* indicates a form of rhetoric that is not appropriate to the present. What it suggests is a reified set of prescriptions in the form of a manual of discourse. Such formulations fossilize quickly, and as they become outdated, give rhetoric a bad name: that of a textbook, quasi-scientific approach. As we indicated as the end of the previous chapter, the metaphor that is more appropriate is that of light scaffolding rather than a body of rules. A *speaker or writer* might be better replaced by the notion of a "rhetor" or "maker" or "composer"—someone who has all the repertoire of resources available and who uses them to communicate a message to someone else (or to a group of people). The gendered "he" is clearly inappropriate, though it probably suggests not only convention but could refer to the supposedly male-centered nature of rhetoric as opposed to rhetorics, which embraces diversity. In this book, we use he/she or he and she alternately to indicate that the rhetor might be anyone—and we address issues of gender and rhetoric in the chapter on power. Finally, *with eloquence* does not do justice to the stylistic range that rhetoric offers. While eloquence might be appropriate in certain circumstances, as clarity would be in many more, the rhetorician is able to choose what degree of eloquence or clarity is appropriate for the purpose in hand. In almost all respects, then, the key terms of the traditional definition are no longer fit for purpose in the twenty-first century.

The pejorative or depreciatory sense of rhetoric has almost as long a history in England, dating back to the fifteenth century, as does the adoption of rhetoric in the more general and positive sense. The second of OED's definitions characterizes rhetoric—perhaps because of its close associations with persuasion—as "language characterized by artificial or ostentatious expression." The distaste for rhetoric would also have been not just a matter of style and linguistic register, but also of the use of rhetoric to persuade for less than worthy purposes and/or to mask a poor argument. Current uses of "mere rhetoric" to mean cant, vacant arguments and flummery date back to this period, and possibly beyond.

A subdefinition, not in pejorative terms, links rhetoric with the "expressive action of the body in speaking" and with the "persuasiveness of acts and looks."

Another subdefinition, this time of the adjective *rhetorical,* refers to the rhythm of prose "as distinguished from metrical rhythm." Arcane and mostly obsolete variations on the term *rhetoric* include *rhetoricaster* (a poor rhetorician), to *rhetoricate, rhetoriously* (with colors of rhetoric), *rhetorisms,* and *rhetory* (cf. oratory). None of these are worth adding to the range of technical terms in charting a new theory of rhetoric, partly because they refer to the outdated conception of rhetoric as a catalogue of persuasive techniques, discussed previously, but also because the new rhetoric does not need such a catalogue of technical terms. Perhaps the only derivative term that is of use is *rhetor,* to indicate that the originator of a message need not be a speaker or writer of verbal language, but may be using the wider range of resources (image, moving image, gesture, choreographed moves, etc.) in seemingly monomodal or actually multimodal combination. *Rhetor* does not sit easily in the diction of contemporary communication. *Composer* is probably the more generally applicable term, except where there are specific modes being used, when *writer*, *speaker*, *designer*, *artist,* and so on are more appropriate.

Preminger, Warnke, and Hardison (1986) give a concise account of the history of rhetoric in Europe. A less objective but fuller account is given by Barthes in his essay "L'ancienne rhétorique: aide-mémoire" (1988), prefiguring the debate between semiotics and rhetoric in the 1970s and 1980s. I will come back to the Barthes essay later in this chapter, and in due course throughout the book, as the discussion of rhetoric is characterized by what Barthes sees as a pivotal moment between "the old rhetoric" and the "new semiotics of writing" (11).

While Aristotle is seen as the father of rhetoric, his take on it is as "the art of persuasion" designed for public engagement and debate in an Athenian society. Three types of rhetoric are posited: one that appeals to the audience's feelings (*pathos*), one that is an appeal to the speaker's character or set of values (*ethos*), and one to argumentational proof (*logos*). The different genres of speech need not concern us here, as they pertain to Athenian social and political structures; nor the largely logical enthymemic micro-structures, which, I have argued elsewhere, do not apply when scaled up to the mezzo- and macro-levels—and which Toulmin (2003) moved away from in *The Uses of Argument*. What is of interest to the contemporary world of communication is the notion of *topoi* or "places" of argument. In *Argumentation in Higher Education* (2010), I focus on *topoi,* particularly with regard to the points of dispute in a discipline, which are the places to drill down to if rich discussion of tensions in any field are to be explored. So while the types of rhetoric and the speech genres of classical Athens can be discounted in a theory of contemporary rhetoric, *topoi* remain an area of continued interest, particularly in educational and academic debate.

The Roman contribution—Cicero, Quintilian, and the *Rhetorica ad Herennium*—further refined the structural categories of rhetoric, particularly with regard to arguments. The division of speeches into five parts was an advance of Aristotle's notion of statement and proof. Thus, *inventio* (invention), *dispositio* (arrangement), *elocutio* (style), *memoria* (memory), and *pronunciatio* (delivery, presentation) were posited and provided a textbook-like structure for the compositions of orators. Of these, invention, arrangement, and delivery, with some reference to style, characterize the contemporary need. Memory is hardly needed, and invention is replaced in the present book by "composition."

Interestingly, Greek and Roman rhetoric generated various formulae for the arrangement of speeches and other compositions: from Aristotle's two-part notion of "statement and proof" (the basis of argumentational structure, as modeled later in Toulmin's "claim" (proposition) and "grounds" (evidence)); through three-part generic structures like "beginning, middle, and end," which have become staple in textbooks; to four-, five-, six-, and seven-part structures, which at their most elaborate contain an introduction, *narratio* (the facts of the case), *divisio* (definitions, a "division" of terms), the propositional core of the argument, evidence to support it, the *refutatio* (refutation of counter-arguments), and a conclusion/*peroratio* (peroration). The four- to six-part versions simply missed out some of the elements—for example, a good argument could be put forward without the *divisio* or the *refutatio*—and even, in some cases, without the evidence if the argument was logically strong enough to support itself. Such forensic power, used in legal contexts as well as public oratory and written arguments of any kind, has general and contemporary relevance as the structures consist of a greater number of elements. As Quintilian remarked, the art is to find the structures that suit the purpose of the proposed communication.

In many ways, the revival of interest in rhetoric in the Renaissance was powered by the invention of the printing press and the wider range of humanistic discourses available as the Church weakened its grip on cultural exchange and on the discourses/genres of human behavior and interaction. Rhetoric was remade with an increased focus on its creative and logical components: invention and arrangement. Logic and dialectic came to the fore, and language began to be separated, reforming around the notion of grammars to teach correctness, clarity, and rhetorical style. We can see in this division a diminution in the power and scope of rhetoric, despite the proliferation of textbooks and grammar schools. Indeed, I would argue that the establishment and authorization of rhetoric in the form of grammar created a fossilization of the discipline and contributed to its decline, at the very moment of its revival. If rhetoric is separated from logic and dialectic, it becomes mere eloquence, mere style, and mere delivery: a theory of tropes and figures.

The reduction in scope of rhetoric continued in the nineteenth and twentieth centuries, first in the separation of literary from linguistic studies in England (the one branching off into the field of 'English Literature' and subsequent variations; the other to historical and synchronic linguistics and its derivatives), and then again in attempted revivals of rhetoric, but from a narrow Aristotelian base, like Burke's (1969) consideration of literature as persuasion. The creation of poetics—discussed in more depth in chapter 9—has been an attempt to build for literary and poetic works an overarching theoretical structure through analogy with rhetoric. But the very existence of a field of study like poetics separates the literary from the documentary, from stylistics and from socio-linguistics, and thus diminishes each. I will argue in chapter 9 that Eagleton's notion of rhetoric as a political literary criticism is a way of recombining rhetorics and poetics.

One could say, in the emphasis on invention, arrangement, narrative, argumentational, and other structures, that the project to redesign rhetoric is an essentially *structuralist* one. Such a view can be refuted by drawing attention to the fact that rhetoric is not only interested in the grammars (at every level) and structures of discourse, but also in their informing social relations (not structures). There is a continual to-ing and fro-ing between the socio-political and the instantiation of such relations in tangible discourses. Rhetoric is no longer interested in a fixed set of structures that can be taught; rather, it is focused on the understanding and use of flexible and multiple structures (cf. fram*ing*) to make meaning. To the extent that it is interested in structures, these would be of a light, disposable kind, intended to make communication effective.

Finally, in this brief history of rhetoric—insofar as it pertains to the thesis of the present book—the emphasis on rhetorical analysis in the twentieth century, particularly as applied to literature, is too narrow in two senses for our present purposes. First, because of its concentration of the literary at the expense of the documentary, despite claims to the contrary; and second, because rhetoric as currently conceived, is both generative and analytical. In other words, rhetoric not only provides tools for analyzing discourse, it actually provides tools and orientations for the production and generation of utterances, texts, and other forms of communication.

Why Now?

Why is rhetoric particularly appropriate now? Why is it needed? Let us go back to the brief working definition of rhetoric as "the arts of discourse." *Discourse* is a useful general term for types of communication, originating in speech but applicable to any form of dialogic exchange. Its more tangible form—text—can be made up of any number of modes in combination or seemingly on their own (later in the book, we will address the question of implied multimodality in the seemingly monomodal). We can accept the fact that discourses range from simple everyday and brief exchanges in speech, text form, email, letter, and so on, to monumental and large-scale public discourses like the meetings between government heads of state and their set speeches and declarations. On another axis, mentioned previously, discourses range on a spectrum from the non-fictional to the fictional, from the literal to the metaphoric. Given the range of different media via which communication can take place across the world, the proliferation of communication is a matter for interest, study, and attention—not least in an attempt to improve its quality. Given, too, that discourse implies power relations (at least in critical discourse analysis, but now in any consideration of discourse), the focus on discourses is comprehensive in its range.

What distinguishes rhetoric from discourse analysis is its emphasis on the *arts* of discourse. That is to say, it is not interested in discourses *per se* in the way that a linguist might be. Rather, it is engaged by how such discourses are made and received, who are the composers and audience, what is the occasion, and crucially *how* the exchange is constructed. These issues are not just a matter of technique but of art (in that sense they align themselves with the notion of *technè* as craftsmanship). They are better classified as art, as opposed to science, as the concentration is on originality, quality, and performance rather than on classification and the discovery of new relations. That does not mean that rhetoric is a matter of people reproducing the same kinds of exchanges along tried and tested routes, fulfilling roles in relations to conventional social schemata and discoursal genres. These patterns will be available but can be reworked, combined, and transformed according to the purposes of the transaction. New forms of interaction can be generated (as they often are, by new media). And, as with some of the arts, *ars est celare artem*—the art is to hide the art.

The arts of discourse, then, are particularly appropriate for global use in the twenty-first century because of the increased communicational possibilities, increased chance of misunderstanding, increasingly fast pace of interaction and increased democratization of societies. The latter point is the most pertinent in terms of the socio-political nature of rhetoric. As social and political structures change, so do rhetorical possibilities. What we might term the *rhetorical imperative* is the need to make sure that communicational possibilities are up to speed with social and demographic change. When they fall behind, and people call on outmoded types of communication to bring about transaction, the process of change is slowed or does not take place. As Gee, Hull, and Lankshear (1996) imply in the prescient *The New Work Order,* fast capitalism brings about fast rhetorical responses and a need for a critical take on these. Not that rhetoric is the servant of capitalism, but that it can and should respond to change in the balance of relations between people at work and in domestic and public spaces.

A First Look at Rhetoric and Semiotics

As mentioned briefly earlier, Barthes (1988) saw a key pivotal moment in rhetoric as the turning point between old rhetoric and the new semiotics of writing. The paper is in fact a transcription of a seminar given in 1964–65. First, it must be pointed out that Barthes has couched his argument in terms of old and new: old rhetoric, new semiotics. In terms of intellectual positioning, we must see this as an ideological move in favor of new semiotics and at the expense of old rhetoric. Indeed, the aide-mémoire is "the manual I should have liked to find ready-made when I began to inquire into the *death* of Rhetoric" (11, my italics). Such a "manual," Barthes claims, did not exist in French at the time. But there is, almost in the same breath, an acknowledgement that a negative attitude to such a manual—in the sense of a list of terms, classifications, and prescriptions for action in discourse—"does not mean that in the course of this study I have not often been moved to admiration and excitement by the power and subtlety of that old rhetorical system, and the modernity of certain of its propositions" (12). What I will argue here is that Barthes, by couching rhetoric as "old" and indeed "dead," and by defining it as a metalanguage—a "discourse on discourse" (13), has constructed a rhetorical argument in which the dice are loaded against rhetoric from the start.

Barthes's argument is nonetheless elegant. He posits a rhetoric that is monumental in scale: a meta-discipline and way of looking at the world that has seen the passage of history "without itself being moved or changed" (15). One that has seen off, as it were "Athenian democracy,

Egyptian kingdoms, the Roman Republic, the Roman Empire, the great invasions, feudalism, the Renaissance, the monarchy, the French Revolution; it has digested regimes, religions, civilizations; moribund since the Renaissance, it has taken three centuries to die; and it is not dead for sure even now" (15). Such an edifice is bound to fall at some point, but what is fascinating about the way Barthes sets up the construction is that behind the metaphors is a notion that "Rhetoric grants access to what now be called a super-civilization; that of the historical and geographical West" (15). This ideological—almost invisible—network of assumptions and verities has provided, suggests Barthes, an immutable background against which successive civilizations—both West and East—have defined themselves. Post-*Orientalism* (Said 1978), we might, from a Barthes perspective, see *rhetoric* as underpinning the values and influences of the West (extrapolating to Europe and America what was originally Greek and European): monolithic, essentially European, invisible, powerful, and pervasive. In Barthes's terms, "a kind of subtly articulated machine, a tree of operations, a 'program' destined to produce discourse" (16).

In a particularly interesting section, the paradox at the heart of Barthes's (1988) analysis is revealed: "Rhetoric is triumphant: it rules over instruction. Rhetoric is moribund: limited to this sector, it falls gradually into great intellectual discredit. This discredit is occasioned by the promotion of a new value [we might say, Enlightenment-induced], *evidence* (of facts, of ideas, of sentiments), which is self-sufficient and does without language (or imagines it does so)" (43). The belief in the power of evidence belies the very fact that evidence is created in language, or in some form that can be constituted in language. If evidence is the touchstone of empiricism, it pushes language and communication to the edges and sees rhetoric as ornament, detail, and elaboration. The paradox is the one that has bedeviled rhetoric from the start: the dialectic between *truth* and the communication of truth. Only the slickest of rhetoricians would turn that dialectic to advantage and say "this is the nature of rhetoric: it both is and is not of itself. It is predicated on the generation of the 'other' and then debates with its *alter ego*." Barthes has a tendency to be attracted by the ludic, game-like nature of the enterprise that is rhetoric, and he pursues the intellectual game of to-ing and fro-ing on both sides of the argument. Here, to drive home the point, is another rhapsody on the theme of ambiguity:

> [T]hese contradictory evaluations show clearly the present ambiguity of the rhetorical phenomenon: glamorous object of intelligence and penetration, grandiose system which a whole civilization, in its extreme breadth, perfected in order to classify, i.e. in order to think its language, instrument of power, locus of historical conflicts whose reading is utterly absorbing precisely if we restore this object to the

> diverse history in which it developed; but also an ideological object, falling into ideology at the advance of that 'other thing' which has replaced it, and today compelling us to take an indispensable critical distance. (47)

But much in the aide-mémoire is helpful: the quick journey through the history of rhetoric, the insightful and fragmented nature of the commentary. One challenge that the present book has to face is the accusation that rhetoric was "diluted by syncretism" (Barthes 1988, 26): in other words, that it has or had become so ubiquitous and powerful as to be weakened and thus ineffective as theory. Barthes points to the fusion with poetics, the breakdown of the distinction between fiction and non-fiction; we could add to that list the blurring of the distinction between action in the real world and the kind of language-as-action ideas of speech act theory. It is a necessity for the present book to draw the parameters around rhetoric so that it does not spread thinly and dilute; to continually police the borders so that distinctions can remain clear and precise; and to delimit the power of rhetoric to the arts of discourse—a large enough territory—rather than the whole of social and interactive experience.

The Urge to Classify

Perhaps because of its quasi-scientific nature and the predilection of those who have championed the meta-discipline through the centuries, rhetoric has shown an urge to classify. It is as if the practice has been defined as the "the science of discourse" rather than "the arts of discourse." Science classifies because its starting point is hypotheses. From this general level of operation, evidence is sought to prove or disprove the hypothesis. But first, science must make sure that its terms and its methods—overall, its tools of operation—are clear, distinct, and fit for purpose. Otherwise the relationship between the hypothesis (claim, proposition) and the evidence (data, grounds) would be questionable. In Toulminian (2003) terms, the warrant for advancement in the field would not be strong enough.

Each of the classical rhetoricians spun a web of classification, based on their particular starting points—or what we would describe today as their ideologies. Aristotle from his conception of rhetoric as "the art of persuasion" and from *technè* (speculative production of what may or may not exist—the generation of propositions and their subsequent proof); Cicero from his focus on oratory in the public (Roman) forum; Quintilian from what Barthes (1988) calls a starting point that "is certainly *technè,* but [that] is a practical and pedagogical *technè,* not speculative; it aligns: *a.* the operations (*de arte*)—which are those of Aristotle and Cicero; *b.* the operator (*de artifice*); *c.* the work itself (*de opere*) (these last two themes are discussed but not subdivided)" (48–49). Quintilian thus may be said to have an ideological position in common with the twentieth-century rhetorician Kinneavy (1971), who posited a three-point rhetorical model with *I, You,* and *It* as the three cardinal points of the triangle of communication, with the text or product in the center; the "product" is the result of the combination of dynamic forces between the rhetor, the audience, and the object of communication. Earlier in the present chapter, it was mentioned that Quintilian was the pragmatist who, eschewing the elaborate classification systems of previous rhetoricans, suggested that in the relationship between *inventio* and *dispositio* (invention and compositional arrangement), the art is to find the right number of elements, in the right order, that suit the purpose of the communication. Such high-level positioning on classification (suggesting that, ultimately, it is not classification that matters but the ordering or arrangement of the elements in any given situation) is exactly the level at which the current book operates, though we will generate a model that is different from Kinneavy's predigital, premultimodal conception. However, one could say that the progenitors of the current theory are not the classical rhetoricans Aristotle and Cicero, nor the twentieth-century social semioticians (Saussure, Barthes), but a line of rhetoricians (Quintilian, Kinneavy) who see the *arts* of discourse as more important than the classificatory obsessions of the more scientifically inclined tradition. The simple reasons for such an emphasis is the need to generate a theory that is both high level and applicable in the discourses of the real world; one that embraces the fictive as well as the ostensibly "real"; is fit for purpose in the digital, multimodal world of communication; and, crucially, has an aesthetic dimension. If the generation of theory at this level is relatively more pragmatic than that of the high rhetoricians, so be it: the book operates at a relatively high plateau of signification, but not high enough to see its peaks disappearing into the clouds.

In short, the temptation to proliferate technical terms and a catalogue of classifications will be resisted in the interests of putting up light scaffolding (to change the metaphor) that is fit for purpose, helps us to construct the building we are interested in constructing, and can be taken down quickly to enable us to get on with the business of the world.

A More Recent Take on Rhetoric

Prior et al. (2013) identify the three key elements of classical rhetoric—invention, arrangement, and style—as "canons" in a rhetorical model that has been influential for two millennia. Because these canons reflect high level maps of rhetorical activity and yet at the same time are practical in their application, they have been associated with rhetorical practice and pedagogy. Prior et al. state clearly what the ideological and practice-based position is for their deliberations: it is the work of writing researchers and practitioners in university level writing programs. The emphasis here is on resurrecting the two elements of rhetoric that had been sidelined by Barthes—delivery or presentation on the one hand, and *memoria* on the other—and seeing these elements as fundamentally associated with the *resources* for communication in the digital age: a range of modes, in combination, and fast network-based means of dissemination. Prior et al.'s argument is that the re-inclusion of *presentatio* changes the whole picture of the model of rhetoric, and requires a re-think of the classical bases for the meta-discipline. In other words, the core classical trio of invention, arrangement, and style is not sufficient to account for the complexities of communication in the contemporary world. What is needed, argue Prior et al., is a rethink of the category of "delivery" to take account of the range of choices or "mediations" and distributions that take place as a speaker/writer/composer chooses how to communicate his or her message to an audience. From another perspective (that of multimodality) we might call the mediations *modes* and the means of distribution *media*. One clear move forward and clarification offered by Prior et al. is that they eschew the notion that the five parts of rhetoric—invention, arrangement, style, memory, and delivery—are necessarily sequential, but that they can be simultaneously operational in the making of an act of communication. Such compression and hypertextual co-presence in the act of communication is accepted—some acts of communication are instant, seemingly spontaneous, and co-incident. Others are composed over years, for example some of the paintings of Howard Hodgkin, the composition of whose works are often dated over a three- or four-year period before exhibition, after which the original resonates in different exhibition spaces, in online and print catalogs, in prints on purchasers' walls, and elsewhere in the memory.

One aspect of rhetoric mentioned by Prior et al., and developed further in the present book in chapter 6 on argumentation, is the fact that classical rhetoric concerned itself largely with monologues. A contemporary theory of rhetoric, however, must—in the wake of Bakhtin (1982)—accept that monologic statements and utterances are, even in their apparent monologic state, part of a larger dialogue. They are responses to the existing body of dialogically produced utterances and statements, whether in everyday colloquial form, in the deliberations of politics, or in the literary world. So, we must bear in mind as the theory is developed, that not only must it address multimodal and digital dimensions of communication, but also the essentially dialogic nature of communication (even when cryptically couched as "when I talk, I listen"—a fridge magnet/post-it example). See also Prior et al.'s (2013) account of the complex scenes of semiotic interaction "which challenge the abstract, dyadic, production-oriented bias that lies at the heart of the rhetorical canons" (11).

Indeed, at the general level at which we are exploring new rhetorical theory in this chapter, a move to genuinely embrace the dialogic dimension might go some way to alleviate concerns that rhetoric is the domain of the speaker/composer/writer/rhetor and that it persuades—even *forces* its will upon—the listener or audience. Let us take the example of a rehearsal performance of two Greek plays—*Oedipus Rex* and *The Trojan Women*—that took place in a studio theatre of one of the London conservatoires in 2012. The student actors, working with an English translation of the plays, rehearsed for three weeks with their director (whose expertise was in voice training). Being actors, their emphasis was on the two elements of rhetoric that Prior et al. argue must be reconsidered in a contemporary theory of rhetoric: memory and delivery/presentation (or, as they couch it, "mediation/distribution") (12).[1] The audience of invited fellow-students and families of the actors were willing participants. Their own suspension of disbelief (characteristic of all public audiences in theatre, excepting those of a Brechtian inclination) was colored by their wish to see their fellow-students and sons/daughters/brothers/sisters in action, but also by their willingness to take part in a rehearsal performance and thus learn from the experience about the process of acting. Such involvement in the process was made more clearly evident by the director stopping the action on two occasions to ask the actors to rerun a section with more concentration, or more intensity. In short, the presence of the director and audience shapes the performance of the actors, just as in any performance with audience, the audience's reactions encourage or discourage the actors. Even the meeting of eyes between an actor and a member of the audience generates an interactive, dialogic moment of recognition or avoidance. The audience helps shape the overall experience, even though it is silent throughout the framed performance.

Prior et al. (2013) go on to sum up the canons of classical rhetorical theory as "a snapshot, a synchronic rhetoric, too situated in particular homogenous worlds and not situated enough in emergent, laminated histories, too centered on the producer rather than the system, too focused on language at the expense of a full semiotics" (17). Without elaborating each of the elements here in the present book, they argue for "remapping the territory of rhetorical activity" (17) in terms of literate activity, functional systems, and laminated chronotopes—with mediation as a fundamental unit of analysis across the three domains. The comprehensive nature of such a conception, taking into account functional *systems* as well as the cultural-historical lamination or *complex multiple framing* of actions (cf. Vygotsky [1991], Bakhtin 1982) is ambitious and beyond the scope of the present book, which concentrates, or rather embodies, these further dimensions in what we choose not to call "literate activity" but *acts of communication* and *textual practices*. But the spirit of the conception is acknowledged in the present book in the attempt to build a theory of rhetoric that is light on apparatus but strong in structure, relevant to everyday and cultural interaction (production and reception), and fit for purpose. The aim of the present book, then, is to design a theory that does not construct its own edifice of theory through terminology and classification, but is grounded, useable, "elegant," and ultimately disposable. The analogy is with the field of light structural engineering, which specializes in temporary structures.

Why are we eschewing the chance to build a more comprehensive model of rhetoric of the kind posited by Prior et al. (2013)? Part of the reason is that we would not wish to appropriate what is an innovative and brilliant conception. The other part is that the particular function of our enterprise is to construct a working theory and model of rhetoric that has parameters and limitations. Its limitations are defined by the edge of *communicative relevance* and its admittedly communication-focused nature. Communication, in the conception of rhetoric that informs the present book, is the heart of the matter. The social and political nature of rhetoric is embodied in acts of communication, and the book makes no attempt to draw a theory of ecology of resource, the economics of time or attention, the sociology of human interaction, or the dynamics of institutional politics, though all of these bear upon the field of rhetoric and the acts of communication within that field. In this way, the aim of the present book is to depict the operation of rhetoric in its full semiotic sense but not encroaching upon the fields of human feeling and experience, disciplinary and inter-disciplinary engagement, or ecologies of the natural and made worlds. Rhetoric has much to say about all of these, but it remains an art of communication as a means to ends, not the ends of thought and/or action in themselves.

Where the conception of a cultural-historical conception does bear upon rhetoric, and where it is hard to exclude a particular perspective from those listed previously as "outside" rhetoric, it is with regard to the economics of attention and the close association of that concept with learning. The economics of attention means the use of, and choices from, the limited resources of attention that any one person has during a day, week, or any length of time (ultimately, a lifetime). Attention means the degree of conscious concentration that is used in response to any situation—from flickering and marginal consciousness at one end of the spectrum to the deep or high (according to the metaphorical take) concentration that is deployed in an act of artistic, sporting, intellectual, spiritual, and/or personal engagement. There is no significant purpose, in such a notion, of separating the conscious from the unconscious: both may be at play in an act of attention. In terms of learning, the economics of attention is crucial, not only in distinguishing learning from other states of being, but also in understanding that transformational learning might well be directly linked to the quality of attention that is brought to the act. Getting people's attention is another aspect of the economics of attention, in that marketing companies, instructors and teachers, the media, and family and friends vie for attention. Some people react by being able to concentrate on activities that require a great deal of undivided attention; others are good at attending to multiple demands at the same time. What is significant for rhetoric in both the economics of attention of the individual, and also for those working to try to attract attention of the individual, is that both are informed by the socio-psychological framings, modal variations, and power relations of rhetoric.

Finally, in this chapter on the limitations of classical rhetoric and the parameters of contemporary rhetoric—its antecedents and its distinctive nature now—we address the question of whether we should be using the pluralistic term *rhetorics* or stick with the singular and overarching term *rhetoric*. Earlier in this chapter, we dealt with the pejorative associations of the term *rhetoric* that occur frequently in everyday discourse and in newspaper, radio, and television media (driven by a journalistic mission to separate the "truth" from "mere rhetoric"). We can learn much from the creation and use—and ultimate demise—of the pluralistic term *literacies*. Coined in the 1990s to reflect the social, anthropological, and political variations in kinds of literacy, and also to refer to different domains of literacy and competence (like computer literacy, emotional literacy, financial literacy), the term *literacies* has been over-used and attentuated to such a degree that it is in danger of losing meaning—and coming to mean mere competence. The balance between unifying and diversifying tendencies in the use of such terms—always remembering that *literacy* implies *literacies* and vice-versa—has been lost as the devaluing of the term *literacies* has washed back to dilute the original singular term, *literacy*. So, too, in the present book we have retained the singular term *rhetoric,* eschewing the opportunity to distinguish between Rhetoric (high, approbational) and rhetoric (low, pejorative) or to pluralize into *rhetorics* (reflecting the diversity of ideology, situation, or application). When "rhetoric" is used in the present book, albeit with its tarnished and battered associations, it is used to imply both high and low associations and to embrace pluralistic versions. Like the field itself, and its principal term, it has limitations.

3

Rhetoric and English Studies

As has been suggested so far, rhetoric is the discipline that has been the basis for theorizing about communication in public since pre-Athenian days—not the pejorative use of the term in phrases such as "mere rhetoric" or "cant, sophistication, and rhetoric." The knife-edge nature of the term makes use of it risky. Nevertheless, the risk is worth taking in relation to the future of English as a school and university subject.

Rhetoric is about who communicates what to whom about what, in which modes and media, how and (sometimes) why—though the latter function encroaches into the territory of philosophy. It can variously be described as "the arts of discourse" or "the science of communication." One of its great advantages is that it does not limit itself to any particular language—English, Mandarin, Spanish—nor to any particular mode—writing, for example—or medium (e.g., on screen, on paper). It includes other modes, such as the still image, moving image, gesture, and sound, as well as the verbal mode, which covers speech and writing. It is not only socially situated but politically situated, too, sensitive to the power relations that inform communication between individuals and between groups, on domestic, local, regional, national, and international levels. (The rhetoric of communication beyond the planet has been wittily dealt with in Edwin Morgan's poetry collection, *From Glasgow to Saturn,* 1973.) It is pan- or multi-linguistic, multimodal, and socio/political and thus—potentially—provides a unifying theory for "English" and other subjects concerned with communication.

"English" seems to be a misnomer. We might be engaged with writing in English from across the world, but we should also acknowledge that such writing may have been cast originally in another language and/or culture—and so issues of translation are at play. We are interested in the evolving history of the English language, in all its hybrid color, but we will be also interested, as a result, in world Englishes and how they are being owned and developed in the twenty-first century. And by "English" we will certainly be interested in fictional, dramatic, and lyrical genres, but also in real-world documentaries, manuals, reports, spoken genres, and other transactional forms of language that go under the broad and strangely negative title of "non-fiction." We will *not* be interested in a narrowly England-based notion of a national literature: there is too much confusion about whether Irish, Welsh, and Scottish writers are included and whether we are referring to "literature written in England," "literature written in English," and/or "literature written as part of a 'national' heritage activity." Equally, as much of world literature in English is composed in the United States, Canada, India, Australia, and elsewhere, and as English as a world language is in the hands of many countries (see Brutt-Griffler 2002), the notion of a narrowly England-based English is out of date by many centuries.

In short, when we use the term *English* are we referring to a language, a country (or nation—and if so, what kind of nation?), or a subject (or discipline)?

The theoretical potential of rhetoric is much needed right now. Its value is clear. First, rhetoric has a long history because every generation has to work out the dynamics of the why and how of who is speaking to whom about what. Second, the re-emergence of rhetoric as a unifying theory for English (and other subjects/disciplines) is much to do with provisionality, democratic pluralism, and socio-economic pressures requiring people to communicate with each other. It does not thrive in an autocracy, other than through propaganda. Third, any remaking of rhetoric has to take into account multimodality and contemporary digital communication in the twenty-first century. We cannot go back to Athenian rhetoric, as Edward Corbett did in the 1960s with *Classical Rhetoric for the Modern Student* (1998) for the undergraduate American market, even though there are some generic truths we would want to apply to our current situation. What we need is *contemporary* rhetoric for the modern student, whether he or she is at primary, secondary, or tertiary levels in the education system. Fourth, we need a theory that will unite fiction and the documentary genres, makes sense of and utilizes the relationship between speaking and writing, acknowledges the reciprocity of writing and reading as well as that of speaking and listening, embraces the other modes and is clear about the affordances of each, and accepts digitization and electronic media.

"English" as we know it will be in decline from about 2020 onwards—as a world language (overtaken by Mandarin) and as a suitable name for the field we are all engaged in. As Bergonzi states in *Exploding English* (1990), it could go on like this for a long time (i.e., in terminal decline), not unified by any theory, fissured, and shard-like . . . and yet still with an assured place in the school and university curriculum. There is an advantage in such looseness of identity. But perhaps more advantageous would be to remake the subject at school and at university levels, underpinned by a foundation of contemporary rhetoric, and called something like "communication arts." Then we could work more closely with film-makers, website designers, artists, typographers, theatre directors, singers, and musicians—as well as with those who teach other languages—to fashion a subject that truly reflects contemporary culture and that students of all ages will find to be irresistibly engaging, diverse, and empowering . . . because it is about the means of finding one's identities and exploring one's possibilities socially and politically.

In terms of remaking the subject at school level, the work of Moffett is worth reconsidering as it appears to be prescient in terms of a rhetorical conception of English studies.

The Work of James Moffett

The revival in interest in rhetoric the late twentieth and early twenty-first century is perhaps the result of a number of converging vectors: the need for an overarching theory of English studies, embracing fiction, documentary texts, multimodality, and the politicization of discourse; the weakness of "English" in the face of right-wing criticisms and the "back to basics" movement; the confusing conflation of English as a school subject, university discipline, world language, and nationality; and a desire to relate communication studies in general to the long tradition that goes back to pre-Athenian democracy in Europe, rather than see "English" as the derivation of a nineteenth-century split between language and literature studies.

The work of James Moffett (1983), operating within the American tradition, may not have experienced such a sense of a split in English to the same extent. His work certainly sits squarely within a long rhetorical tradition. Much of the rest of the present chapter will be devoted to a consideration of his work and its relevance to the thesis of the book overall.

Ostensibly, *Teaching the Universe of Discourse* (1968) was written as a reaction to the "arhetorical" practice, as Moffett saw it at the time, of sentence combining and embedding. Although sentence combining and embedding were themselves part of a 1960s reaction to the formal teaching of sentence grammar (and have continued as practices up to the present—see Abrahamson 1977; Combs 1976, 1977; Lawlor 1980; Ney 1980; and Stewart 1979 for research on the efficacy of sentence combining; plus more recent systematic reviews by Andrews, Torgerson, Beverton, Locke et al. 2004 and Andrews, Torgerson, Beverton, Freeman, et al. 2004), Moffett bracketed them with decontextualized exercises that had little to do with composition for specific purposes. So the very inception of Moffett's project was, by definition, rhetorical. He wanted to situate English within the tradition of the arts of discourse with their emphasis on function (why), motivation (who), the audience (for whom), the substance of the communication (what), and the techniques available to make that communication successful (how).

The use of the term *discourse* also made it clear that this book was more than a commentary or a prospectus on English as a school subject. In fact, the acknowledgement comes early on in the book that "some ultimate context or super-structure is exactly what English as a school subject has always lacked" (3). For "context or super-structure" we could substitute the term *theory*. But Moffett, with characteristic diffidence and modesty, holds back from calling his project a theory: "you are advised not so much to believe these ideas as to utilize them" (v). However, the book could have been subtitled "notes towards a theory of English" because that is exactly the function it fulfils and has fulfilled since its publication in 1968. Despite the fact that Moffett states that he wanted to "recast into the psychological terms of human growth those familiar but opaque academic elements such as rhetoric, logic, grammar and literary technique" (vii), the project as a whole seems avowedly rhetorical in nature. "Discourse" for Moffett means exchange, conversation, dialogue—in print and action as well as in speech—and the "universe of discourse" is the range of communication in action in the real world as well as in the simulated (but also real-world) space of the English classroom.

Another point of reference for the Moffett project is the relationship between teaching the universe of discourse on the one hand, and literature teaching on the other. In the Foreword to the 1983 re-issue of the book, Moffett defends his apparent exclusion of literature from the original 1968 conception. He declares, "I unwittingly threw off some readers who did not recognize just how much in fact I was dealing with literature or how dear it was to me, so different did it appear to them in the greatly expanded context of the *total* universe of discourse . . . perhaps I should have indulged myself more" (vii). Again, what Moffett was reacting to in the 1960s was *too* close an association of literature and rhetoric, characterized, for example, by Grierson's (1945) *Rhetoric and English Composition,* which, although it drew the distinction between rhetoric and persuasion (thus distinguishing itself from the Aristotelian position of rhetoric as the "art of persuasion" and re-broadening rhetoric to include informational, descriptive, and creative writing *and* speech), came across as a mini-treatise and argument for *literary stylistics.* In Harold Rosen's copy of Grierson, he has annotated in pencil the point where Grierson recites the what, who, to whom, where, why, and how questions.[1] Rosen seemingly distanced himself, as Moffett also seems to have done, from the over-literary sensibility, associated with prestige and an élitist take on culture.

Finally, although rhetoric had been revived in the United States through the work of Burke (1966, 1969), Booth (1961), and Corbett (1998), the audience for these works was largely in higher education. In Burke's case, the arguments were made for rhetoric as symbolic action; in Booth's, for an understanding of narrative as rhetoric in literary studies; and in

Corbett's, as a primer in classical rhetoric for undergraduate students' composition.

In summary, then, as a starting position for what Moffett was trying to do in 1968, we can say that he was running against currents of the time that were emphasizing either expressive or literary or technical approaches to English teaching and that his effort was to find new ground for the construction of the beginnings of a theory of *school* English, based on human intellectual, cognitive, emotional growth and on a broader, more contemporary, more generous sense of rhetoric than had been current.

To What Degree is Moffett's a *Rhetorical* Model?

It should be clear from the opening of this chapter that by *rhetorical* I mean "pertaining to rhetoric" in the positive sense, rather than suggesting that Moffett's position is the result of posturing, or that the "model" is itself mere gestural politics within the English field. The source of Moffett's reflections on language development is deeply rhetorical in that it establishes "the ultimate context of somebody-talking-to-somebody-else-about-something" (5) as a level at which it is necessary to make sense of discourses within the English classroom. While it may not have been until 1971 and Kinneavy's attempt, in *A Theory of Discourse,* to establish the approach as theoretical, it is Moffett's achievement to have provided the basis for such a theory.

If "somebody-talking-to-somebody-else-about-something" is the *sine qua non* of discourse, its definition is "any piece of verbalisation complete for its original purpose" (10–11). The nub of Moffett's model then follows: "What creates different kinds of discourse are shifts in the relations among persons—increasing rhetorical distance between speaker and listener, and increasing abstractive altitude between the raw matter of some subject and the speaker's symbolization of it" (11). At the heart of the rhetorical model, then, is dialogue (the word derives from the Greek meaning *through* the spoken word, rather than two people speaking). In most cases, the dialogue does involve two or more people, and this is the way Moffett interprets it. In fact, for Moffett, the existence of two or more people in dialogue is the starting point for discourse: the formulaic version is more accurately "somebody-talking-*with*-somebody-else-about-something." It is this move to the dialogic (in the contemporary sense of that term) that is at the core of Moffett's conception and use of rhetoric. This is not the rhetoric of a single orator expounding to a passive audience; it is the rhetoric of exchange.

Moffett's conception has more in common with Vygotskian notions of social constructionism in the making of meaning and the development of thought than with Piaget's notion of an autonomous biological entity being gradually socialized. And yet it is the Piagetian idea of increasing *abstraction* from the particular that provides the structuring of Moffett's proto-theory, particularly as Moffett believes "that development of symbolic expression depends on nothing less than general mental growth" (18). This is not the chapter in which to debate further the cognitive psychology allegiances of Moffett's thinking (he seems to tend toward Piaget, as suggested also by the diagram on page 68 that has the "biological" as the "largest or most universal context" for determining the individual's language), but it is worth noting that the peculiar concoction of his model is one between dialogism on the one hand and abstraction on the other. It is as if elements of Vygotsky and Piaget are combined, from different perspectives. If we associate rhetoric more closely with Vygotsky and public discourses, Moffett makes the connection between *two* planes: between the *I-you* dimension of "talking with someone . . ." and the *I-it* dimension of ". . . about something." The notion of abstraction emerges from the *I-it* dimension. Abstraction is not the aspect of the conception that we will pursue in the rest of the present chapter. Rhetoric is more interested in the *I-you* perspective.

Nevertheless, the process of abstraction in Moffett leads us to a deeply rhetorical place: the classification of types of discourse based on the dual perspectives of the distance between people in the *I-you* relationship and the abstractive distance between particularities in space and time at the lowest level of verbal abstraction and generalities and theorization at the highest levels. To compress the argument and with a self-acknowledged "tautological transforming" (35), the formula comes out as demonstrated in Table 3.1.

This formula, once it is arranged as a curriculum sequence, sees drama as the lowest level of abstraction and the starting point for all discourses and educational exchange. The natural move is upward from there to narrative, and thence to exposition and logical argumentation. I have rearranged the categories to depict the relative levels of abstraction. But the movement is also the other way: higher categories subsume lower ones and frame or bring meaning to them. Hence the arrows move in both directions. I stress that this arrangement, and the addition of the arrows, is my take on Moffett and not his own representation of the relationship

Table 3.1 A Two-Way Approach to Moffett's Levels of Abstraction

what may happen – logical argumentation – theorizing	↑	│
what happens – exposition – generalizing	│	│
what happened – narrative – reporting	│	│
what is happening – drama – recording	│	↓

and sequence of the different categories; but their mutual relationship needs to be represented by such a depiction.

The advantage of the two-way depiction, with the notion of "what is happening" as the basis of the relationship, is not only that various elements of Moffett's emerging theory are brought together, but also that the pattern as a whole, at the whole-text or whole-discourse level at which it operates, is revealed as rhetorical in the positive sense. We must assume a dimension in which the audience is present in every engagement, whether manifested in other people or in terms of an interior dialogue. What is evident, once we have assumed this dialogic dimension, is that "something of every level is found at every other level," and "likewise, the three main logics—chronology, analogy and tautology—operate at every level" (48). What is more, the fictive dimension (yet another dimension that does not appear in Table 3.1) is a matter of distance, too—not of abstraction and generalization, but of degrees of distance from the perceived world (see Pavel 1986). We had to wait until the mid-1980s to have Pavel's full articulation of the degrees of distance in fictional theory to understand the "mythic" dimension that Moffett refers to (48) but does not fully explore.

Part of the limitation that results from a tendency to adopt Piaget rather than Vygotsky is an underestimate, in Moffett's conception, of the powers and discourse faculties of younger children. The often-quoted statement that "whereas adults differentiate their thought into specialized kinds of discourse such as narrative, generalization and theory, *children must for a long time make narrative do for all*" (49, my italics) seems, in retrospect, contradictory and illogical in a model that posits the notion that "something of every level is found at every other level" (48)—and yet we must remember that Moffett's is a model of growth combined with a rhetorical model of the arts of discourse. He builds in a developmental sequence that is flexible, as in the refinements of neo-Piagetians; and, of course, there is the disclaimer that "this whole theory of discourse is essentially an hallucination" and "heaven forbid that it should be translated directly into syllabi and packages of serial textbooks" (54)—which, ironically, it was, in Moffett and Wagner's *A Student-Centered Language Arts Curriculum, Grades K-12: A Handbook for Teachers* (1991), a "companion volume" that was written alongside *Teaching the Universe of Discourse.*

So, to what degree does Moffett's work constitute a rhetorical model? The answer appears to be that it is a hybrid—part-psychological, part-rhetorical, but ultimately a series of reflections that can act as the spur to an imaginative, coherent, and engaging curriculum for young people and for teachers designing the best kinds of learning opportunities for them.

The Chapter on Drama from *Teaching the Universe of Discourse*

What is distinctive and original about the core of Moffett's book is that he posits drama and speech—what is happening—as "central to a language curriculum" (60). This would not be news to the long tradition of rhetoric, which had its (Western, at least) origins in pre-Athenian public speech and drama. But it *is* news to the hundred years of Scottish and American tradition for which Bain (1871) strikes the keynote at the time when the tradition in England was abandoning rhetoric for the study of literature (and thus leading to an unhealthy split between literature and language study). Bain's categories of narrative, argument, and description *in writing* have formed the template for successive curriculum formations in English, right up to the present. Yet again, the emphasis on speech and drama at the heart of the English project would not be news to those who were advocating speech in the 1950s and 1960s in England (see Hardcastle et al., in press) and who helped to transform, gradually, primary and secondary classrooms into places where talk was valued as a means to learning.

The case for drama is well made by Moffett: in essence, it is primitive, accessible, the "first . . . verbal art to come into being" (64). What is not fully acknowledged is that it is highly framed. Despite its connections with play, drama is one of the arts of discourse that is consciously framed; and framing is a key act in rhetoric. It might be said to be the agent of rhetoric in that without framing, there is no meaning. Let us reveal this connection between framing, rhetoric, and drama more slowly, and then come back to the place of drama in Moffett's universe of discourse. It is clear that framing operates in theatre: there is an edge between the performance by the actors and the space in which the audience sits or stands. That line or frame can be transgressed, but the transgression, for whatever function, is always consciously made. There is also framing in time in that a play lasts for a particular amount of time, during which there is a suspension of disbelief (unless you are watching Brecht or Brechtian-style theatre) or, more positively, a willingness on the part of the audience to engage with the fiction. So formal theatre is highly framed in space and time, and also institutionally in that it involves going to a theatre; it is a social occasion. But even informal theatre, carried out on a street or in a small show by children for parents and friends (and thus close to play) is framed by space and time. There may not be a curtain or even a line on the ground, but the performance is separate from the current of everyday life and demands a different kind of attention. See chapter 7 for further exploration of framing in rhetoric.

The point about this diversion into drama and rhetoric is that Moffett's conception is deeply rhetorical in the sense that dialogue and exchange are at the heart of the English project, but the additional dimension or act of framing is underplayed by Moffett. It would fit well with his overall conception, but, like much of the book, the ideas flow sequentially but not always systematically.

Another connection between the conception of speech and drama at the center of English activity is Moffett's statement "I am asking the reader to associate dialogue with dialectic" (82). Bypassing the nuances and complexities of the etymologies here, the connection between dialogue in everyday discourse and the oppositional, ideological dimensions of dialectic is an important one in terms of abstraction, and specifically with regard to argumentation (which, as a mode of operation in a rationalist universe, is closely allied to the rhetoric of persuasion, but also of clarification, defense, exposition, and delight). What Moffett is implying, I think, is that everyday exchanges, however seemingly insignificant, are indicative of larger dialectical moves: the to-ing and fro-ing of everyday exchange is like the puntal and contrapuntal rhythms of dialectic. Moffett does not expand on this connection, but it is fairly clear that everyday speech has all the hallmarks of drama and dialectic in more consciously framed worlds: the dramatic/dialectic level informs everyday speech and provides the humanist framework within which discourse operates. From thence, the natural curriculum movement is from dialogue to vocal monologue to written monologue and then on to the other forms of written discourse. In English curricular terms, it makes sense, is exciting, and is difficult, for students to make those transitions. In cognitive psychological terms, the sequence is Vygotskian. In rhetorical terms, the addition of speech and drama to the panoply of written forms that derive from Bain—and the demonstration of the connection of speech and drama to those written forms—is a brilliant move that reconnects "English" to the rhetorical tradition, remaking rhetoric for the needs of the contemporary English classroom.

The Section on Rhetoric

Embedded (a key term for Moffett, even though he was reacting against sentence combining and embedding) in the chapter on drama and speech is a section on "Rhetoric." At first, Moffett seems to see rhetoric as "the ways in which a person attempts to act on another" (115). It appears that he thinks that "the tremendously important art of manipulating other people"—let's call this, less negatively, *persuasion*—"is the genesis of rhetoric" (115). But as the argument progresses, it becomes clear that rhetoric is seen as a verbal and nonverbal means of exchange and making things happen in the world: "acting on others through words is merely one aspect of the larger rhetoric of behaviour" (115). What is contemporary about this conception of rhetoric is that it acknowledges the multimodal. Speech and writing (the verbal modes) are seen as mixing with other behavior or modes, and only later are they separated out to be taught as individual and seemingly distinct arts. So in drama, Moffett sees rhetoric in action: a rhetoric of persuasion. Such a conception of rhetoric is Aristotelian ("the art of persuasion"), which tends to put emphasis on one of the specific functions of rhetoric rather than on its myriad forms. If we adjust the notion of persuasion to include a wider range of communicative functions (entertainment, description, exchange, etc.), we could recast rhetoric as the "arts of discourse" and thus marry Moffett's conception of the centrality of speech and drama more happily to his conception of rhetoric . . . and indeed to the tenor of the book as a whole, with its emphasis on the "world of discourse." One of the key links that Moffett makes, however, is to suggest that the seemingly distinct written forms in the English curriculum are all intimately related to the basic spoken and dramatic forms and motivations. The following passage crystallizes the argument:

> Although we enter school already with a rhetoric, it is of course naïve and drastically inadequate to later communication needs. The function of the school is to extend the rhetorical repertory and to bind messages so tightly to message senders that this relation will not be lost in transferring it to the page. What is too obvious to notice in conversation must be raised to a level of operational awareness that will permit this transfer. (116)

Moffett also, by "binding messages to message senders," re-emphasizes one of the main unspoken themes of his book: that there needed to be a rebalancing of the productive arts (speaking, writing, making) with the receptive ones (reading, listening). It is likely, in the literary-influenced English curriculum of the first part of the twentieth and twenty-first centuries, that the productions of school children might always seem second best to those of published "writers" and that the culture is one of deference rather than of coproduction. We still suffer such a deferential curriculum and set of practices now: reading gets more research and policy attention than writing; English teachers are trained by their degrees as advanced readers but not as advanced writers; and even in the age of Web 3.0 and beyond, the authority of the teacher is deemed greater than that of the learner. There is thus a politics of the English curriculum and its relative balances that is implied by Moffett's book, but not fully made explicit. The nearest we come to it is in the wonderful paragraph at the end of the chapter on drama, in the section titled "The Drama of the Classroom," which focuses on pedagogy:

> Instead of creating constant tension between the social motives of the student and his own motive to teach the 'subject', the teacher would

> do better to acknowledge that his [sic] own intellectual pursuits are framed by dramatic relations between him and the world, and to recognize that this must be true for his students as well. Since discourse is ultimately social in origin and function, it seems a shame to fight those forces that could be put to such excellent use in teaching the subject. (119)

For social and dramatic, we could use the term *rhetorical,* as long as we recognize that the rhetorical is intimately tied up with power and thus, more broadly, the political. This "broader discursive context" (186), which Moffett argues is necessary to put the sentence in its place and for the development of narrative in the English curriculum, is the underlying thesis on which the book is based. This thesis is the beginning of a "global rationale" for English, "the lack [of which] has obstructed the alignment of means and ends and obscured the unity of the field" (211). In relation to the teaching of writing, Moffett advocates an environment in which writing is seen like speech, as a dialogic exchange within and beyond the classroom, largely between the teacher and his or her pupils, but also with wider communities and audiences. The alignment of writing with speech and drama gives it significance and function, even within the simulated spaces of the classroom. Although the answer to Moffett's call on the teaching of writing came partly from the creation of the National Writing Project in the United States in the early 1970s, with its emphasis on building up the confidence and repertoire of teachers in writing, there is still a long way to go in persuading authorities, at least in England, that developing teachers as writers is key to improving the quality of students' writing (see Andrews 2008a).

The Relevance of Moffett to Contemporary Rhetoric

Moffett's focus on discourse and rhetoric is one way of working toward a global rationale for English as a school subject (and indeed, English as a university discipline). The twenty-first-century interest in rhetoric, as discussed by Green (2006), for example, echoes much of what Moffett was proposing. As noted previously, Moffett is characteristically modest about the scope of his argument; that modesty, with its eye very firmly on practice and possibilities in the classroom, is partly what makes the propositions attractive and usable. And yet a global rationale *is* needed for the epistemological, social, and pedagogical practices that constitute "English," which continues to fissure as a subject and discipline. Such a rationale is needed because (a) we are literally now experiencing global awareness under the heading "English," which covers a wide range of practices and orientations; (b) "English" seems a misnomer for much of what goes on under its name; (c) multilingualism is the norm worldwide;

and (d) drama, media work, and multimodal perspectives all sit under the umbrella term. As Green (2006) suggests, neither "literacy" nor "new literacies" are the terms under which the range of practices can gather. Partly this is because these terms have been asked to do too much. Instead, he proposes rhetoric "appropriately reworked, as providing a new organising principle for English teaching" (11). That reworking means more than a reworking of classical rhetoric for the present times. Such reworking would need to take into account that making persuasive speeches in public forums is only one small part of what rhetoric might be used for in the twenty-first century; and, furthermore, that the prescriptions, manuals, and *progymnasmata* (exercises in which genres were modeled and then imitated) of Renaissance rhetoric are no longer appropriate.

In exploring the possibilities for rhetoric as a unifying principle or body of theory, Green (2006) discusses Hunter (1997), who proposes a separation of rhetoric, ethics, and literature in the secondary classroom. This separation, it seems, confines rhetoric to something like a contemporary combination of classical and renaissance rhetoric and could lead to a reductive language curriculum.

The larger conception of rhetoric as the *arts of discourse* is one I would want to propose here, not least because it builds on Moffett (1983), Hunter (1997), Green (2006), Kress (2005), and others who see rhetoric, in various guises, playing a role in the redefinition of English as a school subject. To keep the focus on Moffett for the purposes of the present chapter, a further dimension of rhetoric that he does not develop sufficiently (and acknowledges as much) is the aesthetic dimension: the *arts* of discourse. This term also has the benefit (and, some might argue, the disadvantages) of an emphasis on the *technè* (technique as art, craft) of contemporary communication, as well as on the political nature of rhetoric. In addition, rhetoric can deal with communication in any language or combination of languages and in a number and combination of modes, it can handle the difference between the fictive worlds and the real world or worlds, and it links itself to a long but varied tradition of public discourse.

But Moffett's position, as well as fundamentally arguing the case for speech and drama (in practice and as dialogic principles) at the center of discourse in a renewed English curriculum, prepares the ground for such a wider conception of rhetoric. Rhetoric's concerns are essentially simple: it is interested in who is speaking to or with (writing for, composing for) whom, why, what they are communicating about, and when and how they are doing it. These simple questions have complex and wide-ranging answers. Moffett's conviction—that the interchange of speech or drama (an interesting coupling that is not fully exploited for its real world/fictive world potential) realizes a principle that applies to all communication—is deeply rhetorical. From the vantage point of the early twenty-first century, when growth-based, literary, and/or skills-based models of English or literacy no longer seem to convey the excitement or range of contemporary communication, Moffett's contribution as one of the first to challenge the orthodoxy of the written product at the heart of the English curriculum now looks prescient.

In partial conclusion, we could also say that Moffett's contribution to contemporary rhetoric needed further development: in relation to framing theory, dialogism, multimodality, and the fiction/non-fiction divide. What the discussion in this chapter hardly touches on, but what is so inspiring about *Teaching the Universe of Discourse,* is that it continues to be a tonic to any English teacher who is wondering what sequence of types of text to use in the classroom and why, how those types of text are related to each other, and how to engage and negotiate with his or her students.

Rhetoric and Fiction

Without wanting to invoke Booth's work (cf. *A Rhetoric of Fiction,* 1961) at this point (his contribution to thinking about Rhetoric is discussed elsewhere in the book), any chapter on rhetoric and English must consider the place of fiction within rhetoric. Fiction holds a strong central place in English curricula, both at school at university levels. Since the 1920s in England, at least, literature (novels, plays, poetry) has been seen as the central civilizing and humanistic core of the English curriculum, with "language work" spinning off from this literary core. To put it crudely, it is as if the highly framed world of fiction—the fictional worlds created in those literary works—has engineered a space within which students may explore various takes on the world, as well as the relationship between the world and their own inner worlds. In many senses, this engineered curriculum space is a privileged, free space for the individual. It affords the possibility of engagement, immersion, criticality (how do the fictional worlds portrayed compare to other such worlds?), therapy, enjoyment of language, entertainment, and self-realization.

But what is rhetoric's contribution to the understanding of fiction, or, conversely, fiction's place within rhetoric? We can characterize the relationship as having at least four dimensions: a *political* literary criticism, the connection between fiction and the real world via the notion of "possible worlds," the building of a bridge between fiction and non-fiction, and a contribution to the understanding and making of fiction through framing and re-framing.

Political Literary Criticism

Any discussion of a work of fiction from a rhetorical perspective comes close to what has been termed "Marxist literary criticism" (see Eagleton 1976, 1983, 2004). The relationship is close, but not congruent with

Marxism. Rhetoric will ask the following of fiction: Who has been authorized to "speak" by being published? What are the gateways through which the journey to published work has been made? How do the media (literary magazines, list of publications in newspaper supplements, radio programmes, cultural affairs programmes on television, etc.) mediate the fictional work for audiences? Is there a late Romantic cult-of-the-single-author at work? How is the fictional work packaged (e.g., does the contemporary novel have precedence over short stories, plays, or poems in the market?)? If the novel has precedence, why is this? Is it a preference for unalloyed narrative within the population? Again, if so, why does the printed novel (or the novel read on an electronic reading device) hold more status than a story that is *told?* In short, how is power exercised in the literary world?

Such questions give rise to a consideration of the relationship between rhetoric and late capitalism. If fictional, published works are commodified and prepared for the market like any other product, they play a particular role in the life and economy of a society—and indeed, within a global society. A novel is conceived, written, and published. It either falls on stony ground, achieving little in the way of sales and falling off the marketing shelves quickly. It may have a shelf life of a few years, capturing the zeitgeist temporarily. Or it may become a modern classic. In addition to the baseline buying and selling of novels, however, is the creation and maintenance of an imaginative space for readers. Individuals and societies maintain this space as a human necessity: the space for private immersion, "escape" and reflection in a novel; the coming together of people in book groups or reading circles (see Duncan 2012) to share views on such reflection; and discussion of such experiences in literary magazines, chat shows, and radio/TV programmes. The three other dimensions are discussed *passim* in the following chapters.

4

Rhetoric and Composition

Composition, in the United States and U.S.-influenced education systems, sits in a symbiotic relationship with rhetoric: rhetoric provides the theoretical background and the classical models; composition is the practical manifestation. Freshman composition courses are common in the first year of undergraduate study and take various forms, from the generic to the discipline-specific. Their function is to prepare students for the linguistic and discoursal demands of written academic study. Their presence is both remedial and preparatory: remedial in the sense of compensating for shortcomings in writing instruction (and, to a lesser extent, reading instruction) at the higher levels, and preparatory in helping students to read and write academic texts such as position papers, research projects, essays, and dissertations. That rhetoric and composition are seen as closely related is encouraging. At its best, the relationship is one of exploration across a wide range of written genres, of exploration of function and audience as well as form, of the history of composition, and of the possibilities of rhetoric, seen broadly as the arts of discourse and related to the real world as well as to academia. At worst, the relationship between rhetoric and composition is seen in fossilized terms via formulae, as exercises (the Renaissance *progymnasmata*), too heavily dependent on classical models and practices, derivative, and "instructional" and pedagogically primitive. It is therefore no surprise that many students who experience this induction to academic study find the courses dry and irrelevant.

Just as we have looked at rhetoric in new terms in the present book, so too *composition* needs to be looked at anew. Literally, the term means "putting with"—to form by putting together. It is a useful term, because it both denotes an action or process of putting elements together (*composition*), as well as the created phenomenon itself: *the composition*. In that sense, it functions as a term like *writing* or *argument*. Its uses and associations suggest more: it is used not only to describe the act of making a piece of writing, but also the making of a musical or visual work. Indeed, the "composer" is most often used in music. There are other peripheral uses (as far as our present interest is concerned), such as the composition of type arranged for printing, the quality or state of being compound (in chemistry), and the notion of composing oneself in the sense of being free from agitation. All these facets of the term *composition* have a common core: the idea of putting things together into a unified, proportionate, and aesthetically pleasing form.

The term was, and is, used to denote a piece of writing in school: a composition on any topic. In England in the 1950s and 1960s, it was the preferred term for school writing exercises. It fell out of use as more specific terms, denoting text types, emerged: essay, autobiography, story, "descriptive piece." At the same time, more abstract generic terms entered, like "a piece of writing" or the invitation/instruction: "I'd like you to write about . . . ." The term *composition* fell out of use because it was associated with the narrowly rhetorical approach to the teaching of writing. Its composite origin of "putting things together" was lost, and it became a vestigial term to denote the act of writing and the products of writing in the classroom.

What Is Composition?

In contemporary conditions, why is "composition" worth reviving and remaking as the term of choice for teaching writing and other art forms? In the chapter on framing, we will set out the case for the act of framing to be central to rhetorical practice. But within frames, elements are arranged to convey meaning.

Before we focus again on writing, let us look at other art forms. An artist (principally, a visual artist) can create a work in a number of ways. Most conventionally, he or she will take a canvas and apply paint to it, putting together different colors to create a figurative or landscape depiction or to create an abstract painting. The composition may include other resources than paint; it could include found objects, lines drawn in pencil or charcoal, pieces of fabric or tiles, and so on. All of these are *composed* to convey meaning. Someone engaged in communal or community arts practice would go even further in terms of composition. He or she might decide on a site (e.g., a dilapidated building) around which to build his or her compositional project, interview people who have observations and/or memories and/or reflections about the site, take photographs of it, look into the history of the building, record sounds associated with it, take map projections, and so on. In order to convey meaning about the building and its associations, the artist/composer puts a number of elements together—and might do so in an art gallery, in a studio, on location, or on film. All of these remakings and re-presentations are composed for particular effect—or for the audience to make whatever meaning of it that they wish (having brought their own frames of reference to the experience).

Similarly, a musical composer, using a different set of resources, can put together a short work or an orchestral work, or any kind of sound composition, by putting together sounds in particular combinations. These can work in relation to a number of different principles (harmonic, melodic, "serial," rhythmic, via naturally occurring and "found" sounds) used singly or in combination. Within the frame of the musical genre, sounds are put together to make music. Even if the composition is undertaken on a score, without actual sound being made and composed, the act of composition via notation still occurs.

Writing is often underestimated in terms of its compositional nature. Once the system of words; letters (or characters); sounds; the relationship between letters and sounds (the grapho-phonemic relationship); the order of words in phrases, clauses, and sentences ("syntax"); of how sentences relate to paragraphs and other sub-sections of text; and how all these relate to the whole text in a range of genres—and thus to the context and audience—are learnt and become fluent means of expression, their *composed* nature is overlooked. And yet the writer/composer puts together letter with letter, word with word, and sentence with sentence to make a meaningful work. He or she is composing not only with the resources of words, but with the ideas and denotations that these words represent. The composition, then, is more than a technical and aesthetic act of "putting things together to create proportionate and beautiful form"; it is an act of conveying meaning, just as a visual artist or musical composer creates and conveys meaning.

The Act of Composition

"Putting things together" is a general description of the act of composing. What does the compositional process entail; what are its constituent elements and practices? First, it is a matter of the overall *conception* of the piece. That conception may be fully formed at the start of the composition, or it may emerge through the juxtaposition of different and separate elements. In a fully formed conception, the act of composing will be one of seeking the elements to realize the conception and putting them together in an arrangement that matches as closely as possible the original conception. When the work is not fully conceived from the start, there will be a period of collection of fragments, ideas, and materials in a number of media that can be laid out and then put together. Whether the making is fully conceived from the start or emerges in the process of making the selection of elements (which mode or modes, which media, which *resources?*) is crucial.

Their *layout* is also important. Some composers (depending on their preferred and principal medium) like to work on a large table, others on a computer screen, and others on canvas or wood or paper. Directors of theatre productions—to take art forms in the wider sense that includes performance—see the empty three-dimensional space as their frame for composition. The framed space for composition is a key defining feature of the nature of that composition, though we have to acknowledge that the computer screen is itself like a window or panel on to or as part of a scroll. Large computer screens allow for a number of "windows" (usually texts, including images or diagrams and tables) to be open at any one time and thus to be composed—brought together into a new work. Whether on screen, on paper, on a large table, or in a rehearsal space, the *physicality* of composing is felt by all composers.

Next is the art of *contiguity* and *juxtaposition.* Resources have edges. They are brought together, configured, and arranged in order to make meaning. This arrangement may be spatial; it may be linear. But which element goes next to another element is central to the making of meaning. In linear arrangements (most verbal printed works and narratives) the connections between the elements are set out, logically or quasi-logically, and have all the properties and affordances that *sequentiality* gives, including the classical principle of *post hoc propter hoc.* Linearity might also be manifested in time, for example, in the frames of a film that is experienced as continuous motion in time.

(As a further example, although I composed this chapter last in the first draft of the present book and it was originally conceived as coming between the chapter on multimodality and that on digitization, it is placed as Chapter 4 between one on English studies and one on power in order to suggest that composition might be a central concern to expression and the development of a repertoire of genres. Those are concerns about composition in the larger structural sense. As I actually composed it, the to-ing and fro-ing between the larger structural design and the actualities of writing the words on an electronic page, with attention to accuracy of spelling, the make-up of sentences, and the positioning of sections and paragraphs within sections, all took place. Because I was working on a computer, I could move sections, paragraphs, sentences, phrases, and words as seemed to fit my overall intention.)

In two- or three-dimensional arrangements of a nonlinear nature, the connections between elements are more latent that determined. It is the reader, audience, or viewer who determines the connections between the elements, as much so as, if not more so than, the composer. We might read a website by jumping from one framed box of information to another; we might dive down through hypertextual levels, or follow a link to another website. All the time we are navigating the configuration of text and image that the composer has created for us. The experience of reading a website or a multipaneled work of any kind is thus different from a sequential reading, just as the act of composing these different works is different. We deploy sequentiality and other types of configured spatial relations as we see fit *in order to make meaning.*

This act of navigating not only what is within each of the framed texts that we "read" but also the lines of engagement and juxtaposition between them—and any spaces that surround or stand between them—is central to the act of composition and reading. The two sides of the communication act—that of the composer and the reader—are reciprocal, and each construes the intentions of the other. For the composer, the reader is often "within" rather than an actual reader or audience without. That is to say, the composer carries within him- or herself the ability and need to listen to, read, and/or view the work he or she is creating in order to help to make it cohere. In these ways, the act of composition is as much an act of decoding and interpreting as it is an act of making and configuring. And the "meaning" is created in the interaction between composer, reader, and "text"—a space that is filled and put together to enact old meanings and to create new ones. Thus rhetoric is the social mapping of relations between ideas and feelings via the composition of modes, media, and other resources.

What Are the Limits of Composition?

We have already suggested, and will elaborate further in the chapter on rhetoric and framing, that the immediate limits of a composition are its frame. The act of framing—either using existing off-the-shelf frames ("text types," conventional genres in any art form or social encounter) or creating a new frame—determines the boundaries of the composition. To give some quick examples: a painting on canvas that is intended to be framed for exhibition provides the parameters for the composition. There is some leeway afforded the painter as he or she works on the canvas, in terms of the bleeding off of the edges of the composition (which a mount and a frame might cover in due course), but the edge of the canvas is the limit of the compositional space. In another nonverbal example, a conventional piece of music is composed in five movements that fit together in a sequence to create some degree of artistic unity. The "edges" of the composition are defined by the score, spatially, in digital format or on paper. In performance, the work is framed by time, with a clear beginning and end, often marked by a moment's silence and (ritual) applause.

Even in these examples, however, we have defined two kinds of framing that mark the limits of composition: one is the actual creation of the work, and the other is the work in performance (if these two aspects can be separated).

The act of composition is a critical/creative act that works toward a product. That product is a poem, novel, playscript, painting, sculpture, installation, score, or other art form. Each of these is driven by an aesthetic impulse that dictates that the work will have an internal unity, balance, proportion, and elegance that, combined with framing, will distinguish it from non-art. The product can be enshrined in print or digital form (if it is a verbal or musical work), photographed, reproduced, transported, and experienced by an audience. Some of these art forms require performance for their full realization, like musical scores or playscripts. In performance, they take on a different and more multimodal nature and are realized differently each time they are performed. The performances (including recorded performances that are broadcast or recorded on CDs and DVDs) are also "compositions" in the sense that we have been using it in this chapter because they are the result of a bringing together of elements to create a single composition in time. Take the staged performance of Ibsen/Grieg's *Peer Gynt,* for example, that took place at the Barbican, London, in December 2012 and was subsequently broadcast on BBC Radio 3 eight days later. It existed first as a composed score/script. The director of the staged performance worked with an orchestra, a chorus of singers, three solo singers, and six actors to create the performance itself. Following rehearsal of the separate groups in locations around London, they came together for final rehearsals as an ensemble. The coordination of orchestral music, songs, spoken narratives, and choral elements was an act of composition, working toward a two-hour performance (one kind of framing, in time) in a large concert hall (another, in space) in one of London's top arts venues (yet another). Furthermore, the work was recorded by the BBC, mixed and balanced, and broadcast with suitable commentary (further framing) eight days later. In addition to its scheduled broadcast, it was made available for a seven-day period on iPlayer, the BBC's repository of radio and television programs that can be accessed online. These two performances are framed and composed in time, with particular audiences in mind, thus fulfilling the rhetorical/theoretical space that the "arts of discourse" implies.

There are works that are both products and performances simultaneously, such as improvised dramas, art installations, opening/closing ceremonies, and films. These are also compositions in that they require the bringing together of different elements to create a whole "work," in time.

Multimodal Composition

Much of what we have discussed as composition is multimodal, by default. Multimodality and rhetoric are discussed fully in another chapter, but here we continue the exploration of what it means to compose—in this case, multimodally. First, it can be said that *monomodal composition* is rare because each mode (speaking, writing, movement, graphic symbolic languages, still image, moving image) is instantiated physically. The simple act of speaking, even in everyday conversation, is grounded in the physical body, its vocal chords and resonance chambers. Sound waves travel through the substance of air, in various acoustic settings, to be decoded and interpreted by the listener. When spoken conversation is mediated by wireless or telephonic means, a different medium is brought into play; and when recorded for playback on a voice mail or in a speech recording for research or aesthetic purposes, the seeming monomodality of the speaking voice is still mediated through physical means. Equally, a poet working with a pencil on a blank sheet of paper is (a) responding to the size and shape of the paper itself, (b) placing the words of the poem in lines to indicate rhythmic identity, and (c) using the white space around the poem to indicate that the work is framed by space and is thus special in some way. Here, the media (pencil and paper) and the affordances of those media (the identification of surrounding space, the propensity to draft and re-draft) come into play in the act of composition. "Pure" modes are rarely experienced, either as composers or as audience.

Second, multimodal composition operates via *bricolage, juxtaposition,* and *rearrangements* to create communication. Behind bricolage—the gathering together of a seemingly disparate range of modes or materials to make an artistic statement—is the notion and practice of collage. Collage and bricolage both assume a frame within which to work. They bring together material of the same mode/medium, like pieces of fabric for example, or from different modes, like scraps of text that are woven (the metaphor is from fabric again, like the term *texture*) together to form a new whole. A play such as *The Laramie Project* (Kaufman 2001) or a novel such as Ian McEwan's *Sweet Tooth* (2012) uses textual bricolage to forge letters, personal testimonies, third-person narrative, and the authorial detached and reflective meta-voice into a hybrid form: the docudrama or novel, respectively. When more than one mode is employed, such as the combination of word and still image, not only is bricolage at play, but juxtaposition comes to the fore as one of the key elements of composition.

Juxtaposition—the placing of one element not just with, but *next to* another—involves careful choreographic decision making. The exact alignment is important, not only for the elements themselves but for the space in between them and the meaning that is generated by their juxtaposition. The formula *word + image* is not the same as *image + word,* and even such balanced equations do not do justice to the possibilities of two- and three-dimensional juxtaposition. Sometimes the placing of one element next to another is complementary; sometimes antagonistic and critical. Take the mounting of an exhibition of paintings or photographs in an art gallery. There are at least two ways in which word and image combine to create the whole experience. One is in the mounting of the artworks themselves, almost always accompanied by written captions or statements alongside them. At minimum, these statements simply denote the artwork: *Still Life with a Curtain*/Cézanne/1895. Usually, they contain a little more information: the painting "illustrates Cézanne's increasing trend towards terse compression of forms and dynamic tension between geometric figures" (Wikipedia 2013). Sometimes, but more rarely, the plaques or statements contain questions or counterarguments that force the viewer to take a more critical stance toward the painting itself: "Imagine a different set of objects for the still life, or a circumstance in which Cézanne was unable to secure the time for such studies—or was influenced by photography." Each of these challenges suggests a re-framing of the experience in order to encourage the viewer to see the actual framing that has gone on in the making of the piece. In such cases there is a tension and deliberate distancing of the image and its text to invite the viewer/reader to inhabit that intermediate space.

Exhibitions of artworks also usually are accompanied by catalogs. The catalog is a different composition, driven by the exigencies of the printed book with its sequencing and domination of the verbal text. The image then becomes accessory to the text. A narrative and/or argued text is created, and the images are either appended to the end of the book, or set within the text. Only where the catalog is arranged like an exhibition itself, with the images given pride of place and the verbal text accompanying it, does the catalog mirror the exhibition. It is a different experience, requires different juxtapositional/compositional skills (including, traditionally, that of the "compositor" or arranger of text), and is read differently. Interestingly, the computer as compositional tool and the website as accompaniment to the printed catalog changes the compositional dynamic yet again. In these situations, word and image are brought together and can sit in a balanced relation with each other so that neither predominates. The emphasis then is on the reader to navigate the composite, multimodal text as he or she is inclined. Some may read the verbal text first and then look at the images; others may take the opposite route. The experience of engaging with the whole text, however, is a dynamic and changeable one. In compositional terms, the act of making the digital text as a whole is one of finely tuning the balance between the modes.

Rearrangements are commonplace in communicational design. It has already been mentioned that this chapter was written late in the composition of the book as a whole, requiring rearrangement of other chapters in order to find a proper place for it. But the act of composition itself is an act of arranging and rearranging of existing material. Rearrangement, then, is a concatenation of different voices, different modes, and different materials in order to "say something new." The new statement adds to the existing living archive of communication that can be drawn down as material for a further remaking.

Stages of Composition/Drafting and Redrafting/Making and Remaking

Composition takes place in time. The beginning of a composition can take various forms: from a rhythmic signature that becomes a poem or a musical composition; from a phrase that becomes a novel or the beginnings of an dissertation; or from a chance spatial alignment (for example, a colored scrap of fabric next to a structural feature) that becomes a new interior design for an architectural project. There is both transduction (the movement from one mode to another) and transformation (a broader category involving change on a number of fronts) at play in the *developmental composition* of a work.

Almost all artistic creations, including the construction of buildings, are the result of a series of drafts. Once the idea is sparked, the gradual development of the idea is managed over time in drafting and re-drafting. Sketches and small studies become a painting; maquettes and other early forms of modeling become sculptures; jottings and notes become a short story or an article. At the early stages of composition, ideas are brainstormed and marshaled; one idea may inspire another. As the work takes shape, further ideas are either adapted or rejected. The process is managed by the composer, who makes decisions along the way about what makes for unity of purpose and design; what works (in the case of buildings, what engineering factors need to be taken into account to make the building safe, robust, sustainable, efficient, and useable); and what is elegant. Rhetoric, in the stages of composition, is not merely an add-on at the end of the process in terms of performance, flourish, or decoration. It is fundamental to the design of the whole because of the rhetorical choices that have to be made along the way. Rhetorical choices in composition are choices about fitness for purpose, proportion, beauty, available modes and media, available resources, the balance and function of product and performance, the nature of recording and archiving, and location in space and time.

Rhetoric is thus deeply implicated in the act of composition, from start to finish. Whereas composition deals with the actual process of putting things together to make new meaning, rhetoric provides the theoretical framework and resources, and awareness of the wider social, economic, and political exigencies, that make the composition a success.

The Myth of the Single (Romantic) Composer

The composer is often assumed to be a single person. The myth derives from Romantic notions of authorship, and the idea of a single fount of inspiration that engenders and subsequently shapes a work of art. It is, indeed, often the case that a single person is the principal source of the work and that the "creative" aspect of the making of a work is valued out of all proportion to the actual process of making. Thus we see architects credited for landmark buildings Foster + Partners' Hongkong and Shanghai Bank headquarters in Hong Kong, or Renzo Piano's Shard in London ("Renzo Piano's creation, the tallest building in western Europe, finally opens its 69th-floor viewing platform to the public" in *The Guardian*, December 30, 2012), with hardly a mention for the structural engineers and project managers who often are involved with the projects from the start. Similarly, a book is assumed to be authored by a single or joint writer(s), with little recognition for the editors, book designers, typesetters, and others involved in the making of the final work. Visual artists depend on canvas and paper makers if they are painters, developing houses or digital tools if they are photographers, and workshops if they are sculptors.

We can take the principle of collaborative production to the very heart of the single-author myth. We have already referred to Bakhtin's notion of the dialogic imagination, with no new voice being created without reference to the wealth of existing voices in oral and written form. We could extend his argument to apply to all the arts. Every new work takes reference from what has gone before and responds to it. But let us take this idea further, and right back to the stereotype of the Romantic author. Even a lone writer in a garret, penning a poem or a novel in solitude, cannot escape the fact that he or she is part of the social fabric; that the tools of production—pen, ink, paper—are made objects that have been designed, sourced, fashioned, and produced; and that he or she writes for an (hoped for) audience, even if that audience is the writer him- or herself.

Composition is a collaborative act, even when the author/maker appears to be working on his or her own. This is not to say that all aspects of composition, from initial conception through to the final product, are rhetorical. Rhetoric reserves itself for the description and analysis of the social conditions of the arts of discourse, both in their making and in their reception. It does not encroach upon—though it is influenced by—economic issues such as the availability of resource, the choices made about capital, or the cost-benefit analyses of choice.

Composition thus sits firmly within the conception of rhetoric that is being forged in this book. The rhetor, in communicating something to an audience in whatever modes and media, is shaping communicative resources with the help of historical genres, with collaboration from others, and in a full social context. Because the social is implicated in the political and economic, the compositional act is not merely an individual one. Yeats's statement that a poem might be made from "a mouthful of air" is a late Romantic conceit.

Pedagogies of Composition

In a later chapter, the relationship between rhetoric and education is explored. Here, following the discussion of composition and its place in rhetorical theory, we consider the pedagogies of composition. We are not talking of instruction, textbook approaches, or of the psychologies of learning to compose, but rather of the conditions for learning and the heuristics for composition.

A "writing classroom" or any other kind of workshop designed to provide a space for making in the arts is a collaborative space. First, there needs to be a sense of a community of learners who will learn from each other as well as from the teacher. The teacher herself needs to *see herself* and *act* as a learner as well as a teacher, not only modeling practices that might be followed or adapted, but also working alongside the learners as they create, fashion, and finish their work. The learners need to own the space so that their confidence can be established. Such learning takes place in formal institutions, with accreditation leading toward awards and certificates; it also takes place informally in "make spaces." Several of these less formal spaces are springing up across London during the writing of this book: shops in which after-hours workshops take place; spaces where a sewing machine can be rented for one or two hours to work on a particular project; parties where the focus is on making something. In each of these situations there is a collective will to make something and to enjoy the process of doing so.

Second, the actual moments of learning, of transformation in knowledge and skill, are engendered by the conditions for learning described previously, but also by "heuristics" or strategies and devices that make learning come about. These constitute the art of pedagogy and include working individually, in pairs, or in small groups as well as in whole groups; coaching; inventive ways of presenting a topic; making connections; teaching methods for constructing and resolving arguments; problem solving; practicing a new skill; research skills; and the use of various media.

What is distinctive about the pedagogies of composition is that it is accepted that learning is collaborative and that the learner need not be confronted by a blank slate when entering the classroom. He or she brings experience, framings, personal resources, and the connections that provide social resources ("capital") to bear. Others who join the social encounter of the workshop or classroom bring similar resources. The actual materials for composition are provided by the class/workshop teacher, and the aim of the workshop or series of workshops is to collaborate in the making of new knowledge/products, and thereby the development of new perspectives and skills. The alignment of the frames provided by the learner, and the frames provided by the teacher, make for progression within those frames of a compositional nature. The very act of "putting things together" in new ways is an act of learning.

The Economics of Rhetoric

Any mention of resource, (re)making, and choice brings economic as well as rhetorical issues to bear on the matter of composition. To date within the book, we have charted the relationship between communicative acts, rhetoric, and politics, but the economic dimension has hardly been addressed. At a macro- and disciplinary level, what rhetoric and economics have in common is that they provide a way of understanding how choices can be and are made from a limited set of resources for particular purposes. Although the ultimate end of economics may be the health and well-being of a nation, the reasonable distribution of wealth within a nation, or supra-national issues of global production and consumption, one area of common ground with rhetoric is the maintenance of the social fabric. While economics does this in terms of the distribution of wealth and resource, rhetoric does so by ensuring that the channels of communication are kept clear and free-flowing, that communication is fit for purpose, and that ideas, thoughts, and feelings have proper currency and movement within society (locally, regionally, nationally, and globally).

Economics impinges upon rhetoric if the distribution of wealth is unfair or disproportionately unequal, exacerbating social division and damaging social cohesion. Such stratification, with limited means of movement (social mobility), even through the education system, will make for a breakdown in the discourses that connect one person to another. Lanchester (2013), in an article titled "Let's Call it Failure" in the *London Review of Books,* looks at the state of the British economy in the wake of the 2008 crash—otherwise known as "the Great Recession (or, as the Chinese never fail to call it, the 'Western Financial Crisis')" (5). Aspects of this crisis include tax increases, an increase in the structural deficit, a shrinking of the economy, reduction in gross national product(ivity), public spending cuts, and other "austerity measures," as well as a hardening of the attitude toward social welfare. Similarly, in the United States, the beginning of 2013 brought a short-fix agreement to avert the American economy from going over a "fiscal cliff" of tax increases and public spending cuts. Measures included tax increases on the top 2% of American wealth-owners, thus (to a small extent) closing the gap a little between the rich and the not-so-rich and favoring the majority of "working families." In addition to tax increases and spending cuts (on education and the military), the following measures were included: increases in inheritance taxes from 35% to 40% after the first $5m for an individual and $10m for a couple; increases in capital taxes—affecting some investment income—of up to

20%; a one-year extension for unemployment benefits, affecting two million people; and a five-year extension for tax credits that help poorer and middle-class families (BBC 2013).

We are not so much concerned with the surface rhetoric of economic and political discourse, in the sense of the diction used to describe and ameliorate the nature and effects of these financial crises ("recession," "slump," "fiscal cliff," etc.), but more so with the nature of rhetoric in a declining economy. Does a declining economy require better use of rhetoric? Does it damage rhetoric? The answer is that it is the political implications of economic downturn that have the bigger impact on rhetoric: there is less chance of reaching agreement on ways forward; discussions and negotiations at the national and international political level go right up to the wire, often through all-night sessions; the lack of social cohesion makes for discourses that "do not speak to each other"; centrist political parties look weak and helpless in the face of economic downturn, while the extreme left and right gain support as they chart ideological and single-idea solutions to problems; the language of planning, management, and reconciliation becomes less meaningful so that language and discourse are separated, seeming to have little effect on action and actuality. While it might be said that rhetoric is neutral from economics and politics, it cannot help but reflect the social attenuation that takes place in a declining economy.

Back to Rhetoric and Composition

In this chapter, we have tried not only to delimit what is meant by composition, but also to show how fundamental it is to communicative acts in a number of modes and media. Composition is the act of bringing things together to make meaning within framings that are created by the maker and the audience. A rhetorical perspective is essential to understanding the social and political nature of composition; in turn, composition provides the multimodal engine of making in a theory of rhetoric. Composition uses existing materials but adds something new by creating different configurations of the material, different juxtapositions, and different alliances that themselves create a meaning generated from coincidence and/or from tension. The gaps between elements in a composition are as important as the material elements themselves as they indicate a space for the audience to fill.

Thus, learning to compose—and its reciprocal activity, learning to "read" composition—are the key skills for the communicative arts in the twenty-first century. It will no longer be adequate for someone to learn to write in a particular language, or to learn the language of mathematics or music, or to learn the art of photography. Although we may not have the capacity or time to learn to compose in all the various modes and media, we will learn, by necessity, how to read and navigate our way through these different types of composition. Understanding the fundamental principles of composition will help us to do so and also help us to retain the aesthetic sense that is important to clear communication and to due propriety, elegance, subversion, and harmony in social relations. Perhaps, then, composition in all its senses will play an even greater part in social grouping, curricula, and individual well-being than it does in a dis-aggregated, fissured society.

5

Rhetoric and Power

The birth of rhetoric was associated with power. If there is a correlation between rhetoric and the maintenance of democracy, then rhetoric's function is to ensure that argumentation is available in a society and that through argumentation a consensus can be found that will enable action. That power is the power to argue; to marshal words and other modes to make one's case; to persuade; to defend one's position; to hammer out a policy and see it through into action. Rhetoric thrives in a democracy, and a democracy needs rhetoric. It is a mutual relationship. Only in autocracies, tyrannies, and other forms of undemocratic governance does rhetoric not find a place—except when those in power seek to impose their will upon others with the distorted use of rhetoric.

In the present chapter, various aspects of rhetoric and its relation to power will be explored: rhetoric in autocracies; rhetoric as depicted in fictional autocracies (*Nineteen Eighty-Four*); rhetoric in democracies; the abuse of rhetoric and power; minority group rhetoric; and rhetoric and the media.

Rhetoric and Democracy

Why is rhetoric so closely related to democracy? Democracy—the voice of the people—resides in a principle that each individual has a part to play in society and that he or she has a voice in how that society determines itself. In terms of governance, any organization—from a family to a local club, from a regional body to the government of a state, from a collection of states (e.g., Europe) to an organization that is international in reach (e.g., the United Nations)—has to find a balance between the voices of individuals on the one hand, and what and whom they represent on the other. There are other interstices: between the individual and the local organization, between the individual and the state.

In short, living in a democracy means living within a number of frames of different sizes, all of which relate in some way to the individual. Even if the individual were not part of this elaborate series of Russian dolls, there would still need to be commerce between the different levels, or different sizes of organization. But with the addition of the individual dimension and agency, the singular voice finds that it must engage with other people and thus with private (intimate) and public discourses.

Engagement between these various levels of organization requires communication; it requires argumentation to reach consensus as a basis for action; it requires storytelling; it requires clarification through categorization, description, verification, and distinction; it requires dialogue. Although there are set patterns and conventions for behavior, schemata for everyday discourse, and habitual aspects of "getting by" in the democratic world, the other requirement for anyone living in a democracy is negotiation. Examples are the negotiation that takes place in the permission that is sought (and debated) regarding demolishing an existing building and putting up a new one; the negotiation between the doctor and patient as to which medication, if any, is appropriate for a particular condition; the negotiation to get a bill through parliament or Congress regarding a new health care system or a reform to the existing provision for education.

Communication, engagement, negotiation: these are the elements of social interaction, and they are also the elements of political interaction in a democracy. If the values of a democracy are humanistic (and they usually are, given the individual person that defines the unit that makes up a democracy), those interactions function to understand, tolerate, and resolve difference within the social and political system. It is through difference that the democracy keeps alive and "progresses": the status quo is challenged, an oppositional point of view is established, matters are discussed and debated and then resolved. Rather like a Hegelian process of thesis, antithesis, and synthesis, the dynamic process of challenge, negotiation, and resolution provides the socio-political basis within which rhetoric thrives.

If there is no scope for such negotiation, there is no democracy and no rhetoric. Laws are made; they are enacted and observed. Transgression means censure and sometimes punishment.

The particular function of rhetoric in a democracy is that it is the private and public process of negotiation through whichever modes of communication are required by the situation and/or available to the participants. A decision, however small, is discussed by a family and decided upon; a course of action follows. At the governmental level, a bill is proposed; it is debated, revised, reconsidered, and finally passed as an Act, becoming law. Rhetoric is so much a part of the processes of democracy that, for most of the time, we do not see it. The rhetoric is persuasive; but that persuasion (the core of Aristotelian rhetoric—the "art of persuasion") is more fundamental than one person trying to persuade another to his or her point of view. Rather, it is part of a dialogic and often dialectic negotiation of the decisions that are made on a daily basis, such as whether to catch a bus at 9 AM or 9:15 AM to get to an appointment on time, what to spend money on, whether to holiday in a particular year or not, and if so, where? As will be evident, many such decisions take place on an individual basis via an inner dialogue or dialectic. These inner debates, as Vygotsky represents them, were at one time "real relations between people" before they became "thought"; that is, societal and politically shaped actions that determine the lineaments of the higher orders of thinking.

Thus, rhetoric is about human negotiation through the available means of discourse, and the choices made by individuals, groups, states, and international bodies (including relations between all these levels of interaction). Rhetorical choices, and the aesthetic dimension of the way those choices are framed, lead to action founded (ideally) on the best rational and value-based principles and operations.

Minority Group Rhetoric

What happens when a minority group tries to establish a discourse of its own, or with a hegemonic, majority group? Does it have to adopt the majority discourse, or can it develop its own discourse and still argue its corner in a society? A recent book by Banks (2006), working within a tradition of African American rhetoric, makes the case that the digital divide in the United States is aligned with a racialized divide and thus further depresses the chances of African Americans to play an equal part in society. The complex relationship between socioeconomic disadvantage, lack of access to new technologies at home or in schools, and not playing a full part in the digital discourses of new media provides a cocktail of injustice. The argument, put succinctly, is that "rhetorical and technological education must take up all three of [the] axes in theory, pedagogy, and practice with the focus of helping students employ each and all toward access and/or transformation of the spaces they occupy as they see fit" (Banks 2006, 7). Furthermore, "technologies are the spaces and processes that determine whether any group of people is able to tell its own stories in its own terms, whether people are able to agitate and advocate for policies that advances its interests, and whether that group of people has any hope of enjoying equal social, political and economic relations" (10).

Not all commentators on global digitization see a digital divide (see Haythornthwaite 2007), and not all societies see a racial divide as polemically as Banks. First, the "digital divide" can be seen more accurately as a digital spectrum of access and use. There is inequity in access to new technologies hardware as well as to broadband width and to technology. Banks points out that we can define material access (e.g., to hardware); functional access (in effect, use); experiential access, in which we may well have technical access to new technologies but do not actually experience or use them much (perhaps more as readers than as composers); and critical access, in which we are aware of the politics of use. Then, in terms of use, there can be highly competent and inventive users of relatively primitive technologies on the one hand, and very basic and/or partially competent users of state-of-the-art technologies on the other. The "digital divide" is a binary formulation that masks the complexity of the picture of digital access and use.

From another perspective—that of racialized politics—the black/white distinction is an ideological duality: depicted as one of suppression, self-empowerment, disadvantage on the one side and hegemonic assumption on the other. In the United States, the political rhetoric casts Black and Hispanic groups in a power game with the White "majority," but the changing ethnic demographic, the nature of social mobility, patterns of migration that are linked or not linked to ethnicity, intermarriage, and other factors work to variegate the racialized picture, moving it away from a polarized and dualistic conception to one more based on social class than race.

Why is it that those groups that see themselves as "minorities" (of whichever nature) choose to "tell their own stories," to use *narrative* as a rhetorical mode of expression rather than argumentation or other means? One reason could be that the group in question is disenfranchised from mainstream societal discourses, which tend to favor argumentation as the means for exploring and resolving problems. These discourses favor the powerful, as the "ownership" of logic and access to data that converts to evidence when informed by propositions is controlled by (in Toulminian terms) the warrants that allow claims and evidence to speak to each other. These invisible but powerful warrants suggest, for instance, that certain kinds of evidence (numerical data or data drawn from experimental controlled trials in research, or key witness statements and documentary evidence in law) count more than other kinds. If access to and use of these modes of argumentation enable not only participation in the discourses of the powerful, but also a direct influence on actions that arise from such exchanges, then surely such access is desirable for all minority groups. Why, then, the emphasis on telling one's own story, on the power of narrative to transform lives and life-chances?

Narrative does not transform in the same way as argumentation in our predominantly rationalistic, liberal, democratic, and fast-capitalistic world. Narrative empowers, but in a different way. It provides an inclusive, bonding function for groups ("we share the same stories"); it provides counterpoint ("there may be a hegemonic meta-narrative, but we can tell our own story too"); and it cannot be gainsayed: you cannot "disprove" a narrative. It thus preserves a space for freedom of expression and, more powerfully, freedom to define one's own histories and identities. Ultimately, though, the reversion to narrative is a position of weakness because it has accepted defeat in the politics of discourse. It is the resort of the minority to depend on narrative in a world where the powerful determine the grand narratives by which we live and exist.

Rather, access for all via a wide range of discourses and modes of expression taken to the highest level possible, rhetorical dexterity in being able to choose from a wide repertoire the best means of expression for a particular situation and purpose, access for "majority" *and* "minority" groups to the discourses of power, and a critical understanding of the affordances of the different modes of expression and how they best serve a democratic society that is concerned with social justice—all these are prerequisites for rhetoric to be able to thrive and provide the citizens of a country or of the world with the means of communication they need. To add one further dimension to the present argument: it is not only the ability to *read* the range of discourses that is important for citizens and for education to provide. It is also important to be able to create such discourses, whether they are in print or oral format, and/or in digital format. The highest levels of literacy are now those where the rhetor is able to compose in a range of genres, across a spectrum of digital platforms, and in a number of modes.

Rhetoric in Fictional Autocracies

A classic depiction of the power of rhetoric in fictional autocracies is the world of discourse created in Orwell's *Nineteen Eighty-Four* (1949). Not only is the fictional world created by Orwell a rhetorical construction—like all fiction—but this very world has its own discourse, its own rhetoric. Survival in such a world requires adherence to the discourse. On the third page of the novel, after a conventional opening in which the setting—"London, chief city of Airstrip One, itself the third most populous of the provinces of Oceania"—and the main protagonist, Winston Smith, are established, we are introduced to the language of the fictional world, Newspeak, and are directed toward a footnote: "Newspeak was the official language of Oceania. For an account of its structure and etymology, see Appendix." The Appendix, titled "The Principles of Newspeak," sets out the purpose of Newspeak:

> not only to provide a medium of expression for the world-view and mental habits proper to the devotees of Ingsoc [English Socialism], but to make all other modes of thought impossible. . . . Its vocabulary was so constructed as to give exact and often very subtle expression to every meaning that a Party member could properly wish to express, while excluding all other meanings and also the possibility of arriving at them by indirect methods . . . To give a single example.

> The word FREE still existed in Newspeak, but it could only be used in such statements as 'This dog is free from lice' or 'This field is free from weeds'. It could not be used in its old sense of 'politically free' or 'intellectually free' since political and intellectual freedom no longer existed even as concepts, and were therefore of necessity nameless. . . . Newspeak was designed not to extend but to DIMINISH the range of thought, and this purpose was indirectly assisted by cutting the choice of words down to a minimum. (303–4)

The oppression represented by Newspeak is subtle and invidious. Its design is to limit thought itself (and its products) but also the very processes of thought. As the language of Newspeak gradually replaced English in Airstrip One, so the range of thought and intellectual experience would be limited. The exercise of power to delimit rhetoric is itself an act of rhetoric, as any selection of diction of the "language of the tribe" would be; but in this case, the reduction of language to one level of meaning only (no metaphorical and/or abstract usage) is a highly political act that deprives its subjects of the power to think or create. In such a world, where vocabulary and expression are so limited, rhetoric ceases to have any influence.

There are other such dystopic worlds in literature, all different and all depicting some aspect of the control and oppression by the powerful on language itself, and on the freedoms it affords: for example, Pinter's *Mountain Language,* or satirical pieces like Swift's "A Modest Proposal."

What these linguistic dystopias help us to see is that rhetoric functions freely in a democracy, where matters are to be contested, where there is no limit on the generation of ideas, where communication between people at every level is highly prized and protected. Rhetoric is therefore an agent of freedom, a necessary dimension of human operation because it not only gets the world's work done, it also allows thought and cogitation to take place.

Rhetoric and the Media

That the political world is perceived through the lens of "the media" is no great insight: newspapers, online news, television news and radio, carrying their individual and distinctive mixes of modes (printed and/or spoken word, image, moving image, sound), frame and reframe our experience of the world every day. Scandals happen from time to time (see, for example, the Murdoch empire case regarding the media and the British government, 2011–12, resulting in the Leveson Inquiry into press freedom and the undue influence of the media on political decision making). But mostly, the influence of the media on our perception of the world goes unnoticed. Subliminally, we accept that the media control our news.

Let us take an example from the *New York Times* on an ordinary day in the first part of the twenty-first century (in this case, Wednesday, August 15, 2012). There is a small section, "World Briefing," that sits at the foot on page 6 of section A (the national and international news section) of the paper on that day. It is divided into four world sections: Europe, the Middle East, The Americas, and Asia—chillingly like the division of the world in *Nineteen Eighty-Four* into Oceania, Eurasia, and Eastasia, always with one part of the world at war with the other two who were in alliance. Under Europe, there appears a headline, "Serbia: Cousin of Genocide Suspect Draws Sentence for Harbouring Him." The Middle East section has as its headline, "Egypt: 14 Sentenced in Sinai Attack." For The Americas, "Ecuador: President Denies Decision to Grant WikiLeaks Founder Asylum." In Asia there are two stories: "China: Self-Immolations Continue" and "Japan: Cabinet Minister Visits Shrine." Two of these five stories are from the Reuters agency; the other three by individual special reporters or freelance journalists. The common element that makes up serious news is there: conflict, often relating to war or some other form of physical conflict or potential conflict. Such drama and difference from the everyday run of events (largely harmonious) makes up news stories precisely because they are not run-of-the-mill. Of the five, "Japan: Cabinet Member Visits Shrine" seems the least contentious until you read on:

> A Japanese cabinet minister visited a Tokyo war shrine on Wednesday for the first time in three years, a move that could add to already heated exchanges with neighboring South Korea over history. The visit by Jin Matsubara, the National Public Safety Commission chairman, was the first by a cabinet member to the Yasukuni shrine since the Democratic Party came to power in 2009 with vows to build closer ties with Asia. Mr Matsubara, an outspoken conservative, told Kyodo News that he visited the shrine to Japan's war dead as a private citizen, ignoring a request from Prime Minister Yoshiko Noda not to go. The visit comes as Tokyo and Seoul have clashed over compensation for World War II-era sex slaves and over disputed islands. (A6)

Although this is hardly a story in itself, the symbolic significance of the visit to the shrine and the fact that the visit "*could* add to already heated exchanges" makes it newsworthy. As we read on the wider significance becomes clearer: this is the "*first* by a *cabinet member* . . . since the Democratic Party came to power in 2009 with vows to build *closer ties with Asia.*" "First," so it is different from the ordinary. A "cabinet member," so a person of authority and status and a representative of the elected party—of the people in a democratic state—and thus significant in that respect. The fact that the visit is set against the background of a pledge to build closer ties with the rest of Asia could jeopardize that pledge and, what is more, dishonor the pledge made by the Party in the first place. We know that Mr Matsubara is "an *outspoken conservative,*" so on two counts he is running against the grain: he speaks out (those who speak out usually do so individually and against the accepted line), and he is a conservative, so (we assume) a nationalist and against wider ties with Asia. There is further conflict that Mr Matsubara's action ignores a request from the Prime Minister not to go. Finally, we get the yet wider picture: this action and its immediate context are set against the clash between "Tokyo" and "Seoul" (the personification of the two capital cities being a rhetorical figure in its own right) about World War II–era compensation regarding *sex slaves* as well as disputed islands . . . a sensational ending to a short and seemingly innocuous story.

Let us pan out from this particular section "World Briefing" to the half-page or so that is separated from the rest of the International page. Just above the short news items of "World Briefing" there is a more substantial story concerning the expediting of applications to help Iran's earthquake victims; the "Names of the Dead" (a sad, regular feature in the *New York Times* during the war in Afghanistan); an advertisement headed "Rock Stars" from Windsor Jewelers Inc.—"Today more than ever before it's important to feel confident and comfortable when it comes time to sell your jewelry or precious stones. With over 30 years of experience and integrity, Windsor Jewelers customers are always met with personalized service, unsurpassed expertise, and consistently higher process—offered right on the spot." In a smaller box at the foot of the page is one of the *New York Times*'s own advertisements: a philanthropic invitation to donate to education via the newspaper itself. The two main articles on the page—at the top—are "Crashes Underline Uganda's Spotty Record with Helicopters" and "Israel Names New Minister to Oversee Home Front."

The article we have focused on earlier is thus framed on the page by other international news, some deemed more important than others; a ritual acknowledgement of the dead in an overseas war; a commercial advertisement; and an invitation to donate. We can tell, from this page alone, that the *New York Times* aligns itself with relatively wealthy readers who might trade in their jewels or donate to a good cause and that Iran and Israel are preoccupations for the paper and its readers.

The Wider Textual Context

Within the paper as a whole, the page we have been considering sits within Section A—the main section of the newspaper. As page 6, it sits in the International section between the front page (where there is no dominating story on that day); page 2, which acts like a Contents and information page ("Inside the Times" and "The New York Times Information Directory"); page 3, which has carry-over stories from the front page; and the latter half of the main section, which shifts to national news, a campaign update (this is the year of a Presidential election), obituaries, and a New York section. There is a page devoted to Weather, some lighter features, an editorial opinion page, and, to end the section, some serious features and commentary by leading journalists. Interspersed between the news stories throughout are advertisements, large and small. To give a flavor of the market that the *Times* is reaching, advertisers include Louis Vuitton, Tiffany and Co., MaxMara ("Stegola Bootie in Black Suede $680") and other luxury goods companies, Macy's, Hilton Worldwide, and reputation.com. Their advertisement is worth quoting in full as it sheds light not only on the rhetorical audience, but also on the nature of information in the twenty-first century:

> **Private person?**
> Want to make sure you stay that way?
> Having your personal information publicly accessible on the Internet exposes you and your family to very serious and potentially costly risks. It compromises your personal privacy and increases your odds of identity theft. Luckily, we have a proven technological solution.
> Our executive concierge service starts suppressing your unprotected personal information online in as little as three minutes.
> Stop making your personal information so easy to find.

Sections B, C, and D of the newspaper are devoted to "Business Day" (though that section also includes "Sport"), "The Arts," and "Dining," respectively (the *New York Times* varies its sections, day by day).

Let us take the advertisement for reputation.com first, as advertisements pervade the paper as a whole. It indicates that the readers of the *New York Times* are likely to value discretion and privacy and protecting whatever wealth they have. The language of the advertisement has a hook to get the reader interested, in the form of the two opening questions. The first main paragraph consolidates the catch: you, your family, and costs. But the "technological solution," the "executive concierge service," and the protection of your online personal information "in as little as three minutes" drive home the point of the advertisement and are at the heart of its clever selling message. You might well accept its invitation to call now for a free privacy assessment ("normally $150 value"), persuaded by the rhetoric of the text.

More broadly, in rhetorical terms, the nature of this advertisement points to the balance between private and publicly available information that the Internet has brought about. Private communication in the form of emails, entries on social networks, and other kinds of personal engagement can be made publicly available. The borders of the private and public are blurred, so rhetoric has to deal with the extension beyond the public (its original function, at least in Europe) to the private. Borders or framings then have to be built (this company sees a business opportunity at exactly that borderline) to manage the balance between the two states of communication. The advertisement and its company play on the fears that the private may be made public.

The others sections—B, C, and D—cover the mix of news and magazine material that is typical of a contemporary newspaper. The daily paper is also available online in an e-edition, in large print weekly, or via your cell phone. There are contact details for advertising in various formats; for learning dimensions of the operation of the paper; for schools, colleges, and via "The Learning Network"; and for rights and permissions, including academic use and photocopy.

In short, the *New York Times* is more than a daily newspaper; it is a communications hub and a community, both in the United States and worldwide. It sells itself via its brand and its reputation and the continued high quality of its reporting. As a community, it is a *learning* community. It has learnt that not only does involvement in education help develop the next generations of the *New York Times*'s readers, it also signals a philanthropic and therefore morally responsible ethos, as well as extending the community more widely than its daily readership. In rhetorical terms, its power derives from the breadth, depth, and quality of its product and of its readership. Its politically left-leaning credentials, its New York cachet, its motto ("All the news that's fit to print"), and its commitment to high quality typography and accuracy as well as to the content of what it does are all part of the package.

Rhetoric, Ethics, and Power

Newspapers and their attendant modes and media are one way in which a democracy is kept alive: through challenging the orthodoxies, through a pursuit of the truth (however tentative and provisional that truth might be), through investigative journalism that explores the corridors of power, and through the presentation of conflict and debates that keep the argumentational side of human discourse at the forefront. In what other ways does rhetoric function within a democracy and support its values of free speech, maintaining the balance between the individual and the state? Can it be said to abuse power and/or be a negative presence as well as being used for democratic and largely benevolent ends?

The positive aspects of rhetoric are clear. Not only does rhetoric oil the wheels of democracy, it also enables the audience to distinguish between political cant and rhetoric on the one hand (language divorced from truth) and rhetoric in the service of truth and reasonable exchange on the other.

Rhetoric thus has an ethical basis in that it operates for the common good. It aims to aid communication so that exchanges between people can be clear, cast in the best possible way, and understood. But we need to understand rhetoric in order to see how it works and how it is being used to aid communication. It is necessary to reveal the arts of discourse in order to see the limitations of the art, the limitations of discourse itself, and the different ways in which communication can take place.

There is thus an ethical imperative to be aware of rhetoric and of its power. We also need to be resistant to influence from advertisements, political campaigns, and other highly persuasive genres of communication so that we can act in accordance with what we see as the proper course, rather than being unduly influenced by others. The important fact to recognize regarding rhetoric, then, is that it operates alongside the conduct of the world; even in speech acts, it is there carrying out the business, rituals, and exchanges of the world without any reference to physical action as we know it. It does not operate for itself, so manuals that reify its existence seem inappropriate and help to earn rhetoric its negative connotations. Rather it operates invisibly, for the most part, in the service of society. That is where it gains its power.

There are instances where rhetoric is used with negative intent. A political campaign might aim to attack another candidate by concentrating on his or her personal characteristics or history. Here the rhetoric can be "turned up," but the source of the negativity is never rhetoric itself but the intent and the substance behind it. However, rhetoric—like the messenger—can be "blamed" unfairly for the negative feel or consequences of such an approach. If rhetoric itself becomes disproportionate or inappropriate in a situation, then rhetoric itself must take the blame.

We have suggested earlier that rhetoric may have no place in an autocracy where a single voice dictates the actions of individuals in the state and the very nature of the discourses that are allowed. In such cases, rhetoric can be deployed by the autocracy to circumscribe the nature of discourse, as we have seen in fictional terms in *Nineteen Eighty-Four.* Key to such hegemony is the closing down of dialogue and debate, the appropriation of public media to serve the ends of the autocracy and to pump out good news about it, the vilification of opponents to the state, and the relentless promotion of the virtues of the leader and of the state itself.

Conclusion

There is power without rhetoric, but there is no rhetoric without power. The critical literacy and critical discourse analysis programs built in the dimension of "power" into their deliberations about the nature of literacies and the function of the powerful voice in discourse analysis. Their fundamental insight was that there is no communication that is not lop-sided in some way; in which one party holds greater power than the other.

This notion of inequity in any form of dialogic exchange requires closer examination. It is clear that in hierarchical social situations, the power resides with the "higher" party (as the metaphor has it) and the relative lack of power with the "lower" party. Take the conversation and repartee that ensues when a cleaner arrives to clean an office in which the incumbent is working, or is just arriving or leaving work. It is *usually* the office worker who has the upper hand and who initiates and closes the conversation. He or she *frames* the exchange, setting its length, the topics of conversation, the degree of intimacy, and so on. I emphasize *usually* because there will be occasions when the cleaner might initiate and frame the conversation, especially in work situations that are less hierarchical and "flatter" in management terms.

However, can it be said that a conversation between two parties who are equal, in every possible respect, is lop-sided and has power relations at play? I think it is possible to say in a situation like this—for example, two friends meeting for coffee or for a drink in a bar—that there is either no power play, or that the power that is deployed is balanced and equal. In rhetorical terms, if we wish to propose that there is no rhetoric without power, we could say that the power is finely balanced. It could easily lurch from one side or to the other side, even within a conversation, and it could be the case that what seemed to be an even, balanced conversation develops into a lop-sided one. Let us imagine, for example, that two friends meet and that at the start of the conversation, all aspects of the conversation are equal and balanced. There is a mutual exchange of greetings, of stories, of questions about each other's recent experiences. But soon it appears that one of the parties has a problem he or she wishes to share: say, for example, a relationship problem of some kind with a third party. There are then two kinds of power at play: the power of the proponent who wishes to give a prolonged account of the problem (and who therefore might "hold the stage" for minutes at a time), and the power of the listener, who might, to varying degrees, be skilled at asking the right question at the right time in order to elicit the problem from the other person. This latter kind of counseling ability can be very powerful in its own right, even though the number of utterances may appear to be small in relation to the narrative insistence of the other party. These two kinds of rhetorical power might shift backwards and forwards during the conversation and, in a mutually supportive conversation, might work in complementary fashion to point toward action or a therapeutic outcome. We would—as would the participants—be clearer about the rhetorical contribution if the conversation goes wrong, and if one side asserts more power than the other. Such an outcome would leave the weaker participant with the feeling that the discourse had not gone well, that matters seem unresolved, and that there was rhetorical inappropriateness at play. The more aggressive participant might not see a problem at all, blinkered as they might be to the effect of their own abuse of rhetorical power.

Rhetoric thus acts with the same aim as economics: to understand the *balance of power* that is the goal of human relations (as opposed to resources).

At a more public level, rhetoric too cannot act without power. A politician giving a speech at a convention or rally will deploy rhetorical devices—even if the speech is in simple, direct, heartfelt terms—to convince the audience of his or her position. This is the field of classical rhetoric: the influence of the orator of his or her audience, including not only the technical dimensions of topic, arrangement, and delivery but also that of the invocation of emotion and the moral character of the speaker. In at least two ways the politician draws on power in his or her speech: first, in terms of the choice of language, and the pace and rhythm of the delivery to persuade the audience. But at the same time, the politician's aim is both to gain power and/or to maintain it.

If rhetoric becomes divorced from the substance of the speech, or from the possibilities of real action in the world, then the pejorative connotations of the arts of discourse come into play. Words are separated from acts. Promises seem unfulfilled. Language—or whatever combinations of modes of communication is used—becomes empty and even devoid of meaning and thus of significance. The rhetoric becomes "mere" rhetoric.

But because rhetoric is fundamental to human discourse, the broader, more generous and comprehensive sense of rhetoric is seen to be deployed everywhere and, wherever it is deployed, stands in relation to the balance or imbalances of power in human social and political relations. In contemporary terms, and as distinct from the narrow political deployment in classical rhetoric, rhetoric is seen to pervade even the most intimate personal conversations and also thought processes, if we accept that (post-Vygotsky) thought derives from inner speech and inner dialogue. Part of the function of power in rhetoric is to argue out and restore equilibrium in human relations. That is why rhetoric is so important to the conduct of personal, social, and political discourse.

6

Rhetoric and Argumentation

Rhetoric is the theoretical basis for the practice and study of argumentation. The "court of appeal" in a democratic society is, as Habermas (1984) puts it, argumentation: "The rationality proper to the communicative practice of everyday life points to the practice of argumentation as a court of appeal that makes it possible to continue communicative action with other means when disagreement can no longer be headed off by everyday routines and yet is not to be settled by the direct or strategic use of force" (17–18). Everyday life in a democracy is a matter of negotiation. Although some practices will be habitual and thus seemingly "unthinking," these habits will be the result of a process of decision making informed by thought and argumentation. To take a mundane example from a fairly arcane practice in England: I decide to put out the empty and washed milk bottles for the milkman/woman to collect as he/she delivers new milk. I have previously decided when the best time to do so is, both for the deliverer's convenience and for my own and my family's. At the precise moment when I put out the empty bottles, I could well have been doing something else; but, no, I decide this is the moment to do it. All my actions are informed by weighing up the pros and cons of my timing in the balance of my day and in "the grand scheme of things." If things go wrong—someone knocks over the bottles, or I miss the milkman/woman's round—then "argumentation can act as a court of appeal," and I can work out, rationally and in collaboration, how best to do things in future.

This almost absurd instance from everyday life demonstrates that minute-to-minute decisions about what to do, and also the more engaging issue of the economics of attention, are determined by choice. Take more substantial examples: the decision to proceed with a certain intervention in the medical treatment of a patient; the advice given to a student in school who is struggling with her/his writing in the very act of composition; larger moral issues about life chances (should that banker receive a large bonus?); and large-scale national and international issues (Should we bail out a country whose economy is collapsing? Should we go to war or not?)—all these are informed by the same principles of argumentation.

It is no surprise, then, that academic life—often involving the discussion of such issues in abstract mode—should also be informed by the same principles.

For the classical theorists, rhetoric and argumentation were almost synonymous. Argument was focused on the public forum and the debates about how to live well, what action to take in a state on behalf of the individual, or which moral path to take. It was principally, we assume, oral in nature and application. Even more narrowly for Aristotle, it was a case that rhetoric was the "art of persuasion"—an epithet often used to define argument and argumentation. As is made clear elsewhere in the present book, neither rhetoric nor argumentation are seen today as merely to do with persuasion; that is just one of many functions of argument, which also clarifies, defends, amuses, and resolves, yet also fulfils other functions.

We also need to separate rhetoric from argumentation for the purposes of the present book. Argumentation is one field of rhetoric. Rhetoric also covers other meta-genres of communication, such as narrative, description, lyric poetry, everyday (non-argumentational and non-argumentative) discussion and exchange, and the distinction between fiction and non-fiction. Our definition, in opposition to that of Aristotle, is of rhetoric as "the arts of discourse" and argumentation as "a meta-genre of communication where a person takes a position and gives logical (or quasi-logical) reasons and/or evidence for his/her views." In other words, the emphasis in these definitions is on the communication and how it is informed by purpose, context, politics, motivation, and so on; not merely on the function of persuasion or any other specific function.

Why is argumentation important in—indeed, essential to—a democratic society? In a tyranny, argument is closed down and not tolerated. There is an orthodoxy and a way of conducting oneself and one's actions. Life is monolithic. Argument—for example, the questioning of the hegemonic authority—can lead to imprisonment and/or death. It can also induce in the population a fear of expression, of taking opposition to ideas, or of debate. In a (truly) democratic society, on the other hand, the understanding and, if possible, resolution of difference is essential. Such resolution has to be reached, often by difficult argumentation, in order to reach consensus and thus to be able to act. Such a process applies to individual lives and relationships, to local issues (such a planning permissions and objections), and to national and international government. Such a process does not exclude one possible outcome of argumentation, which is to "agree to differ." But such an outcome does not usually lead to action because consensus is not reached. Rather, it leads to impasse.

Why has argumentation risen to public consciousness again, after a period in which is seems to have receded?

Part of the answer is in reaction to a period in which narrative modes of communication—storytelling, life histories, narrative methodologies in social science research, media predilections for "a storyline"—have dominated. Narrative, in a sense, allows no response other than another narrative. It is not subject to testing (other than to "real life"), and you cannot argue with it. Only if the narrative is proposed as a theory or as part of an ideological position—as in the narrative of a particular period of history, for example—can it be seen as a quasi-argument and thus questioned and opposed. The notion of narrative as a primary act of mind or a human paradigm is understandable but only tells part of the story. Lyricism (the celebration of a moment), description (the depiction of a state or place or person), and argument (a logical, rather than chronological mode), as well as other modes of communication, all need to be taken into account in theories of mind or paradigms for human action and consciousness.

Another reason for the rise in argumentation is a return to a rationalist, re-enlightenment moment in history. Clifford and Leslie Siskin of New York University are leading a Re:Enlightenment project: one that brings together academics and public figures from a range of social science, humanities, and arts disciplines in a Re:Englightenment Collaboratory. Key to the conception is the notion of enacting re:enlightenment through public engagement and through a re-evaluation of institutions, epistemologies, genres and social practices, new technologies, and their inter-relationship.

Another part of the answer is that there has been an international rise of interest in democratic representation, both in societies where previously democracy has been a distant, "other" notion and in digital social networking. Often the two are related. First, one should say about the rise of interest in democratic action that there is skepticism about the promotion of democratic values and systems by the "West." In a declining American and European economic context, it is somewhat ironic that these countries should be promoting and advocating "democracy" to countries that are doing better economically and that have different political systems. The drive to democracy, from this more skeptical perspective, is intimately tied in with materialism and—not surprisingly, but no less inappropriately—with the interests of big business corporations and the selling of their wares to non-democratic countries. At worst, this advocacy looks like a last-ditch attempt to shore up failing economies. Nevertheless, in some countries the prospect of democracy is intimately related to personal freedoms, to the free exchange of ideas, and, indeed, to economic growth. Here, as in the "Arab spring" of the first part of this decade, the desire for the democratic turn is accompanied by argument and the need for more argumentation, sometime spilling over into violence where it meets the uncompromising force of the state. In cases such as the “emancipation” of Tunisia, Libya, Egypt, and Syria in the period 2010–13, the argument takes on physical forms of resistance and aggression, resulting in internal political strife, conflict, injury, injustice, and death. These results are not what Habermas (1984) meant by argumentation as a court of appeal where disagreement was “not to be settled by the direct or strategic use of force” (18). These are cases where argumentation has either not been allowed to take place, or has been suppressed, thus resulting in recourse to force and, sometimes, violence. Or, indeed, where the argument has reached such a degree of pitch and non-resolution that words can no longer contain the need for change.

The rise of interest in argumentation, then, is a result of a complex combination of factors. A further dimension is digitally driven social networking innovation. By reference to this social phenomenon, we mean not only social network sites such as Facebook, but also means by which academics and the general population come together to solve problems online. Crowdsourcing, specialist interest groups, blogs, Wikipedia, and online colloquia are examples of such networking that operate outside the institutional framework for the generation and production of knowledge. One could criticize these innovations for working toward a weak consensual view of knowledge that is the result of the accretion of different views and perspectives, but the grit of argumentation in the production of knowledge is evident in questioning, challenging, and refinement of accepted truths. Perhaps more positively, the realization of the provisional nature of knowledge and its grounding in dialogic exchange is testimony to the live, argumentational nature of knowledge production and dissemination.

To return to the wider theme of the relationship between argumentation and rhetoric, we could say that the increased interest in argumentation in demotic, academic, professional, and governmental contexts puts an onus on rhetoric to sharpen the tools of argumentation so that debate is clear, based on evidence, logical, understood in its wider social and political functions, and fit for purpose. Rhetoric thrives when it is *needed.* It is a means by which to make sense of the function of argumentation in societies, so as a theory it need not build up a bank of devices, a set of *progymnasmata* (exercises), or an orthodoxy of approach, but rather oil the wheels of democracy by providing the following: an awareness of the power and limitations of communication in whichever mode or modes, a sense of the affordances of each of the modes, an understanding of the relationships between modes and media, and a critical perspective on communication and action and how they work in relationship to each other. Nor are rhetoric and argumentation to be seen as purely intellectual, rationalist activities; passion and feeling are as much part of the everyday and political dimensions of rhetoric. A *contemporary* rhetoric must acknowledge the range of thought and feeling that goes into communication.

If rhetoric can be considered as "the arts of discourse," which arts are employed in the development and maintenance of good argumentation?

Argumentation and Learning

Again, we can use Habermas (1984) to start the exploration of the importance of argumentation to learning: "Argumentation plays an important role in learning processes as well. Thus we call a person rational who, in the cognitive-instrumental sphere, expresses reasonable opinions and acts efficiently; but this rationality remains accidental if it is not coupled with the ability to learn from mistakes, from the refutation of hypotheses and from the failure of interventions" (18).

The first assumption here is that we would (like to) "call a person rational" in a reasonable society: one who not only expresses reasonable opinions and acts "efficiently" but who also can listen to and appreciate others' opinions and arguments. What follows is more relevant to our developing argument that rhetoric and argumentation are essential, not only to society but also to learning in contemporary societies: "this rationality remains accidental if it is not coupled with the ability to *learn from mistakes, from the refutation of hypotheses* and from the *failure of interventions*" (Habermas 1984, 18). The refutation of hypotheses is the most obviously central characteristic of argument, linked closely to the freedom to oppose, to refute, and, indeed, to rebut refutations. Such refutation can be in relation to various elements of an argument: to use Toulminian terms, refutation can be of the proposed relationship between a proposition or claim and its "warrant"; it can be between the evidence, data, or grounds and the warrant; and it can also be between the "backing" and the warrant; that is, in the very assumption that a particular set of values or disciplinary practices require a certain set of warrants (for this, read methodologies and methods) to validate them.

But "learning from mistakes" and from "the failure of interventions" are also key to argumentation within rhetorical theory and within democratic societies. As I write, a bill to reform (indeed, to marketize) the National Health Service is currently going through the UK parliament. It is facing problems and has already come back to parliament with 136 revisions to the original proposal. However, there is criticism from all political parties that the fundamental principles of the bill are flawed and that the government needs to go "back to the drawing board," to first principles. Learning from this "mistake" could be costly to the government, not only in time and resource, but also in reputation. It may take a surface approach and attempt to see through the bill, with some further amendments, on the basis of its majority in parliament—this might be seen as a "purely rhetorical" approach. A more deeply rhetorical approach would be to engage democratic principles—not just its democratically elected majority in the parliament—and admit the failure of its intervention, learn from its mistake, and rethink the whole problem. The reasons politicians are usually reluctant to learn from mistakes is that they are driven, ultimately, not by the good of the nation but by their desire to stay in power.

Argument is itself a contentious term. It refers to everyday arguments—tiffs, spats, rows, argy-bargies—that take place in domestic, professional, and public contexts and that at the same time appall and fascinate, divide and unite us. But it also refers to the most highly prized type of academic discourse: something that is deemed essential to a thesis, to an article in a research journal, to a dissertation, essay, and to many other kinds of writing within schools and the academy.

When the whole range of definitions of argument is considered, there are a number of aspects of argument that are highlighted: the two broad definitions cited previously, but also "the working out of a third point from two given points" in logic and in mathematics and astronomy. More specifically, with regard to mathematics: "the angle, arc or other mathematical quantity from which another required quantity may be deduced." *Argument* also meant to Swift and his contemporaries a synopsis of the plot: each of the chapters of *Gulliver's Travels* begins with a short "argument." The argument in this case is pure chronicle, the bare bones of the narrative. Embodied in such a definition is the notion that a narrative can signify an argument and that what follows in a time sequence or narrative sequence (not always the same thing) somehow is a causal result of what came before: the principle of *post hoc ergo propter hoc* (after this, therefore because of this). Parables and fables are examples of compressed narratives that are clearly and explicitly argumentational. But, if you accept the *post hoc* . . . principle, all anecdotes, all stories, and all novels are arguments to one degree or another. The two meta-genres, narrative and argument, simply operate in different ways: the first, largely inductively, and the second largely deductively.

A final aspect of argument is the process of argument: argumentation. This is a technical term, distinguishing the processes of argument from the phenomenon, the product, the thing itself.

The Importance of Argument in Society

In a January 2009 issue of *The New York Review of Books* (Link 2009), China's Charter 08 was translated into English with a preface and postscript by Perry Link. Charter 08 was composed in 2008, conceived in admiration of the Czechoslovakian Charter 77. As Link says, it "calls not for ameliorative reform of the current political system, but for an end to some of its essential features, including one-party rule, and their replacement with a system based on human rights and democracy" (54). The charter sets out the historical context, a set of fundamental principles, and a section on "what we advocate." In other words, it is radical, polemical, and, in an authoritarian context, highly risky. Link records in his post-script that a number of signatories of the charter were, in the days running up to its announcement on December 10, 2008, visited in their homes by the police for what is described as a "chat" and threatened with prison. "Do you want three years in prison," they are quoted as saying, "or four?" Even in that short sentence, the uncontestable power of authoritarianism is present. Indeed, Liu Xiaobo, one of the first signers of the charter and a veteran of Tiannanmen Square in 1989, was taken away by police on December 8 and in late January 2009 was still in detention "somewhere in the suburbs of Beijing." My point here is not so much about the politics of China as about the importance of argument in an authoritarian society even when it is denied.

Not that democracies are pure when it comes to detention, nor the free passage of argument and argumentation. We only have to consider the war against terrorism, the reasons proffered for the invasion of Iraq, and the establishment and use of Guantánamo Bay to find actions taken without argument and without the application of valid evidence. The proposed closing of Guantánamo—the very first act promised by the new president of the United States—seemed like the act of a *deus ex machina* until we remember that it is the result of a democratic process and that the dismantling of Guantánamo and its supporting infrastructure of fear and, more importantly, a proper legal and judicial review of its detainees will require a great deal of patient, detailed, and passionate argumentation. By 2013, however, it had not taken place.

Democracies, in general, are seen to be the natural home for argument because they are in tune with change: creating, understanding, tolerating, and resolving difference, where possible. Argument is prized in true democracies, just as it was in the crucible of pre-Athenian and Athenian democracy. It is seen as the *sine qua non,* the very life-blood of democracy in action. Behind the centrality of argument in such societies is the notion that "truth emerges from the clash of opposites" or that the quality of life can be enhanced by arguing out the best way forward; that by, at first, polar opposition and then by degrees, refinement of a proposition takes place until it becomes workable law and practice. This is the function argument has within democratic societies. One has to accept that, in the end, the decision on how to move forward may be taken by one person, or that he or she may be the leader of a party that has a numerical majority, but the base of the iceberg of that process is argumentation.

Imagine, for a moment, a world without argument. It would either be an authoritarian or tyrannical state, or like the island of Tennyson's lotus-eaters, where "All round the coast the languid air did swoon/Breathing like one that hath a weary dream"—a land where intellect and difference are suspended. So simply to wake up, to be fully conscious, is to be ready for argumentation; for discussion "with edge." You might think Buddhism worked toward a state where there was none of the pull-and-push of Hegelian dialectic, no division, a melting of self and the world—and so, in essence, it is, but of a very different kind from Tennyson's One of the most interesting strands in the International Society for the Study of Argumentation conferences, which happen every four years in Amsterdam, is on "Buddhist argumentation." Buddhists enjoy argument as both a space in which they can play at dialecticism in which the world is trapped, or use it to break through to higher ground.

Back in the world, and more locally, negotiations over a curriculum, or debates about what should go in a core module for a new Masters program, require argument. In our professional lives, argumentation plays an important part because, again, it is a means of resolving difference, a way of exploring an idea to its logical conclusion, and a means by which a range of views can be expressed, arrayed, clarified, and then used to form the basis for a decision, based on the best available evidence. You may not end up agreeing with the way forward in a particular situation; but if you have had a chance to express your views, challenge existing orthodoxies, and make a difference to the outcome, you feel enfranchised and engaged. You can sidle off and grumble if you lose the argument, or you can marshal your resources and re-enter the argumentational fray. Those who can see the process for what it is worth, who can see the limitations of power and see that argumentational exchange is a force for good, can sometimes prize the process more than the outcome. There is a danger in that position, of course, because you can end up winning the arguments or enjoying the argumentational process, but losing the battle for *what happens* once a consensus of sorts is agreed.

Even more locally, arguments take place in everyday life, in domestic and personal circumstances, from time to time. Sometimes, it has to be admitted, the generation of an argument can lead to division and estrangement, even to violence (though it is hoped that argumentation, in both personal and political settings, would be a key way of resolving difference without recourse to violence). In most cases, however, arguments or tiffs, spats, and rows have a number of functions. They are often triggered by something that is not the real cause of the difference. The real causes emerge during the course of the exchange, but the functions include clarification of position, catharsis, recognition, discovery of the truth, and defense of your position. Rarely does a personal argument end up doing what the participants think it does: persuading the other party to accept your point of view.

In fact, argument and argumentation are not the same as persuasion, despite Aristotle's definition of rhetoric (one of argument's principal theoretical frameworks) as "the art of persuasion." Advertisements persuade, physical presence sometimes persuades, but they don't always argue their case. Persuasion can be seen as one of the functions of argument, alongside clarification, catharsis, amusement, defense, attack, and winning, as well as the discovery of ideas and the creation and resolution of difference. Having separated the phenomenon of argument and its process, argumentation, from the function of persuasion, there is one other ground-clearing act that needs to be done before we can go on to explore the theoretical hinterland of argument in education. Argument, while properly associated with rationality, is often opposed to passion and feeling. As suggested earlier in this chapter, rather than accept such an easy polarity, argument and rationality can be seen as deeply implicated in passion and feeling. There are many examples of this close relationship in personal and public life. One such example centers on the notion of *intuition:* you will hear people say "I decided that intuitively" or "My intuition told me that . . ." Rather than see intuition as diametrically opposed to argument and argumentation, it is possible to see it as *high speed rationality*.

Theory of Argumentation

There is a long history of the theory of argumentation, mostly associated with rhetoric from pre-Athenian times to the contemporary rhetorics of Burke (1969), American composition theorists, the visual/verbal explorations of W.J.T Mitchell (1986) and Lanham (1993) (the Chicago school), and Gunther Kress, Theo van Leeuwen, and colleagues' work on multimodality (e.g., Kress and van Leeuwen 2001). The battle between philosophy or logic on the one hand, and rhetoric on the other, has waged throughout that history, with sometimes one in the ascendancy, and sometimes the other. They appear to be symbiotic: logic needs rhetoric and vice-versa. To compress the debates into a simple equation: logic and philosophy are concerned with substance and method; rhetoric is concerned with process and communication, with the arts of discourse in personal, political, and aesthetic contexts. For the particular purposes of the present chapter, the focus will be on two figures that provide a backdrop to the interest in argumentation in education: Vygotsky, a social psychologist, and the philosopher Habermas. Neither is a rhetorician, though both bodies of work draw on communication and the arts of discourse and have implications for the fields of rhetoric and argumentation. Both have key things to say about the relationship between argument and education, from pre-school through to university level and beyond.

Vygotsky

The most extraordinary and significant statement from Vygotsky's work with regard to argument is the connection he makes between reflection and argumentation. With characteristic (not always empirically founded) logical verve, he writes,

> there is an indubitable genetic connection between the child's arguments and his reflections. This is confirmed by the child's logic itself. The proofs first arise in the arguments between children and are then transferred within the child . . . The child's logic develops only with the increasing socialisation of the child's speech and all of the child's experience . . . Piaget has found that precisely the sudden transition from preschool age to school age leads to a change in the forms of collective activity and that on this basis the child's thinking also changes. 'Reflection,' says this author, 'may be regarded as inner argumentation . . .'
>
> If we consider this law, we will see very clearly why all that is internal in the higher mental functions was at one time external . . . In general we may say that *the relations between the higher mental functions were at one time real relations between people* . . .
>
> We might therefore designate the main result to which we are brought by the history of the child's cultural development as a sociogenesis *of the higher forms of behaviour.* (Vygotsky 1991, 32–41)

The excerpt is quoted at length to demonstrate the steps via which Vygotsky comes to the conclusion that argumentation was once external. Much of the thinking is informed by Vygotsky's well-known theory of the ways in which cultural and historical patterning informs cognitive and conceptual development. But there are a number of striking connections made in the previous statement that shed particular light on argumentation.

First is the connection between arguments and reflections. Putting aside whether the connection is indubitably genetic or not, the link suggests that reflection is more than a miasmic, static read-off from experience. Rather, it is seen as dynamic mental space informed by social arguments (the sociogenetic aspect); furthermore, it is in itself a dialectical operation in which the dialogue is both with experience/the outside world on the one hand, and with ideas themselves in the internal process of reflecting/thinking.

Second, Vygotsky's statement that "all that is internal in the higher mental functions was at one time external" can be broken down into two propositions: one, that there are relations between the higher mental functions; and two, that these relations "were at one time real relations between people." We need not spend too much time on the notion that there are relations between the higher mental functions, except to say that hierarchical ("vertical," "synchronic," and " paradigmatic") and relational ("horizontal," "diachronic," and "syntagmatic") thinking is fundamental to subject and disciplines in various combinations and with varying emphases. Not all these higher mental functions are grounded in verbal language; some are based on other languages, such as dance, the visual arts, architecture, and music. Most are multimodal in their actual operation in the world. Nevertheless, these hierarchical and relational connections are central to and critical to the operation of learning and teaching in disciplines in higher education. Learning your way across a grid of such relations is learning to become competent (and thus worthy of the award of academic degrees) in the various disciplines, subjects, and fields. The development of the higher mental functions is associated with the entry to and success within higher education.

The proposition that such interconnections "were at one time real relations between people" is the astonishing idea. The logic follows from earlier propositions in the previous quotation and in Vygotsky's work more generally about the formation of thinking in young children. At the higher education level, let us consider the implications of the statement. Part of the underlying justification for the statement is that the development of disciplinary practices, historically, is the result of "real relations between people." The birth of English Literature as a university subject in England, for example, arose from a dialectical need expressed, over a number of years, by workers' educational associations and particularly by women studying within and beyond those associations, for an alternative to classics as a central (but male-only) humanities discipline at The University of Oxford and subsequently elsewhere. The history of that evolution is well documented in Dixon (1991). As the emergent subject established itself in the university repertoire, discussions between academics, students, and others would determine its development. Specifically, patterns of expectation and convention, for example, what counts as a good argument in the discipline, the nature of the canon, the *modus operandi* in seminars, the journals created, the discourses and Discourse of the discipline—all these would establish themselves and be adapted further. Thus, the lines and conduits along which thought and argumentation take place are determined, distinguishing the discipline from others. When these conduits for thought and argumentation become too over-prescribed, a reaction sets in that changes, with Hegelian inevitability, the nature of discourses that are "allowed" within the disciplinary framework that has been established. Such "real relations between people" are largely mediated by speech, social power, and economics.

A case like the emergence and development of English Literature in England has 150 years of history, and Vygotsky's phrase "at one time" can refer to far-distant history (too far to be evidentially researched and validated) or to a more compressed time-scale. In a much more specific way, Bazerman (1988) charts the development of the experimental article in science, demonstrating how a vehicle for argumentation in a meta-discipline like science emerged from social interactions between people, and relations between people and the material world.

To give a much more contemporary example, consider the relations between a student on an undergraduate course and his or her lecturer/teacher. The student submits a piece of writing. Explicitly and/or implicitly, the lecturer proves feedback in spoken or written form that suggests to the student how he/she might "improve," that is, might get closer to and exceed the expected discourses of the discipline at undergraduate level. Such interaction, at its best, is specific, extensive, formative, and positively critical. Whatever its quality, it is *always* part of a set of institutional and personal power relations. Thus "real relations between people," different in nature from the previous two examples of the birth of a discipline or the creation of the scientific article, determine the operation of the higher mental functions.

Habermas

At the core of Habermas's work is the notion that communicative competence is more than being able to generate and understand utterances and sentences. He suggests that we are constantly making claims. These claims are often implicit, and often they are not backed up by evidence; but the exchange of claims appears to be part of the fabric of human interaction. As McCarthy puts it in the introduction to his translated edition of Habermas's (1984) major work on rationality and communication, *The Theory of Communicative Action,*

> we are constantly making claims, even if usually only implicitly, concerning the validity of what we are saying, implying or presupposing—claims, for instance, regarding the truth of what we say in relation to the objective world; or claims concerning the rightness, appropriateness, or legitimacy of our speech acts in relation to the shared values and norms of our social lifeworld; or claims to sincerity or authenticity in regard to the manifest expressions of our intentions and feelings. (x)

Claims do require evidence—or at least they need a degree of validation that might come from logical consistency, the character of the speaker, the nature of the context, or via methodological support—and they are more likely to be accepted if they are supported in a number of these ways. At the same time, they can be challenged, defended, and qualified. As suggested previously, claims might be strengthened by being subjected to challenge. Indeed, the very nature of making claims (one ingredient in the making of an argument) is that they invite counter-claim. Habermas's particular contribution to the thinking about communication is his insistence that mutual understanding without coercion is the basis of rationality and of human consensus and social action.

Thus, to varying degrees, and in contexts ranging from the everyday and seemingly mundane at one end of the spectrum to high politics at the other end, argumentation is part of the fabric of human existence. Its status as a "court of appeal" suggests that it can be made explicit and raised to a level of social consciousness where the best way forward can be debated. But it is also implicit in the conduct of human interaction, even when it is not acknowledged as such. Such a fundamental and central role for argumentation is important for the thesis of the present chapter. For example, tacit and implicit practices in higher education often need to be made more explicit in order to help teachers understand what they are asking students to do and, in turn, for students to understand what they are being asked to do.

Like Vygotsky's statement on the genesis of the higher mental functions, Habermas's insight into the centrality of a process, argumentation, which is at the heart of primary, secondary, and tertiary education, is a crucial one. Being rational means being able to learn from mistakes, from critiquing half-formed hypotheses, and from the failure of interventions in experimental and non-experimental situations. Such openness to learning via the process of argumentation is one to which teachers, lecturers, and professors, at their very best, are amenable; and one that pupils and students have to learn to develop if they are to progress within their chosen subjects, disciplines, or fields of inquiry.

Visual Argumentation

There is no doubt that images can persuade, and there are countless examples from advertising through photojournalism to fine art that could be cited. But can still images, sequences of still images, and moving images *argue* without words? If so, how do they operate? And is it the same kind of argument that Toulmin (2003) would find to be argument, with claims, evidence, rebuttals, warrants, and backing as part of its armory, its architecture? Some would argue that visual argumentation is just not possible.

It is, however, important to consider the possibility of visual argumentation in thinking more generally about the importance of argument in education. Here, education is taken to be the whole sum of education—not just schooling. Consideration of visual argumentation is important because it is ubiquitous, subliminal, sometimes (like words) insidious, visceral, and engaging, as well as consciously designed, a language and semiotic of its own, and a universal agent of communication. We need to be aware of the ways it operates so that we can accept it via a suspension of disbelief, or resist it, and/or *transform* it in some way (the key act of learning and education). By visual *argumentation* as opposed to visual *persuasion,* what is meant is a focus on the way the visual articulates, or is articulated, in order to communicate and possibly persuade.

The first example combines the visual with the verbal. It is simply a photograph of a kettle alongside verbal text.

The verbal text of the advertisement is a mini-argument in its own right:

> We've been designing products for over 30 years and we're constantly looking at ways to perfect them. Out latest creation is something special. The kettle's unique double wall jacket retains heat, so once you've boiled the kettle, any water left inside stays warm for longer. Which means, next time it's boiled you'll use less electricity, saving you money and helping save the environment. More tea anyone?

In fact, it is not just a good piece of advertising copy; it follows classical structuring possibilities of the kind mapped out by Aristotle, Quintilian, Cicero, and others. The appeal to trust to establish the position ("We've been designing products for over 30 years . . ."), the future-looking vision and commitment (". . . and we're constantly looking at ways to perfect them"), the distinctiveness of the case ("Our latest creation is something special"), the *narratio* or facts of the case ("The kettle's . . . stays warm for longer"), development ("Which means . . . helping save the environment"), and, finally, the *peroratio* ("More tea anyone?"), answering the cleverly nuanced invitation of the title ("Anyone for *green* tea?"). There is no need to labor the effect of the verbal language: it's witty, directed at a certain class of people (those who perhaps have been thinking of switching to a healthier tea, or those who want to do something for global warming), concise, fleeting, and persuasive.

The words could probably carry this advertisement on their own, but they are articulated with, joined with, an image of the kettle in question. Words and image have the same stylish economy; the elegance of design; the simplicity. Probably, the image could not, in this case, carry the burden of the argument, nor fulfil the function of persuasion. In this case, the image appears to function as an illustration but also as a bit more than that: as an icon, as the object of desire. It could be said that the highlighting of a domestic image like this does give resonance to the kettle. It is framed in a particular way, photographed in isolation from its packaging, its kitchen counter, its users, and thus given a prominence and life it does not usually have. It infers and suggests an argument but does not quite deliver an argument in the Toulminian sense of a claim, or series of claims supported by evidence. But it *stakes its claim to be recognized* as worthy of consideration. It is, in a sense, a *proposition.*

But can the visual argue without the help of words? Consider the famous photograph of Jean Shrimpton at the Melbourne Cup in 1965. It has been used before (Black and Muecke 1992) and is easily accessible.

The suggestion here is that certain single, still images can embody an argument through the tension between two elements in the image. In this case, Shrimpton, in her state-of-the-art London look of 1965, is foregrounded against the background of the conventional race-going look for women in Melbourne at that time. Her very presence at the Melbourne Cup caused controversy in the Australian press: it was a provocation, a counterpoint, an invitation to do something not only about dress, but about the associations of femininity and womanhood implied by this particular dress. Shrimpton, both at the occasion and in the photograph, is the antithesis to the middle-class race-goers thesis—except that they did not realize they were the thesis until she came along. This is "discussion with edge" of a cultural kind. Furthermore, the photograph is symbolic, not only of a moment in fashion and identity, but also of a pivotal moment in culture, suggesting a tension between constraint and liberation, propriety and impropriety, Melbourne and London at the time, and sets of values underpinning those positions.

There is an equally famous, or infamous case of two photographs alongside each other. The photograph, titled *Legs,* is by Mike Wells and shows two billboards in London, around the late 1970s, early 1980s. The one on the left is an advertisement for Aristoc tights; and the other is a Christian Aid advertisement showing what appear to be an old man's withered and bony legs. Whether the two advertisements were deliberately juxtaposed by the advertising agency, or whether it was the photographer himself who framed and captured the irony of the contiguity, is not known. The point is that two images alongside each other, with similarities and, in this case, stark differences, set up a tension that appears to suggest argument. If the two images were to change places, there would be no significant difference in the proposition: that comparisons of this kind make one reflect on inequity, on the ravages of age, on the unfairness of where you were born, and your lot in the world.

The suggestiveness and openness of the visual—its openness to interpretation, its refusal to be defined by words, its seemingly direct communication, its instantaneity—are contained to a degree by a *sequence* of images, where the *post hoc, propter hoc* principle comes into play. A well-established genre in this kind of visual argumentation is the photo-essay, often of a journalistic kind. Sometimes the photographs are accompanied by small or large captions or by a verbal essay, but the images can stand on their own and provide their own argument. In doctoral research with 12 and 13 year olds (Andrews 1992), using photographs that were used to sequence narratives and arguments, students said that once they were committed to a narrative sequence, it would change the narrative to change the sequence but that it was possible to move the sequence around if the photographs were depicting an argument. This perception that the *post hoc, propter hoc* principle only goes so far in argument is a significant one, where an extra level of abstraction enables composition and recomposition of a sequence of particularities designed to convey the argument.

From the point of the photo-essay, it is an easy step to the multimodal slide sequence, as in Sam Strickland's brilliant *Engladesh* (2008), designed as a final submission for a masters in photojournalism at City University London, which combines sequences of photographs with voiceover, music, and some words, but with the images as the central spine of the narrative and arguments; and thence on to moving image: film and television.

In summary, as far as visual argumentation is concerned, it is clear that images can be used as evidence for claims and propositions. In this role, they go beyond illustration to providing evidence in a court of law, as incontrovertible "fact" in support of a thesis, or as a diagram of a process that is to be followed and that is based on a procedure that has been expressed verbally. But images can fulfil the function of claims and propositions themselves because of their multiple signification, and especially if they are juxtaposed with other images and/or they are set in a sequence that allows logical or quasi-logical connection. Their articulation constitutes an *argument* rather than merely persuading.

The Importance of Argument and Rhetoric

Argument is important because it rehearses in public life the various sides to a problem or a point of dispute. Its very identification of the sore points, or the points of tension in a culture or an individual's emotional life, is the first stage of solving a problem. By drilling down at the point of dispute, which is what school and academic life at their best are very good at doing, the elements and dimensions of the tension and dispute are laid bare: their "backing" revealed; the sets of values, theories, and ideologies underlying their very characterization made transparent; and the possibilities of reconciliation and "moving forward" are laid out.

The next stage is the mapping out of those possibilities, the arguing for this plan of action of that plan; for selecting from a range of possibilities the best one—the one that marries short- and long-term objectives, the one that is for the greatest good of a community, an institution, a department, a nation, and/or a personal life trajectory.

If we were to slow down the process of decision making so that the lineaments of each micro-decision were made visible, as well as the more protracted passage of major decisions, we would see a process of argumentation at work. Helping young people, old people, people of indeterminate age to understand those processes, to give them power to challenge received ideas and generate new ones, to appreciate and compose arguments that are monomodal or in mixed modes . . . this is what education can do, and why I think that argument and argumentation have a very important part to play, not only in education, but in the reasonable progress and renewal of social and political relations more generally. As such, argumentation is a crucial component of a theory of contemporary rhetoric.

7

Rhetoric and Framing

In *Re-Framing Literacy* (Andrews 2011) the case was put forward for an accent on *framing* as a key critical and creative act for the composer, as well as for the reader/audience, in any communicative transaction. Framing is especially salient when it comes to the arts, where the composer and the audience are particularly conscious of, or at least draw attention to, what is framed and how it is framed. If we were to depict rhetoric in allegorical and idealized terms, framing would be one of the key twenty-first century tools in its armory. It is a modest element or device, too, often not drawing attention to itself; and yet it operates in every act of communication in important ways, defining the social and communicative *parameters* of the exchange.

Framing is not a theory. It's a device operating as part of a theory. The point of the present chapter is to illustrate how framing operates within a theory of rhetoric, and why framing is so important to rhetoric.

Why "Framing" and Not "Frames"?

Goffman (1986) and subsequent education theorists and practitioners have developed theories of framing that build their thinking on the tangible notion of *frames*. These are close in nature to *schemata*. Although some schemata are intangible and invisible in that they are socially conventional constructs that guide the operation of behavior, they are nevertheless phenomena or entities. Similarly, the notion of genres as social action (Miller 1984) comes close to the idea of frames. What these phenomena have in common is that they are socially situated patterns of behavior that have linguistic and other modal characteristics. The emphasis on defining such phenomena is akin to an emphasis on nouns: these are things, notions, constructed ideas, or phenomena that can be defined and classified.

The accent of *framing* in the present theory of contemporary rhetoric is significant. It moves the debate about communication toward *process* rather than (albeit sometimes invisible) product. The focus of interest is on a verb; indeed, a present participle. The suggestion is that rhetoric is always in motion, relevant to, and informing the acts of communication in the past, *present,* and future. The emphasis on the process of framing for both rhetor and audience allows the theory of contemporary rhetoric to be both simple and elegant. It does not have an architecture that is unwieldy and more complicated than the phenomenon it is examining. On the contrary, it is akin to light scaffolding, or to sketches of a building that can run through to fully fledged designs and plans. The important thing is the communication itself, not the theory that informs it.

Some Examples

To begin the discussion of the relationship of framing and rhetoric, here are three examples of social and communicative encounters. Each requires a different kind of framing; each sits within an overarching theory of rhetorical choice and delivery.

First, a public lecture at a university. A guest speaker is invited and flies around the world to give the lecture. The occasion has already been framed in a number of ways, partly to define its nature and partly to encourage an audience to attend. The means for the initial framing are posters advertising the lecture, located in the university and in the students' union; online notices and reminders, conveyed via email and on intranets as well as on the internet; and formal individual invitations, some of which are printed on a card and require a response. Behind these formats are the fact that this lecture is one of a series of three "public lectures" held by a faculty at the university and expressly intended to welcome and include anyone and everyone who wishes to attend. There is an important element of institutional framing in this fact because—in effect—the university is inviting anyone to attend the lecture without payment. The move is part of a general trend to "public engagement," thus reaching out beyond the traditional frame of the university (bound by regulations, fee payment, registration, degree-awarding powers, etc.).

Once the invitations are out and the speaker confirmed, the occasion itself is framed in particular ways that enhance its social dimension. Tea is served beforehand. The lecture itself, and the lecturer, are introduced, setting them within the aspirations of the Faculty, the university, and its international work. The lecture, once over, is followed by a question-and-answer session from the floor, monitored by the chair, who decides how long that part of the proceedings is to take. The whole lecture, plus Q&A, is followed by drinks and canapés to encourage further informal discussion and social bonding. Food and drink serves an important purpose here: not only to keep people going through an end-of-the-day occasion, but to forge social interaction and to welcome members of the public to the university. There are other frames that we could cite that are at play in such an occasion as this, but these are the immediate ones that help to shape and define the event.

What of the actual lecture itself? The particular lecture in question was on rhythms of social justice and the place of hip hop in literacy development, and on the relationship between in-school and out-of-school activities in this regard. The speaker[1] began his 45-minute lecture with an autobiographical account of his early life and why this pertained to the theme of social justice. The *narrative* and *autobiographical* nature of this introduction served a number of purposes, rhetorically. It established the speaker in relation to his audience; it provided a rationale for the personal drive and momentum of the issues at stake; and it was engaging, as good narratives are, and thus served to "draw in" the audience to the argument that followed. In these senses, narrative operated with argumentational function (see Andrews 1989)—what we might call the *narratio* of classical rhetoric, or the laying out of the facts of the case—and partly engaged the audience through its personal and emotive import. The opening narration was followed by a more conventional academic presentation, with interspersed video clips of hip hop in performance. But that academic delivery was infused with commitment, passion, and energy, particularly at points in the lecture that moved beyond the conventional academic frame into committed and informed *invocation* for the audience to subscribe to the argument. The exploration of the rhetorical frame—or to put it more dynamically, the creative and critical *framing* of the talk—was a talking point for the audience as they enjoyed the frame-breaking, inspirational nature of the occasion. Given that the audience was mixed, involving students, faculty staff (both academic and professional), honorary guests, and members of the public, the pitching of the talk and management of such diversity was critically important.

Following the lecture, requests for audio versions, or of slides, were attempts to capture vestiges of the occasion itself. These residual texts are traces of what happened. They give a partial window on to the occasion and on to the multiple meanings generated by the lecture.

Second, the speaker from the public lecture series was invited to undertake a "lunchtime conversation" with an interlocutor at an art gallery. This occasion was part of a series titled "Culture Now." Apart from the publicity online and in the gallery, and via its networks with schools, there was little in the way of framing apart from (a) a chance to eat an informal lunch with the audience beforehand, (b) an opportunity to meet gallery staff who were setting up and filming the conversation, and (c) a brief introduction to the conversation from the host. The actual event, attended by 40 or so students and members of the public, took place on the stage of a small cinema in the gallery. The seats were arranged to face each other and the audience. In an hour's session, 35 minutes were devoted to the two-way conversation, and 20 minutes or so to questions-and-answers.

The framing for this occasion is clear. Rhetorically, the occasion is interesting in that it sets an ostensibly informal *conversation* on a more formal stage. The genre is more like a live radio or television interview. The confines of the genre did not prevent some breaking of the frame: a rap included in one of the "answers"; the tables turned in the interviewer–interviewee relationship at one point in the conversation. Indeed, "conversation" manifested itself more in the American sense of a semi-formal dialogue on a particular matter rather than an informal, improvised conversation. What was captured is the apparent (and, to a degree, actual) improvised nature of the exchange, based not on a script, but on a few topics agreed before by the participants. The order of these topics, and the way the exchanges flowed, was improvised. In research terms, the nearest genre would be "semi-structured interview." Audience questions were given more time than in the public lecture, leading to a more in-depth and more extensive conversation between the audience and the interviewer/interviewee. But after an hour, because of scheduling, the occasion was brought to a close, continuing afterwards, as with the lecture, in entirely informal conversation.

Degrees of formality are important to rhetoric and framing, not least in *performances* that are more highly framed than the two occasions described here. In the rhetoric of music performance, a recent concert by the London Symphony Orchestra of two works by Stravinsky[2] will serve as the third example in this exemplification of the role of framing within rhetoric. It is, in many ways, typical of classical music concerts worldwide, although it is acknowledged there are variations on such framing. Taking into account the publicity, posters, programs, and attendant build-up to the actual concert—including the fact that it was part of "Gergiev's Stravinsky Festival" that spring in London—the concert is immediately framed by the location and timing: in one of the main concert halls at the Barbican, and, like many framed events, at a particular time. The framing is accentuated by entry to the concert hall, with its orchestra stands and instruments laid out on stage. Seats are numbered (unlike the other two occasions described previously). As the audience fills the seats, the musicians wander on stage and take up their positions. The beginning of the concert itself is signaled by the arrival on stage of the first violinist, the leader of the orchestra. He (in this case) bows to the audience, they applaud, and he proceeds to lead the tuning up of the orchestra—a sonorous cacophony of sound. After a moment of two of silence, the conductor walks on stage, acknowledges the orchestra, bows to the audience, and shakes the hand of the leader of the orchestra. More silence ensues before the music itself begins.

Even the musical performance itself is subject to rhetorical framing, notwithstanding the internal structural and compositional elements of the piece itself. In some countries, it is customary to sit in silence through the performance; in others, not. In some, the breaks between movements are an opportunity for applause; in others, a sacrosanct silence obtains. Yet further, particularly pleasing and/or moving parts of the composition itself can be applauded in some contexts (even triggering reprises or improvisations), and yet not in others. The variations in convention are important to understand for composer, conductor, player, and audience alike. At the end of the piece, it is customary for the conductor and principal violinist to walk off stage together and to come back two or three times (or more) to applause, until it dies down. An encore or two might be demanded and played. Finally, the conductor and first violinist leave the stage completely, signaling (with or without house lights) that the performance is over, and the rest of the performers and audience leave the auditorium.

The formality of such an occasion is unlike the lecture or "conversation" described earlier. And yet each is framed in particular ways, on a spectrum of formality-informality that requires understanding and interpretation.

The framing is partly determined by power relations, partly by convention, and partly by an agreed contract between the "performers" and the audience—or, more broadly, the rhetor and the audience. *Composition* is a term that is helpful in this regard because the communication takes various modes and media but is always informed by a composer. In music, that term is reserved for the author of the piece to be played, the "writer" of the score. And yet, despite their role as interpreters of the score, the conductor and his or her musicians recompose the piece for a particular occasion and/or for a recording. The term *composer* is used generally in the present book as an alternative to *rhetor* given the archaic nature of the technical term from rhetoric. There is a reason for this choice in the twenty-first century: composition needs recognition as the central act in the creation of communication. "Composition" requires, as has been suggested in chapter 4, the putting together of a number of elements in an arrangement that is intended to make meaning to be conveyed to another, or to others. It can use elements that have been used before and include quotations and other material that has previously been used. But essentially, it will be new in the sense that the context, the arrangement, and the particular intent have not been instanced before. This "making new" is essential to a theory of rhetoric because it not only demands a theory that can account for such social, creative communication, but also grounds the theory in the actualities of present demands for communication.

Visual Metaphors, Analogies, Actualities

The window allows one to link the outside to the inside of a room. It provides a frame through which insight into a room, or from a room to the outside, is made. This apparently simple building device, with its functions of letting in air and light to a room, defines the borderland or the frame between the interior and the exterior. Such abstraction enables us to think of the implications of that distinction: interiority/what is "other" or outside; what is familiar on the one hand, and what is less familiar on the other. These binary generalizations soon become unworkable as exceptions to the rule can be easily found. For example, when looking into an unfamiliar room from outside (as a fox or a stranger may peer into a room) one can be on familiar ground. Equally, a perspective from the inside may be just as familiar as one from the outside, for example in looking out from a kitchen window to a well-loved garden, or from a New York apartment window to a familiar view.

However, the inside/outside distinction is valuable in that it allows us to see how one perspective opens out on to another. It certainly "frames" the view each way, as the window is finite and (usually) rectangular; built in wood, steel, or other durable material; and a permanent fixture designed for viewing one space from another.

The window itself is a membrane, a plane of transparency between the two worlds: a means of transference, of passage for eyesight, air, imagination.

The window provided inspiration and a recurring motif and framework for a series of paintings by Bonnard, Matisse, Manguin, and Camoin, brought together in an exhibition, "Bonnard et son amis" at le Musée Bonnard, Le Cannet, in 2012. A subsection of the exhibition was devoted to "Variations on the window." As the catalog suggests, "The window, situated somewhere between reality and imagination, draws out of this duplicity an inspirational power and contributes undeniably to the construction of an aesthetic, poetic and symbolic space" (Navas 2012, 93).

Let us draw out, in general, the qualities of paintings with windows. First, the *canvas* (a term we will use to convey the ground on which the painting is made, whether it is paper, canvas, or other material) is limited and rectangular in shape—a frame unto itself. (Later, this canvas will be further framed within a wooden frame to be transported, hung in a gallery, stored, etc.). Second, the painting itself incorporates a window, or part of a window. The inclusion of the window often gives the painting its title: for example, Matisse's *Open window at Collioure*, Bonnard's *The Window*, Camoin's *Open Window at Cannes*, and Manguin's *By the Window*. Through the window we see a landscape, or darkness, or elements of sky, or even abstract designs, that are always figured in relation to what is inside the room. Almost never in this collection of paintings does the interior or the exterior merely serve as a neutral framing or lack-of-commentary on the other. Almost always, the one comments on, reflects in some way, or is a version of the other. Furthermore, there are structural properties in windows that assist the structuration of the compositions as a whole, for example, in Camoin's *Lola on the Terrace of the Hotel Bellevue in Toulon* in which the shutters of the window provide the vertical framing, and the balustrade on the balcony provides a strong horizontal line, dividing the painting into a third sky, two-thirds seated figure and table; or in Bonnard's *Vase of Flowers* (circa 1922), which uses the upright frame of the window to separate a painting of vases of flowers into two distinct panels.

What does this combination of framing and windows suggest? One message is to draw attention to the act of framing itself. The artist frames what it is we see. He or she selects from an infinite range of possibilities and presents us with a selected viewpoint. By including windows within a painting, the artist is saying: "I am in the business of framing, and here, included in my painting is recognition that this act is central to my creations. I hereby acknowledge and reveal to you part of the secret of my art." Another is to set up the relationship, symbolically but also in sheer textural and color form, between the inside and the outside. Yet another is the actual technical challenge that is demonstrated: often the window is at a different angle from the view of the painter him-/herself, for example. Another is the "geometry of framing": the provision of a grid, a form of structuration, on the canvas via which the various elements can be arrayed and brought together to interrelate with each other. Perhaps most importantly, there is an aesthetic and emotional connection between what is outside and what is inside. Matisse, in a letter to Teriadeune, stated:

> If I have managed to reunite in my painting what is outside, that is to say the sea, with the inside, it is because the atmosphere of the landscape and my room are one and the same . . . I don't have to bring the outside and the inside together, the two are reunited in my emotion. I am able to associate the armchair that is near me in my studio to a cloud in the sky, to the stirring of the palm tree on the sea front without having to differentiate their locations, without separating the different elements of my motif that are one in my mind. (Navas 2012, 93)

In terms of how one looks at these paintings,[3] questions arise: What do you look at first? What is through the window? What is inside the room? What is the nature of the whole composition in terms of framing? It is probably fair to say that what is inside the room is the least foregrounded element. Of the two remaining "framings," the whole picture is most likely to be the first framework of attention, followed soon after by what is perceived through the window. The eye then returns to the room and from there to the whole picture again. Finally, one can say that the presence of reflecting glass in the windows or shutters, or indeed of mirrors in the room, further complicates the perspectives that the artist brings to the composition—and the reception—of a work. In a very different way from the multiple angles of Cubism, the window as a motif in paintings seems to suggest the multiplicity of ways of seeing, bringing the invisible to the visible, recognizing the complexity of vision, and using framing to focus and refocus, as well as to negotiate the relationship between inside and outside, the unconscious and the conscious, the human/constructed and the relatively unconstructed.

Transgressing and Breaking Frames

One of the most challenging aspects of a theory of contemporary rhetoric is this: how does rhetoric account for three-dimensional space? We have already seen that two-dimensional, or roughly speaking, "flat" forms of communication, such as print, digital signs on a computer screen or smart phone, paintings, and films, can be accounted for well by multimodality and/or digitization. Even time-based forms of communication such as films, narratives of different kinds, videos, radio plays, and other programs can be accounted for in terms of the temporal dimension of rhetoric.

Space, however, presents a particular problem and challenge. Let us think, first, in terms of the rhetoric of sculpture. Works by any sculptor exist in three dimensions, even if they begin as drawings/sketches on paper or screen. A recent exhibition at the Gagosian Gallery[4] at King's Cross, London, placed a number of Henry Moore's large forms within the white space of the gallery. There were no words or other distractions to mediate the experience of the sculptures, other than the space and spaces they inhabited and their relation to each other within the gallery space. Perhaps the only other mediating factor was that of people looking at and through the sculptures. Notions of rhetoric are thus extended to include not only "who is speaking to whom about what?" but also to "how": In what medium (e.g., bronze)? In what mode(s) (e.g., sculptural form)? And crucially, *where*?

The location of sculpture is critical. Its immediate context is a space that informs the way the specific sculpture is seen in that space, in terms of angle, distance, background, ambience, and whether there are other people around. Seeing Henry Moore sculptures of this scale in the Gagosian Gallery, London, in a converted, white-painted warehouse gallery, is different from seeing them, for example, in Yorkshire Sculpture Park in rolling countryside. There are analogies of form with people in a gallery or an outside space; but there are different analogies that offer themselves if the sculpture is located in a rocky landscape.

Even more site-specific in terms of sculpture is the work of Andy Goldsworthy (e.g., 2004). In *Passages,* for example, Goldsworthy records sculptures made from natural materials, or found patterns in nature—all based around actual or metaphorical journeys or passages (also of time).

What is distinctive about Goldsworthy's work is that it is so site-specific that it is often allowed to change, decay, and disappear in the natural course—for example, if an artwork is created on a beach between tides, or is made of ice that melts, or decomposes in natural weather conditions.

Site-specificity can also be applied to the use of verbal language and is a key dimension to be considered in contemporary rhetorical understanding and composition. A joke does not always work the same way with a different audience, or in a different space; Eliot's *Four* Quartets and Fitzgerald's *Tender is the Night* might read as different works if (a) read at different points in one's life or (b) read on location, as it were, in Burnt Norton, East Coker, The Dry Salvages; or respectively on the Côte d'Azur in the south of France. *Situated* language theory suggests much the same: "context" has considerable bearing on the meaning and interpretation of signs. The key question as far as *context* is concerned, however, is what exactly do we mean by "context"? Is it the immediate time-space intersection of a particular place at a particular time? Is it the same location/space over a specified period of time? Is the "location" the immediate one (say within human reach of the phenomenon) or some other parameter, extending to a building, a landscape, a country, the world, the universe?

Such elasticity of context brings us back to the notion of framing as a powerful tool in contemporary rhetoric, for both the composer and the audience, in determining the range and significance of the work in question. There are no set, definitive frames. Frames can always be set within other frames. The key question is which frames do we wish to bring to bear on the act of communication? Which frames are at play, are suggested by the work (act of communication) itself, or impinge upon the work itself? Who has agency to determine which frames are deployed?

Another example of framing in space and time is a rehearsed "showing" of *Measure for Measure* in a London theatre/drama school—that is to say, an undergraduate level academy or conservatoire for the performing arts. Rehearsed showings are not public performances: they are part of an education in acting and direction in that they are shown to a limited and invited audience (tutors, fellow students, parents, and close family) as work in progress or unpolished rough-cuts. The intention is to give the students experience of learning, rehearsing, and performing, but also to minimize production values and to invite feedback. In this particular case, one of the rehearsal rooms was set up in traverse fashion, with the performing space set between two banks of seating for the audience, each facing the other. At the two open ends of the acting space were screens to mask entrances and exits from the "stage."

In a modern dress version, the actors wore costumes to suggest a boardroom setting in a (potentially) corrupt state. Action proceeded as in a fully fledged production, with an interval in the middle of a roughly two-hour performance. At one stage, the director intervened to ask the actors to re-do one of the parts of scenes. Clearly, this intervention broke the "suspension of disbelief" and magical absorption in the production—however provisional—that the play induced. What is the nature of that engagement in the fiction of the play? Live theatre or drama can be seen as engagement in the present moment, enacting in the moment a particular vision that draws on reference to the past and future. But the very *presence* of the actors—their physical proximity, their delivery of lines, their movement in relation to each and to the audience—reinforces the sense of abandonment or suspension in the *present*.

There is one more aspect of space that needs to be addressed, and it pertains to a key question or two in relation to rhetoric: where does rhetoric not operate? What are its parameters? Because rhetoric is broadly defined in this theory as the arts of discourse, it should, by definition, not operate where there is no discourse (as in all discourse there will be an *art*, whether conscious or unconscious, evident or hidden). There is usually discourse, wherever people congregate, even if that discourse is not verbal. But space in which there is no discourse moves us into the territory of uninhabited landscape, or its equivalent in the mind: Zen, transcendence of the human condition, ecstasy, the sublime.

Let us deal with uninhabited landscape first. Putting aside the philosophical question of whether it "exists" if there is no human perception or recognition, we can say with confidence that in one or more senses it does exist—people have seen it, experienced it, and bring reports back from it; maps that have been charted by explorers, though symbolic and rhetorical representations in themselves, have recorded it; and landsat and other photographs from space prove its scale, nature, and existence. But within a mountainous region or a great forest, or any wilderness region, there is no rhetoric because there is no human communication. Poets, using rhetoric in a transformed and metaphorical sense, can talk of the rhetoric of the forest as if there is a network of communication and rhetorical possibility in the ways that the ecosystem operates. But it can be said that, unless there is a single person in the wilderness who is talking to him/herself or others, there is no real rhetoric.

In the internal *tabula rasa* that is characterized by great stillness and silence, as in moments of ecstasy, spiritual enlightenment, catharsis, or *sartori*, and also the less grand states of meditation, peace, and quietude, rhetoric also ceases to operate. There is no communication *per se*, other than in religions where there is a deified higher presence and assumed or imagined commerce with that being. Such communication with a higher being itself is worthy of study in rhetorical terms, as an inner dialogue is projected by the rhetor into an outward form of communication. One could say that rhetorical moves are those that are employed as a means to an end, as scaffolds for the real building that is being constructed. But as soon as the spiritual or religious experience interfaces with the real world and the world of ritual, rhetoric is brought back into play. Rhetoric is the great mediator between humankind and the rest of experience, as well as the principal engine of humanism.

How Does Framing Sit within a Theory of Rhetoric?

Framing, the topic of the present chapter, is a tool in the application of rhetorical theory. The theory of contemporary rhetoric can be described as the overarching (or underpinning, according to metaphorical preference) set of ideas that enables us to (a) make connections between different kinds of communicative experience; (b) place rhetorical activity in relation to philosophical, actual, and other kinds of activity; (c) provide a social and political dimension to communication; and (d) define an aesthetic and design dimension to communication. Framing is not a theory. It is a "servant" to rhetoric in that it is (a) the activity via which meaning is made and communicated; (b) a creative and critical resource for the rhetor and the audience; (c) a lightweight form of "scaffolding" that, once the meaning is communicated, becomes invisible and superfluous to need; and (d) flexible, adaptable, breakable, and transgressable.

It is almost impossible to conceive of a theory of rhetoric without the operational function of framing to enable meaningful communication to take place. The *what, why, when, where,* and *how* of rhetoric are enacted and shaped by framing. Similarly, when a reader or viewer is accessing a work or on the receiving end of communication, he or she is using these same devices to make sense of the signals that are coming through; communication thus becomes a dialogic act.

Equally, framing acts in a vacuum unless it is informed by functional purposes that are defined by rhetoric. Power relations, social relations, equities, and inequalities in communication are accountable in rhetoric. Although the act of framing looks to be a neutral act, it is always informed by the rhetor's intention and the audience's preparedness.

How Do We Teach the Notion of Framing?

Framing is often invisible or hard to see. The way the present book has been framed—by the publisher, by the stages of preparation that have been undertaken, by the individual, as well as the collaborative and collective endeavor that has gone into its making—are not made explicit. Indeed, the fact that a book is as much a collaborative act as the making of a film is not recognized in the "credits" in quite the same way. This invisibility or partial visibility in creation and production makes it difficult to give a full account of the framing that goes into the production of such a form of communication.

In such a situation, and in cases where the way in which an act of communication is framed is not always evident, the best way to start to teach a notion of framing is via clear and concrete examples of framing: a painting in the visual arts, a garden design "framed" by walls or the parameters of the space, a theatre or dance stage on which the action takes place, or the place of a poem on a page, surrounded by white space and bound by conventions of rhythm, rhyme, meter, and shape on the page. How the communication fits the frame is the first stage of understanding its nature: what is inside and outside the frame; what happens, and what is implied when the frame is transgressed; what the actual design of the material inside the frame is like. The important next stage is to demonstrate that received and conventional frames (schemata, frames, genres) are only temporary manifestations of an act of framing. The frames themselves are a result of framing—but it is a chimera to believe that the frames can be taught without a considerable loss of flexibility in communication.

It is through awareness of the concrete operations of the act of framing that a sense of the power and possibilities of framing as a rhetorical device can be built. Rather than build an impossible edifice of "frames within frames"—which do exist but are not a useable or useful analytical tool—the emphasis has to be on the *act* of framing that brings about such frames.

In very simple pedagogical terms (there is more in Chapter 13 on rhetoric and education), the *what, where, when, why* questions are followed by the key rhetorical question: how? This question is *key* in the sense that rhetoric is concerned with *how* communication takes place. The why question tends toward philosophical justification; the what, when, and where are concerned with substance and with the temporal/spatial dimensions.

Conclusion

Framing has been neglected in rhetorical studies, other than through the work of Tannen (1993) and Goffman (1986) in their respective fields, all of which could be seen as drawing on rhetoric in some respects. Its dynamic possibilities, revealed by making the move away from fixed and concrete frames to the act of framing, reconnect it to rhetoric and to the moves that take place in everyday life to enable communication to take place and for the world to proceed (cf. Habermas). Framing thus plays a key part in the formation of a theory of contemporary rhetoric—and more so than it did in classical and medieval theories of rhetoric. This is necessary because the manifold possibilities of communication in the contemporary world—via media, modes, and in "flattened" social structures—require some means of determining how meaning is to be constructed and how meaningful communication can take place. That is why framing takes a central role in the present book: it sits between chapters that set out the lineaments of a theory of rhetoric on the one hand and chapters that explore rhetoric's application in various fields on the other. It is this generative function that enables rhetoric, through framing, to ground itself in real world situations and thus make it a powerful theory of communication. Without framing, rhetoric could be seen as ethereal, academic, and irrelevant to the operation of the world; with it, rhetoric becomes closely connected to all forms of human communication, from the literary and artistic to the mundane, from operatic scores and their realization in theatres to the exchange of tickets on a bus or train. If rhetoric is to have credibility in a fast-changing world, the way in which framing operates to shape the problems that are encountered, the debates that take place on them, and the solutions that are generated that in turn lead to consensus and action is crucial. Framing is the engine and principal operating device of rhetoric in the twenty-first century. It makes rhetoric happen.

8

Multilingual Rhetoric

This chapter uses a collection of initial case studies—of the nature of doctoral students' work—to set the scene for discussion later in the chapter on multilingual rhetorical theory.

There are increasing numbers of Asian students in universities in the UK, the United States and Canada, and western Europe. Equally, there are increasing numbers of "Western" students in universities in China and east Asia. It is often assumed that the approach to argumentation—a quality highly prized in essay and dissertation composition in the West—is different among Asian students brought up in the Confucian-heritage education systems.

The aims of the research presented in the present chapter are to examine this assumption, asking the following questions: to what extent is it justifiable to suggest that the models of argumentation and rhetoric are different between East and West? Are the differences, if they exist, one of product or process? Are there similarities in approach?

These questions are addressed by reviewing existing research by Watkins and Biggs (1996), Andrews (2007, 2010), and others; by examination of new written texts; and by the undertaking of in-depth interviews. Furthermore, cultural assumptions are examined, leading to questions of how the postgraduate learner sees him- or herself in terms of developing and using argumentational skills. The research situates itself within multilingual rhetorical theory, which takes as its starting point that social and political notions of identity and practice manifest themselves through writers/composers and do so in different languages and cultures. The substrands to which the chapter would lend itself are intercultural communication and teaching and learning from a cultural perspective.

The findings suggest that students from east Asia have more in common with their Western counterparts than has been assumed and that such commonalities include a desire to reach the "truth" of the matter through intellectual enquiry, whether that truth be objective knowledge or postmodernist in nature; a common understanding of what good argumentation looks like as a *product*; and a desire for success in academic inquiry *through argumentation*. Differences are more likely to occur in *processes* and approaches to argumentation, including a deductive as opposed to an inductive approach, some degree of difference between explicit and implicit argumentation, and different notions of what it means to be "critical." Differences are noted within approaches in the West (e.g., between U.S. and UK approaches to argument), which may also exist within east Asia, thus suggesting that a simple East/West divide is neither accurate nor appropriate.

The number of students who study abroad for the whole or part of their undergraduate and/or postgraduate studies continues to increase at a rate of 12% (BBC 2012). Although figures are hard to quantify and to validate, UNESCO statistics for 2009 show that international students rose from 2.96 million to 3.43 million over a year. The measures are many and varied, but the overall estimate from UNESCO suggests that numbers of overseas students have risen by more than 75% since 2000. Currently, the most popular destinations for students are the USA, Canada, the UK, and Australia—in other words, there is a migration from developing economies to so-called Western countries with highly developed undergraduate and postgraduate provision.

The largest exporter of overseas students is China. In 2010, there were 284,000 Chinese students abroad; in 2011, that figure had risen to 440,000. Current estimates are that, in total (given that the increasing trend is for Chinese students to stay abroad), there are somewhere in the region of 1.27 million Chinese studying overseas. However, there is also an increasing trend for Chinese students to return to China after their studies. In 2011, for example, 186,200 Chinese students returned home by the end of 2011, an increase of 38% on 2010's figures. In addition to this rising figure of returning students, China is planning to rapidly increase the number of overseas students coming into China, with an ambitious plan of 500,000 places. One can see in these plans a wish to match the flow of exporting students (440,000 in 2011) to the number of students coming into the country. The reason for the increase in returning students, and the planned increase of overseas students in China, is to ensure that China increases the quality of its intellectual firepower and that the economy continues to internationalize; that, in short, its knowledge economy does not fall behind that of the West and that there is no "brain drain" from the country.

The UK, on the other hand, is a bigger importer than exporter of students—it is the second biggest destination for overseas students, after the United States. Figures released from the British Council in 2011, however, show that there are more overseas students taking UK degrees in their own countries than traveling to the UK to study. In 2011, there were 340,000 students taking UK courses in their home countries, either through partnerships between UK and local universities or through branch campuses. More than 150 branch campuses are open in 50 countries, mostly by U.S. universities. Furthermore, online degrees can only increase the numbers of students living in one country, but registering for a degree in another. The University of London International Programmes, for example, have been running in one form or another since 1858 and currently register 50,000 students in 190 countries for the University's degrees.

There are thus three kinds of international student: (1) those who travel overseas to register for a full-time program; (2) those who register overseas but who study in their own country; and (3) those who undertake online distance programs.

The cultural assumptions of international students are often underestimated. In particular, the academic conventions of the host countries in relation to the expectations and practices of overseas students are an area where there can be problems, or at the very least, a period of induction and transition is required so that the expectations of the host institution can be met by the overseas student, and vice-versa.

Rhetoric and Argumentation in Higher Education

At the cutting edge of student experience is how to compose academic argument. Success in Western universities, in all disciplines (though manifested in different ways), is predicated upon the ability to argue a case by taking a particular stand on an issue, or simply to argue academically by weighing up the pros and cons of a situation (see Andrews 2010). Although the criterion of argumentation in the assessment of student essays and other forms of assignment is not always explicitly stated, it is always there—at undergraduate, postgraduate, and research degree levels. That criterion can be best represented, in general terms, as the ability to present a coherent argument, that is, to present a logical or quasi-logical set of propositions or claims, to support these with evidence and/or with intellectual (abstract) justification, and, through the combination of statement and proof, to put forward a proposition and stand by it.

The ability to argue is also closely connected to criticality in students' work. Criticality manifests itself in a number of ways (Andrews 2007), all of which are essential to success and which help to sharpen and develop argumentational skills. These include weighing up one source against another; developing a logical or quasi-logical sequence of ideas; testing the propositions against evidence, and, furthermore, questioning the relationship between propositions and evidence according to the "warrant" (Toulmin 2003) that validates the relationship; developing one's own "position" on a topic; operating via a skeptical intellectual approach rather than by compliance or deference to existing ideas and/or to lecturers, professors, and other "authorities"; and not taking the "truth" for granted, but questioning accepted truths in order to reach a higher and more accurate sense of the truth of a case.

What is often missing from debates about rhetoric, argumentation, and criticality is the question of intercultural influence and emphasis. In the present chapter, attention turns to the East Asian learner and how he/she deals with the expectations of the Western conventions of argumentation and criticality. In order to do so, we will first look at existing research on the Confucian-heritage learner, then compare three East Asian doctoral students with three European doctoral students to see how rhetoric, argumentation, and criticality manifest themselves in their work.

The Chinese Learner

A significant publication, emanating from the Comparative Education Research Centre at the University of Hong Kong (Watkins and Biggs 1996), suggested that the success of Southeast and East Asian students in Western academic contexts was a matter not only of hard work based on a strong work ethic, as well as competence in achieving proficiency in English, but also of the adaptability of such students to "read" the demands of Western academic conventions and practices. Such conventions and practices can be characterized as having developed from a personal-psychological model to a socio-constructivist model. That is to say, there is a core of personal development theory at the heart of approaches to learning and studying in the West, but that core has been developed in the twentieth century by a strong sense that learning is not only personal and "psychological," but an effect of community; a socially generated act; a social, political, as well as personal transformational process. To link this model of learning with the previous section on rhetoric, argumentation, and criticality, it is not enough, in the West, to learn "facts" or to make measurable advances in relation to interventions within a psychological paradigm. Rather, learning in the West is defined by a complex interaction between deduction and induction; between the development of new ideas and propositions in relation to evidence; and via engagement, critique, and debate. In a mistaken deficit approach, some Western academics have assumed that, because East Asian learners do not share the Greco-Roman origins of rhetoric, argumentation, and criticality in European and Western thought, they are somehow "deficient" in being able to argue, to be critical, and to attain the highest grades in academic assignments.

Lee Wing On (1996) presents the East Asian Confucian perspective with a caveat that, although "east Asian societies such as China, Taiwan, Hong Kong, Singapore, Korea and Japan share an obvious Confucian tradition" (26), it cannot be taken for granted that the presentation of Confucian ethics and practices is the same in all of these countries. We know, too, from a recently successful PhD at the Institute of Education, University of London (Zhu 2012), that Confucian thinking itself is highly contentious within East Asia and that, within China itself, Confucius goes in and out of favor according to the political climate. Nevertheless, the Confucian influence in East Asia is considerable, particularly in terms of higher education approaches. Lee Wing On points out that the "Confucian tradition is characterized by discourse and debate on learning—why learning is significant and how it is to be carried out" (27). Among the tenets of Confucian thinking are that everyone is educable, that motivation (intrinsic or extrinsic) is more important than innate intelligence, that "everyone can be come a sage" and attain a degree of perfectability through effort, and that reaching a purely rational state of being, to be applied in decision making in the world to the moral betterment of the self and society, is a worthy goal. The important aspect to note with regard to the discussion of rhetoric, argumentation, and criticality is that Confucian approaches suggest that learning must be "deep"; in other words, surface approaches to learning are to be the subject of critique. Self- and public knowledge of the truth comes from deep reflection on propositions and existing states of knowledge. More specifically, with regard to reflective thinking, "we should not take for granted that what one reads is correct. We should suspend our judgement for the time being, then read more in order to gain a new view" (On 1996, 35, in citing the work of Zhu Xi). The sequence of learning consists of memorizing, understanding, reflecting, and questioning—not just of memorizing or close reading. Indeed, the supposed emphasis on memorization in East Asian learning is a chimera—first, it is not possible, given the information explosion; and second, it is often misunderstood, and refers principally to the initial and close engagement with "reading."

Are there significant differences between Western approaches to rhetoric and argumentation on the one hand, and East Asian on the other? If these differences exist, are they principally matters of product or process? Are there similarities in approach that are masked behind the apparent surface quest for difference between West and East?

In order to examine the question of whether it is justifiable to suggest that the models of rhetoric and argumentation are culturally different, a small research study looked in depth at the work of six successful doctoral students: three from Europe and three from China. While this sample is small and opportunistic, the study was in-depth and consisted of three elements: a close examination of the supervision and examination of the students, a study of their final dissertations, and interviews with all six. The limitations of this study are evident: it is small in scale, all the degrees were examined and awarded in English universities (Exeter and the Institute of Education, University of London), and the field is Education studies. It is therefore intended as an initial study that might lead to larger scale comparative and international work on doctoral thesis composition from a perspective of rhetorical, argumentational, and "critical" concerns.

Six Doctoral Students

All six students agreed to having their work cited in this chapter, so we can be explicit about their work. They are outlined in Table 8.1.

First, it can be said that there is little or no difference between the awarding universities. Both have a set of criteria for the award of PhD that includes the following: that it makes a distinct contribution to

Table 8.1 Research Students and Their Theses

Student	*Nationality*	*Title of Thesis*	*Awarding Body*	*Date*
Frances Bodger	British	Coming to an understanding of children's transformation of their own syntactic and textual approach: longitudinal, small-scale research into sentence- and text-level changes in the later years of primary education	Institute of Education, University of London	May 2010
Annabel Watson	British	L1 English teachers' beliefs about grammar, and the relationship of espoused beliefs to pedagogical practice	University of Exeter	June 2012
Evanthia Tsaliki	Greek	Intercultural education in Greece: the case of 13 primary schools	Institute of Education, University of London	July 2012
Hazel Chiu	PRC/Hong Kong	Grammar teaching concepts and practice in the task-based secondary English curriculum of Hong Kong	Institute of Education, University of London	December 2010
Ching Ching Lai	PRC/Hong Kong	Hong Kong secondary school students' uptake and perception of enhanced and unenhanced recasts on their past tense usage in spoken narratives in English	Institute of Education, University of London	March 2012
Wengcheng Zhu	China	Confucian themes and China's high school language and literature textbooks in the Reform era	Institute of Education, University of London	August 2012

knowledge; that it *affords evidence of originality by the discovery of new "facts" and/or the exercise of independent critical power;* that it is *an integrated whole and presents a coherent argument;* that it describes the method of research and its findings; that it includes a discussion of those findings and how they advance the study of the subject; and that, in so doing, it demonstrates *a deep and synoptic understanding of the field of study . . . and a capacity for judgment in complex situations.* There are other criteria that are not so closely linked to rhetoric, argumentation, and criticality.

The commonalities between the students are best represented in terms of the structure of the six theses, outlined in Table 8.2.

There is a high degree of homogeneity in the structure of the theses. If we take structure or the classical *dispositio* (arrangement) to be one of the key rhetorical aspects of argumentation, we can see that the practice here is to undertake a seven or eight-part argument. All have an introduction and a conclusion. All have a literature review and a chapter on methodology. All move from the Introduction through the Literature review to the Methodology and on to the results or findings, before reaching the Conclusion. We could say that there is a clear genre within which all the students couch their thesis: in education and social science studies, this genre assumes that, at the highest level of academic achievement, the student is making a contribution to knowledge by reviewing existing research, telling us how she approached or undertook the new empirical research, presenting us with the results, discussing the overall outcomes, and framing the whole with an introduction and conclusion. The regulations, guidance, and criteria for the award of PhD at the two universities concerned do not specify such a genre—they are couched in more general terms.

There are variations between the students. Those with eight chapters rather than seven have needed the extra chapter to provide two chapters of literature review, or three chapters of results (the norm is two). In the case where there are nine chapters (Wengcheng Zhu), the five chapters that constitute the "results" are arranged in a thematic fashion, more like a book than a thesis. They provide the framework for a *discussion* of the topic from five different perspectives. One cannot say, however, that this is a particularly East Asian trait; it is just as much a convention in humanities and social policy work in Europe as in Asia. Indeed, the reason for the thematic arrangement is probably more to do with the fact that the thesis was supervised within a Faculty of Policy and Society than within a faculty that emphasized empirical and pedagogic aspects of education. Finally, all students incorporate discussion in their theses. For some this is embedded throughout; for others it appears in a separate chapter, after a more descriptive account of the data (and thus modeling the conventional scientific journal article, albeit in a scaled-up version).

Table 8.2 Structure of the Students' Theses

Student	*Structure of the Final Thesis*
Frances Bodger	1. Introduction 2. Literature review 3. Arriving at a conceptual framework 4. Methodology 5. Data set 1 6. Data set 2 7. Data set 3 8. Discussion and concluding chapter
Annabel Watson	1. Introduction 2. Literature review 3. Methodology 4. Teachers' espoused beliefs about grammar 5. Relating beliefs to practice 6. Discussion 7. Conclusion
Evanthia Tsaliki	1. Introduction 2. Literature review 3. Context 4. Methodology 5. Presentation of main findings of the questionnaire 6. Presentation of main findings of the interviews 7. Conclusion
Hazel Chiu	1. Introduction 2. Literature review 1: Grammar in second language acquisition 3. Literature review 2: Teachers' role in curriculum implementation 4. Curriculum interpretation in grammar teaching materials 5. Research design and methodology 6. Findings on individual teachers' grammar teaching concepts and practice 7. Discussion on curriculum materials and teaching practice 8. Conclusion
Ching Ching Lai	1. Introduction (short) 2. Literature review 1 3. Literature review 2 4. Methodology 5. Quantitative data analysis 6. Qualitative data analysis 7. Discussion 8. Conclusion
Wengcheng Zhu	1. Introduction 2. Literature review: Confucianism and modernity 3. Methodology 4. Educational policy reorientation in the Reform era 5. Benevolent governance in the Syllabus Edition textbooks 6. 'Submission to authority' and patriotism in the Syllabus Edition textbooks 7. Confucianism and the 'defects of character': Lu Xun's work 8. The 2004 Curriculum Standard Edition textbooks 9. Conclusion

The differences between students are more evident in the research questions and methodologies. It is here that the argument sets out its starting point and works out *how* it will address the question. In each case the focus is on the main research question(s), outlined in Table 8.3.

Table 8.3 Research Questions and Methods Used

Student	*Research Question*	*Sample and Methods*
Frances Bodger	How are children's transformations of their own syntactic and textual approaches best understood?	Analysis of a small sample of pupils. Textual and longitudinal analysis.
Annabel Watson	What beliefs do teachers espouse about the value of teaching grammar for writing? What different pedagogical approaches do teacher stake when teaching grammar? What is the relationship between teachers' beliefs and pedagogical practice in grammar teaching?	Part of a larger Economic and Social Research Council project that investigated 31 teachers. This study looked in depth at three schools, using observation, stimulated recall interviews, and an analysis of the broader set of data.
Evanthia Tsaliki	What are teachers' and headteachers' perceptions of the nature of intercultural education? What are their perceptions of its implementation within the intercultural primary schools in Greece?	A study of 13 intercultural schools, with 133 questionnaires and 39 teachers interviewed, plus 11 headteachers.
Hazel Chiu	How is grammar teaching perceived and practiced within the task-based secondary curriculum in Hong Kong?	Eight teacher participants. Two lesson observations and two interviews for each.
Ching Ching Lai	Are recasts feasible within the context of Hong Kong schools? Are salient recasts effective in facilitating Hong Kong learners' learning? How to balance both the communicative and form focuses of recasts?	Three intact classes of Cantonese speaking 15 year olds. Two experimental and one control group spread across the whole sample, which totaled 89 pupils Narrative discourse, stimulated recall (question prompts), audio and video taping.
Wengcheng Zhu	What have been the influences of the different portrayals of Confucian themes in the school curriculum? How has the changing treatment of these themes reflected shifts in the broader social, political, cultural, and economic context of contemporary China?	Not a sample of people as such; rather, an analysis of education policy and textbooks at three points: 1983, 1992, and 2004.

What are the differences between the approaches taken by the six students, and are they culturally influenced or informed?

The first point to make is that, in general, research questions are pivotal to doctoral research and theses because they not only encapsulate the substance of the investigation, but also shape the methodological approach (Andrews 2003). For example, Frances Bodger's formulation of "*How* are children's transformations . . . best *understood?*" opens up the investigation to consider a number of ways in which such syntactic and textual transformations can be interpreted and appreciated, and which of these ways is the best. A further issue is raised by the technical term *transformations*, the definition of which will form part of the study. In another example, Hazel Chiu's "*How* is grammar teaching *perceived* and *practiced* . . . " allows the student to look at a number of ways in which such teaching is perceived and practiced—with the implication that there will be comparison between perception and practice. It should be noted that a number of the theses cited here (Watson, Tsaliki, Chiu) use teachers' *perceptions* as a focus of attention and research.

It is better to have a single research question, as the question provides (to change the metaphor slightly) the keystone of the study. This single question can be accompanied by subsidiary questions whose answer can precede or follow the answer to the main question, but the subsidiary questions should not determine the structure, nature, or argument of the thesis as a whole. It will be noticed that Watson, Tsaliki, Lai, and Zhu all ask more than one main question—and even Bodger and Chiu have a double aspect to each of their single questions ("syntactic and textual," "perceived and practiced"). In rhetorical, argumentational, and critical terms, the single question is better because it is more focused and can be used to determine the structure and methodology of the thesis. There is no logical sense in which a single question can be complicated or diffused by another main question.

Second, in relation to the samples, methodologies, and methods used by the six students, three of them (Bodger, Watson, Chiu) use small samples and generate qualitative data and analysis. Tsaliki provides a medium-sized sample. Zhu has no sample at all, but proceeds via analysis of policy documents and textbooks. Lai provides a classic experimental study in combination with narrative discourse, stimulated recall, and audio and video taping (but no video analysis). In short, a variety of samples and methods is used.

There is no clear pattern that has emerged regarding Eastern as opposed to Western approaches to argumentation, rhetoric, and criticality. The three East Asian students perform just as well, and across a range of approaches to research question formation as well as to sampling and methodology. Deeper investigation, beyond structure, research questions, and method, is unlikely to reveal any further cultural difference. In four of the six cases, the language used is a second language. Again, there are no differences in quality or approach. Perhaps we could say that in this particular small-scale and initial study, the sample itself was small (six), purposive, and opportunistic. One could also say that the fact that five of the six students are all working within the regulations and guidance of the Institute of Education at the University of London, and therefore it is no surprise that there is a degree of homogeneity in their productions. All that is true. Nevertheless, the hypotheses generated from such an initial study can be useful for further research: that there is no difference in rhetorical, argumentational, and critical preparedness in students from Eastern and Western backgrounds, and that the academic genre in which students are working, and the precise framework provided by university regulations, are more likely to influence the nature of the composition than any other factor.

There is clearly more research to do: first, in scaling up the study to include a larger sample of students. Second, in undertaking more in-depth and comparative studies of university regulations and the way in which they determine or influence the academic genres in which students write and are assessed; and the extent to which students and supervisors and examiners are on the same wavelength in terms of their understanding of the parameters of the genre in which they are working.

Pedagogical Implications for Cross-Cultural Studies in Argumentation

What are the implications for this study in pedagogical terms? As far as doctoral supervision goes, it is clear that for students from any background, explicit consideration of the rhetorical and argumentational requirements of undertaking a thesis is essential, at an early stage of the process.

First, a look at the requirements as set out in the university's regulations and guidance is important so that the immediate assessment context of the study is clear. If such guidance or even the criteria for success specify that a "coherent argument" is required, the two elements of that term need to be discussed. An argument will require the student to present his or her work in a logical sequence—whatever the logic of the particular discipline requires. Conventionally, in the humanities, the sequence starts with an introduction and literature review, then moves through methodological considerations to the presentation and discussion of results, and then on to a conclusion. Behind this conventional sequence is the assumption that the work will contribute to an existing field through the presentation and analysis of new data and/or new theoretical configuration (and sometimes also by a contribution to methodology). Logic can be suspended or resequenced if there are other paradigmatic forces at play, for example, if the work is presented as a website, or if it is being conducted in paradigm that challenges the conventional argumentational forms. For example, if the thesis is being undertaken in a digital and/or multimodal context, considerations of the particular nature of argument need to be addressed (see Andrews, Borg, Boyd Davis, Domingo, and England 2012).

Related to the overall structural issues are the fact that the thesis, by its very nature as a *thesis* (a proposition, a set of ideas, an argument), needs to show that it is arguing a *position.* The position takes time to emerge: if it emerges early at all, as it does in scientific studies, it will be in the form of a *hypothesis* (a hypothetical proposition). Once established, the position will need to be defended, both in the thesis itself and in any oral examination that follows.

Second, each part of the thesis, however structured overall, needs to have a strong argumentational and critical flavor. Students from Europe and China often miss the fact that the introduction and literature review need to be driven by a skeptical intellectual attitude; the doctoral student is not expected to be complicit, but must look for ways in which he/she can find gaps in existing thinking and research and therefore exploit these gaps by adding to knowledge. Other related approaches include critique, the weighing up of one source against another, and the questioning of secondary sources by reference back to primary sources (and thus a re-interpretation of the particular argument presented). The methodological chapter(s), for example, can be given a critical dimension by comparison to other methodologies and methods that have worked or not worked, by drawing a distinction between the methodology chosen and the specific methods chosen within that methodology (and whether they mesh well together), by the interrogation of one method by another, by a precise account of the proposed nature of triangulation by time or method, and by a discussion of the strengths and weaknesses of the methods chosen.

Lastly, at a more micro level, argumentation must be embedded in the writing of the thesis at the level of the paragraph (or subtextual unit—see Table 8.4) and the sentence. Such micro argumentation can be superficially signaled in the use of connectives, such as "however," "nevertheless," "on the other hand," and "despite," each of which marks a turning point in the micro-argument. More importantly and more deeply, these surface signals are informed by the choreography of argument that is taking place in the mind of the writer as he/she composes the argument of the section or chapter.

The overall aim is to move beyond mere exposition and compliant thinking.

Multilingual Rhetorical Theory

This particular small-scale study of six doctoral students' work situates itself within an overarching sub-section of rhetoric that we might term *multilingual rhetorical theory,* overlapping with *intercultural rhetorical theory.* So, although framing—explored in chapter 7—is the principal device via which such similarities and differences in practice can be analyzed, it is the multilingual and intercultural dimensions that give rhetoric a more varied and colorful range. Indeed, the singular term *rhetoric* has been reframed as *rhetorics* to indicate the pluralistic dimension. Like the debate on *literacy* and *literacies,* these are seen in the present book as simply the unifying (centrifugal) and pluralistic (centripetal) sides of the same phenomenon, so *rhetoric,* in all its cultural forms, continues to be used as the preferred term.

The key starting point in multilingual rhetorical theory is a point that is shared by rhetoric as a whole: it is not aligned to any particular language. This point is crucial, as we are not in the field of "English" studies, nor focusing on English as a second, foreign, additional, or world language. Rather, the interest for rhetoric is how language policy manifests in a globalized education context (the politics of language); how particular languages represent aspects of experience and how they culturally determine how its users experience the world; how languages combine in terms of code-mixing, code-switching, and code-sharing; how families and education systems make decisions about which languages to use for which purposes; and other aspects of comparative language study, including language learning (e.g., the function of "grammar" in foreign language learning). Intimately connected to language use are questions of identity and culture: how does an individual person define himself or herself in terms of language, dialect, and accent? How are identities negotiated, developed, changed, and consolidated? There are significant studies in the field (e.g., Cummins 1996; Block 2009), but the purpose of the present chapter is not to contribute to knowledge in those particular fields, but rather to step back and consider how a theory of rhetoric might contribute to clarification both within the field and in terms of its relation to other areas of cultural and linguistic study.

All languages can be characterized in terms of an interlocking and mutually dependent set of levels at which the language can be described. For example, in English, as in many other languages, there are (starting with the most general categories) issues of social and political context, individual concerns and motivations, and framings of various sizes and kinds that bear upon the construction of meaning between the rhetor and his/her audience. At the next level down, communication takes place in one or more modes and via one or more media. Those modes (note that we have already moved beyond "the English language" into international modes, such as the still and moving visual image, sound, and spatial movement) and media determine the resultant levels at which further description takes place. Staying with the verbal mode for the moment, the situation, with all its factors, is reified in the substance of the text. The "text"—whether mono- or multi-modal—can be described and analyzed in terms of its coherence and cohesion, to borrow terms from Hallidayan linguistics. Subtextual elements such as paragraphs, sections, and stanzas can be determined, and "below" that level, the sentence or other mid-level unit of meaning can be described. This mid-level area is the field of syntax and syntactic studies in English. It is followed, further down, by subunits of the sentence such as the phrase and clause, and then by lexical (word) and sublexical levels: the morphological, phonemic, and phonetic levels, with their attendant relationship with letters on the grapho-phonemic plane.

A comparison between Mandarin and English is summarized in Table 8.4.

Table 8.4 Mandarin and English Comparisons

Level of Description	*English*	*Mandarin/ Putonghua*	*Comments*
Above the level of language or any other mode of communication	Situated within a neo-liberal and post-Romantic set of democratic values	Situated within a neo-Marxist and pragmatic (possibly neo-Romantic) set of values	"Meaning" is constructed in the society through a set of shared values and a number of modes of communication
Immediate contexts	All social situations	All social situations	
Whole text	"Texts" in the language can be oral as well as written, and usually contain other modes, at least implicitly. Genres are "text types."	*wen ti* 文体 = genre, in writing or speech, e.g., *xiao shuo* 小说 = fiction, *shi ge* 诗歌 = poetry *wen ben* 文本 = text	Issues of cohesion and coherence in English and in Mandarin
Subtextual elements	Paragraphs, stanzas, sections, etc.	<u>*duan luo* 段落 = paragraph</u> <u>*zhang jie* 章节 = stanza or section</u>	
The sentence	Studies in syntax	*ju fa* 句法 = syntax *ju zi* 句子 = sentence	Studies in "grammar" in English are usually focusing purely on sentence grammar, i.e., syntax and parts of speech

(*Continued*)

Level of Description	*English*	*Mandarin/ Putonghua*	*Comments*
Subsentential levels	Elements of the sentence, such as clauses, phrases, etc.	*duan yu* 短语 = clause, phrase	
The word or character	The lexical level: studies in whole words, vocabulary acquisition, etc.	*ci hui* 词汇= vocabulary, consisting of characters	In Mandarin, a "word" could be made up from more than one character
Sublexical or character levels; the morphological level	Prefixes, root words, suffixes, and etymologies; grammatical subunits of words	*bi hua* 笔画 = stroke *zigen* 字根 = root words *zi* 字 = character	This is where the two languages are quite different, in that English is grapho-phonemic, based on the alphabet; Mandarin is ideographic.
Phonemic level	Meaningful sounds in the language	*Tone* = *yu qi* 语气, *sheng diao* 声调 *yu qi* 语气 focuses more on emotion and feeling *sheng diao* 声调 focuses more on meaning-making (normally first, second, third, and forth tones refer to different "sheng diao" 声调)	In English, the phonemic level meets the alphabetic on the grapho-phonemic plane; the phonemic and phonetic are often confusingly conflated under the term phonics and translated into a pedagogic concept: "systematic synthetic phonics" or "analytic phonics."
Phonetic level	The study of the wider set of sounds that are used in spoken language	*Yu yin* 语音= sounds in the language	

Conclusion

The tentative conclusion of the small-scale study described in this chapter is that there is more international agreement on what represents good argument, in the forms of its *products,* than there is on the *processes* via which argumentation, rhetorical, and critical operations take place in the development of a doctoral thesis. If there is a difference in approach between the European Greco-Roman approach and the Chinese

Confucian-inspired approach, it is that the former operates deductively, and the latter inductively. In other words, to posit a generalization that requires further research, it is the tendency of Western students to begin with ideas and hypotheses (even if they are not scientists) and move toward proof via the seeking of empirical or purely logical evidence. It is the tendency of Eastern students to build toward hypotheses and more secure forms of truth from the gradual accumulation of evidence. Each approach is valid; each is dependent on the other. The latter approach could be aligned with the practice of "grounded theory," while the former is more abstract and more "scientific" in its initial conception. Both are ways of bringing together propositions on the one hand, and data (which becomes evidence when informed by propositions) on the other. It is also the case that different disciplines will operate differently in relation to the deductive/inductive approach.

Related to this mutually complementary distinction between deductive and inductive approaches is that between the degree of explicitness that is customary in the presentation of the thesis. It is now conventional practice in the West to be highly explicit in the writing of a thesis and in the presentation of all aspects of its production. For example, a literature review could be accompanied (perhaps in an appendix) by a search strategy that sets out how the particular literature review was conducted which keywords were used, which sources were investigated, and which languages the search was conducted in. Because of increasing uncertainty about theoretical bases and a widening range of paradigms in which research is conducted, students have felt impelled to make explicit what choices they have made and why. On the other hand, in some countries in East Asia (notably Japan), being explicit about the grounds and processes of argumentation within a thesis can be thought to be inelegant and even inappropriate.

The argument of the present chapter is that preparation for advanced academic study in the East or West needs to include an introduction to argumentational practices and conventions (in effect, the rhetoric of academic discourse in each location) so that students can adapt quickly to what is expected of them. The need is just as great for lecturers and professors, who need to be aware that the conventions by which they operate are often so much a part of custom that they have become habitual and are taken for granted. As students increasingly build international experience into their studies, whether by taking whole degrees overseas, by registering for degrees in other countries, by spending part of their study time abroad and/or by online study, such preparation will become all the more important. In short, they need to learn the rhetoric and discourses of the situations they find themselves in so that they can make a success of their international experience.

9

Rhetoric and Poetics: The Place of Literature

What can rhetoric offer poetics and literary studies? What place do they have in a theory of contemporary rhetoric? Rhetoricians have always been attracted to the field of poetics—the study of literary form and a close partner of stylistics—as the literary appears to hold a powerful place in human consciousness and in social disengagement: people are reading novels on the train, in isolation, in "their own world," in cities—and reading them in books and on electronic tablet devices like Kindles and iPads. But although the literary appears to hold sway and to generate and satisfy *private* passions, it also maps out possible worlds and the consequences of action within those worlds.

To begin an exploration of the relationship of rhetoric to poetics, we need to start at the level of the function of the poetic, then move down to individual genres (the novel, the lyric poem, the play), and then to the deployment of verbal language in its multimodal settings.

A discussion of the function of the poetic—of the *place* of the poetic in a universe of discourse—has to ask the following question: the function of the poetic within what kind of construct? The starting point within the current book is that the construct is rhetoric: the arts of discourse. So, to follow the logic, if the arts of discourse is our primary concern and reference point, what kinds of arts does poetics represent, and why do we need it? What function does it play? There are a number of answers.

First—and to borrow the concept of framing—poetic communication is different from everyday discourse because it creates a frame around itself. In the case of poetry, the frame is the white space on the page that requires a different kind of attention to the words within the frame, in their rhythmic organization. In the case of the novel or short story, the text is bound by narrative conventions (and sometimes finds itself in the medium of a bound book) and most obviously creates other possible worlds through the elements of place, character, action, and time. In the case of plays performed in the theatre, the framing is not only literary (the script), but also realized in the shape of the theatre, the direct connection between the actors and the audience, the thin line that separates the two (and is sometimes transgressed), and the beginning and ending of the performance within institutional and social conventions (the theatre building itself and the practice of "going out to the theatre"). To summarize this first set of characterizations: poetics charts a world of discourse that is highly framed. It is consciously framed so as to draw extra attention to what is inside the frame. The "extra" attention is a demand on consciousness and makes the assumption that what is inside the frame is coherent and informed by principles of unity (cf. Aristotelian poetics). In these senses, the poetic space is different from the rhetorical space because rhetoric is always maneuvering in the wider world of public discourse, where frames are less evident and less consciously defined.

Second, poetic communication invites a step back from the action of the everyday world. It invites absorption and reflection. It holds up "a mirror to nature" so that we can see ourselves in relation to wider patterns of social engagement and/or states of being. Poetic communication provides these spaces, which we assume commuters on trains, solitary readers on park benches, and readers of fiction anywhere are enjoying. The accent on enjoyment of such spaces is important: the poetic space allows the reader to "escape" the "real" world, to inhabit another world, and to compare that other world to the world or worlds he/she habitually inhabits. The key text on this topic is the under-rated *Fictional Worlds* (1986) by Thomas Pavel (initially discussed in chapter 3 of the present book), which posits the notion of *distance* between the real world and different types of fictional world. Each of the worlds as represented in fiction (principally the novel, though any fictional work can fulfil these functions) is a *possible* world with its own boundaries and its position in relation to the real world (e.g., a novel in the realism tradition like Zola's *Germinal* is close to the real world; *Lord of the Rings* is further away). The further away the fictional world is depicted, the more general its reference to the real world, and the more "escapist" it appears; and yet (cf. the *Harry Potter* phenomenon) it can be populated with detail from the real world. If we use the classical notion of the "mirror held up to nature," we can see that the degree of distance from the real world presents a different image: "distant" reflections may draw general lineaments of reference to the real world and yet be populated with detail that "creates its own world" (a parallel world as well as a possible world). Reflections that are closer will concentrate on representing the *detail* of everyday life: like figurative painting, it will represent what it sees and feels; it will attempt to record a *true image* of what it is observing. The seeming paradox of the distant worlds as depicted in fiction—the worlds of fantasy literature that nevertheless are populated with details from the real world—creates a magical alternative and parallel world: a world that is radically elsewhere, and yet is comfortingly familiar.

Third, poetic spaces invite the delineation of feeling/affect. As worlds, fictional and possible, they are defined by, and define the *structures of feeling* (cf. Williams 1977). These affective structures are the key elements of what holds fictional/poetic worlds together. They may ostensibly take the form of plot, narrative time, character, rhythmic shape, linguistic intensity, and so on, but these elements are merely the constituents of a map that charts an emotional landscape. If we, as readers, wish to explore the consequences of feeling, we turn to fictional works like plays, stories, novels, and poems, which have charted those territories for us. They answer the question: *what if?*

Fourth, all the assumptions in the previous discussion have been that there is a commonly experienced "real world" and alternative "fictional" or "possible" worlds. It is a matter of philosophical debate as to what extent what any one person considers as the "real world" is indeed the same as another's perception of that "commonality." Such commonality is hard to prove. Rhetoric as a discipline is more pragmatic than philosophy in this respect: it assumes a degree of commonality—enough to define a communally agreed space that we can call the "real world" and that can serve as a reference point for social and political engagement. This does not mean to say that rhetoric takes *perception* for granted. On the contrary: it accepts that perceptions may be different, but it explores these differences through the lenses of framing, through the channels of communicative modes and media, and through the relationship of the rhetor to his/her audience. The assumption of a degree of commonality moves rhetoric as a discipline closer to social theories of being, like Marxism, in which the actions of any one person in a social network or system affects others. Rhetoric both traces these communicative actions and in fact *generates* them. This closeness to the real world of communicative exchange may explain why Eagleton (1976, 1983) described rhetoric as "political literary criticism"—literary criticism that was aware of its place in the world, not in terms of a simplistic distinction between "reality" and "fiction," but in the filigrees of connection between words on a page and the realities that those words represent and convey.

There is one further aspect of the relationship between the poetic and the rhetorical that must be noted: the dialogic nature of literary production and the further dialogic nature of the rhetor/audience relationship. Bakhtin (1982) is the source of much of the debate on these issues, particularly on the first of the two. If, as Bakhtin suggests, no work of literature is created without being in response to existing works, and that new works position themselves in response to the "voices" that have come before them, then the production of new poetic works is essentially dialogic. New works "answer" existing works. To take a further step—steps taken by reader response theorists in particular—the reader or the audience plays as much a part in the creation of meaning as the author/rhetor. In other words, the relationship between writer and reader (to use these terms for simplicity's sake in the argument) is a mutual, reciprocal, and dialogic one. The "work" created by a novelist, poet, or dramatist, like the score of a musical composition, has no realization until it is "re-created" in the mind of the reader. Such a poetic is deeply rhetorical, in that it accepts that communicative exchange is a social act and that both the writer and the reader bring a hinterland of references and assumptions, manifested in framings, to the act of communication.

Let us now turn from the high level relationships between the poetic and the rhetorical to questions of *form*. Putting aside differences in genre for the moment—the novel, the short story, the poem, the play—the focus in the first instance will be on the supposedly most intense literary form: the poem. The *intensity* comes from the close attention to form and what that represents. The fact that some refer to poetry as the *highest* literary form is merely a wish to erect a hierarchy of forms and aesthetic experiences that creates an élite—and all the cult of celebrity and *faux* excitement that such élites engender. For the purposes of the current argument about the place of poetics within rhetorical theory, *intensity* is a better indicator. To put it another way, the intensity comes from a *highly framed linguistic construct* that constitutes, in the discourses we are exploring, "literature"—reading matter.

Take the following poems, all on the topic of reading and all commissioned as part of an "auction of promises" to raise funds for scholarships for postgraduate study for developing countries across the world.

Recovery

Lost without it, I found myself
piecing together a difficult jigsaw
of letters and sounds; one of the more
cryptic sets; and even more than this,
one in which I needed to make sense of the world,
speak to my friends, understand myself.
Not until I had help with this puzzle
did I start to see the pattern.
The picture formed slowly; images rose
from the developing tray. I could not say
what the process was like, except
that this was no ordinary game.
Now I can hold my head up with others:
recovered, insightful, happy, *the same.*

Fictional worlds

Each story takes me to a different place.
The journey's fast, my whole self's hurled

into distant landscapes; I see faces
I've never seen before, in new worlds.
Yet all seems, safe, intriguing, familiar.
I walk alongside some figures
that speak to me; others, though similar
to me in other respects, are mere characters.
Some locations seem distant, others close;
the itinerary's clear. The room's re-arranged.
I come back to this world of ghosts
and feel I've been away, my outlook's changed.
So reading is my travel guide.
As it was for Dante: with Virgil at my side.

On photographs of readers

A girl is absorbed in a book.
She sits in a window frame
not cognisant of a passing train
or of the photographer's look.
An old man sits in a magazine stall
in Kabul or Fez, his customers
all preoccupied too; his trust in *us*
is a precondition to reading at all.
A riverside picnic near Paris:
after lunch, the party rests
while some pursue their interests
in turning pages, oblivious
to the coming of the new century.
All lost in print they substitute for memory.

Discovery

Once I learnt to read, I felt myself
seeing more in people than I knew was there;
a smile in solidarity, a degree of care
that seemed to come encased in binding on a shelf.
Then images opened up to me:
they sat with print, or stood alone
in frames on people's walls at home,
all colour, form, line and sanctity.
it is as if a window had been opened
Letting in the air from the sea;
what was closed to me was now evident
and full of scope; and,
although I like its complexity
comes like a force nine gale, now imminent.

The first point to note is that they are set on the page differently from the rest of the text of this book (in its prose-based, discursive, argumentational mode). They are instantly recognizable as poems in that they are consciously surrounded by white space, the words do not go up to the right hand edge of the page, and they are the product by a rhythmic sensibility that finds the form and the nature of the lines within that form a medium for the characterization and "setting" of internal and relative rhythmic relations. Such differences from everyday speech, or the discursive writing that surrounds them, can prompt those who read the works aloud to take on a different "voice": more distant, more Oracle-like, more toneless, and consciously rhythmical than everyday speech. On the other hand, an actor reading them might take on a more unevenly paced, colorful, and varied delivery in his/her attempt to "convey the meaning." Whichever way we look at these works—even if they try to emulate the colloquial, as these poems do—they are different and distinct from the everyday.

All are sonnets, in that they all consist of fourteen lines. If we take the sonnet form as one of a number of poetic forms designed to capture a sociological niche (in this case, the "little song") as well as representing a tradition running from Petrarch through Shakespeare to, say, Robert Lowell, we can state that the form is often used to make an argument, either of a general nature or of a directly persuasive kind (e.g., from one lover to another). The arguments are condensed, eloquent, and carefully constructed. The form is instantly recognized, even on a page from a distance, in that the 14 lines (with longer lines than those in the previous examples) often look like *a square of printed text* on a page. This visual recognition of a sonnet is instant: the assumption of the sonnet form is sometimes played with by poets who provide 12 or 15 lines of blocked poetic text, but generally many such recognitions are correct: the author wishes you to know that he/she is using the sonnet form, with all its associations. Differently, if we experience a sonnet aurally rather than visually, for example in a reading on the radio, we are caught up in the formal sense that not only might the voice sound different from everyday speech, but the intensity of the delivery takes 30 seconds to a minute; we are asked to, in Coleridge's terms, suspend disbelief for that short period and frame that brief period for contemplation, enjoyment, and reflection.

However, although all the previous poems are sonnets, they experiment with different types of the form. The first is Lowellian, in that it operates in free verse, unrhymed except for the resonance of "game" and "same" in the twelfth and last lines—a way of bringing about closure. The punctuation—as is the case with the other sonnets—invites the reader to move from line to line in a more colloquial way than a more tightly conceived metrical form, even though the unit of rhythm, as in most free verse, is the *line*. Without the accentuating support of rhyme in individual line endings (suggesting "this is the end of a line"), and the structural support of a rhyme scheme in the work as a whole, which sets up a musical pattern that underpins the words, the rhythm has to be carried by the "*sense* of a line ending," which is built up by the overall sonnet form, once perceived. All the lines are roughly the same length, and the line length provides an underlying measure (Hughes suggested poetry was a "dance in words") or rhythmic template within which the words move, even as they define the template. Within such a "free" form of the sonnet, syntax gets more profile, and we attend to the rhythms of the demotic, everyday voice more closely than if it had been highly framed for us in musical terms. The impression is of a casual voice, speaking directly to us in informal terms; the actuality is that the voice is part of a constructed artifice that is giving the appearance of informality.

The second sonnet takes the Shakespearian form that we are familiar with from *The Sonnets,* with a rhyme scheme of ABAB, CDCD, EFEF, GG. The alternating rhymes in the main body of the poem are wrapped up in the rhyming couplet at the end. What is distinctive, too, about this form is the series of three quatrains followed by a couplet. Shakespeare uses this form to argue a case: three propositions, some of them including "evidence," followed by a concluding statement. The third one is slightly different, in that rather than alternating rhymes in the body of the poem, each quatrain operates in a more enclosed way with a rhyme scheme of ABBA, CDDC, EFFE, GG. Here form dictates a slower, more deliberate build up to the conclusion with less argumentative momentum.

Finally, the fourth sonnet uses yet another pattern: ABBA, CDDC, EFG, EFG. The effect of this pattern is to distinguish the octet from the sestet—the first eight lines from the next six. The "feel" of such a form, or the "structure of feeling" implied by the form, is of one statement followed by another—a two-part argument.

Considerations of form and of formal variation, as in the previous four sonnets, are typical of poetry and of poetics more widely. They are about something tangible, which in most cases is about rhythmic patterning—not only in explicit and ostensible forms like the sonnet, but also on larger canvases like the novel or the play, divided as they usually are into chapters and acts/scenes. The rhythmic patterning is subtle, and in many cases we do not notice it; it simply works at an affective level, providing a substratum of shaping within time that determines for us the structure of feeling. That structure of feeling is different from the perception of time that is either lived through everyday experience, in relation to diurnal rhythms and/or the clock; rather, it is a rhythm that builds on and varies repetition, thus saying to us: this experience moves you out of linear time into a moment of layered time, or timelessness, that asks you to consider the *quotidien.* It is a mechanism that, as in music, lifts the reader or listener on to a different plane of experience, but one connected to the everyday world through the conceptual content of the words. Furthermore, it engages the physical: rhythm is felt physically, in dance, movement, and within the body throughout heartbeat and pulse.

Thus poetics always sits in relation to the wider rhetorical imperative of communication through the arts of discourse. Its functions are to provide a different perspective on experience; to use its devices of rhythm, framing, intensity, and compression to distinguish itself from everyday communication practices but, at the same time, to keep connections strong between the everyday "real world" and the possible worlds it creates as lenses to view the real world.

One of the awkward dualities that a rhetorical perspective can illuminate is that between "fiction" and "non-fiction." We will navigate between this apparent Scylla and Charybdis, and then consider the place of narrative within a theory of rhetoric.

The contemporary novel has challenged the notion of itself as a purely fictional genre by the inclusion of documentary material. While such inclusion may be seen as a sleight of hand on the part of the novelist, incorporating *realia* in order to persuade the reader of the veracity of the fiction, another—more generous—view of such inclusion is that the *possible world* created by the novelist is a hybrid, a crossover space in which "reality" and "fiction" meet. The novel is such a capacious genre that hybridity can be accommodated: think of *Tristram Shandy,* or the short stories of Jorge Luis Borges. Such hybridity can include letters ("the epistolary novel"), fragments of found material, other documents, references to real world events and/or actual people from history who become "characters," or political references (e.g., references to Thatcherism in *The Line of Beauty*). The distinction between fiction and non-fiction becomes more bizarre when we consider that a vast swathe of text and discourse is classified by a "non-" category. This distinction appears to favor fiction as a gold standard, hegemonic, and even élitist meta-genre, and the rest of discourse as somehow defined by the fact that it is *not* of that nature. Perhaps the establishment of fiction as a cultural measure reflects the desire on the part of a middle class or middle/upper élite to be party to a world of possibility, of ideas, and of abstracted fictional life that marks them out from the tedious routines of the real world? The plethora of book reviewers, the adulation of the "creative writer" and the courses in such writing, book groups, and the cult of the author all suggest an industry and a class group geared around fiction, with the novel as the primary genre via which that group and industry define themselves.

Having established that not all novels are entirely fictional, let us look at the category that is classed as "non-fiction." This category includes manuals, guide books, encyclopedias, letters and other forms of correspondence, speeches, reports, academic writing, and briefings of all kinds. This is not so much a single category as a broad spectrum of different genres, all currently defined and united by the fact that they are not fictional. Most of these genres have a function in the world and are valued for the fact that they are a *means to an end* rather than an end in itself: they are generally seen, to use a term from discourse theory in the 1970s, as "transactional" rather than "poetic." But a closer look at these genres suggests that they, too, are the product of creative activity; they, too, can be subject to critical analysis (e.g., notions of unity, imagery, or style); they too are the product of imaginative thinking; and they also chart possible worlds. The term that might be preferred is *documentary* rather than *non-fiction,* which tends to diminish their cultural value.

Let us return to Pavel's (1986) notion of possible worlds in order to shed light on the problem of the fiction/non-fiction categorization: the possible worlds created by the novel, for instance, are sustained possible worlds in which all the elements are shaped within an overarching conception of a possible, parallel, imagined world. Actions, characters, and other elements of fictional novels are no less "real" than actions in the real world, other than that they exist in a potential state. They are subject to narrative, emotional logics, just as actions in the real world are subject to these. The possible worlds created by documentary texts, on the other hand, are linked to the actions of the real world in a different way: they chart not whole, sustained worlds as such, but operate as guides and pathways to the real world, such as a recipe, a travel guide, a manual on how to tune a radio, or an investment portfolio report. As suggested by the philosophy of modal logic, every act within the real world is a matter of choice, and possible worlds are available all the time to each and every one of us, even in the most straitened of circumstances. Rhetoric, it might be said, has weaknesses because it does not take responsibility for the actions of the world that it might lead to; but its boundaries—that of the arts of discourse and communication—preclude it from direct influence on the world other than through speech acts. On the other hand, its deployment can prevent the deterioration of human action into violence, war, and tyranny.

A mode of discourse that the novel draws on for its linear power is narrative: a mode that embraces storytelling, autobiography and biography, chronologies of various kinds, and personal accounts. It can be seen from this list of examples that narrative genres include the fiction and "non-fictional" or documentary. Classical to nineteenth-century conceptions of rhetoric afforded narrative—alongside argument and description—central status. These were ways of arranging discourse, but they also conveyed dispositions and functions of different kinds: narrative, as well as its obvious telling and relating functions, has the association of inclusion, of unarguable record, and of sequential pleasure. Argument tended to be associated with persuasion, with the establishment of different ideologies and positions, with operation in democratic and public spaces as well as in personal life, but also with clarification, the management of abstraction (claims, propositions), and the "vertical" relationship between such propositions with evidence. Argument, then, was a mechanism for debate about how to change the world, whereas narrative was more of a record of how the world was or how it was perceived. Description, though with strong classical antecedents, now seems more of a school genre: an artificial genre for recorded observation or non-sequential, non-vertical discourse. It is thus seen as a lesser partner of narrative and argument, the two main modes of discourse. Much has been written about narrative, but in rhetorical terms, the best way to see its relationship to argument is to envisage narrative as operating on a horizontal, sequential axis, managing aspects of time and rhythm, with argument operating on a vertical, hierarchical axis in its exploration of propositions in relation to evidence. Both have vertical and horizontal properties, though we say on the vertical axis that argument tends to operate deductively, while narrative tends to work inductively. On the horizontal axis, narrative is clearly driven by a temporal principle that links character and action, whereas argument links propositions in a logical or quasi-logical sequence.

Why is narrative so compelling as a form of discourse? Its inclusiveness; its closeness to everyday lived experience of time, sequence, and action; its "natural" similarities to the passage of lives as well as of days, weeks, and years; its ability to create "worlds" that are not easily questioned, other than through the creation of counter-narratives . . . all these properties favor narrative and its adoption as a *modus operandi,* or even a "human paradigm." Argument looks more difficult: it requires logical sequencing, more careful arrangement, the engagement and persuasion of others, and connectivity to the real world in terms of valid and reliable evidence and the manufacture of consensus for action. Argument—and its more technical process, argumentation—was the focus of chapter 6 of the present book. The reason that narrative has been a principal focus in the current chapter is that it is not addressed elsewhere in the book.

Finally, in this chapter on rhetoric and poetics, we turn our attention to a micro-level of classification that classical (and especially Renaissance) rhetoric excelled in and that twentieth-century literary stylistics explored in considerable detail: the science or art of "prosodic and poetic terms likely to be encountered in many areas of literary study" (Preminger, Warnke, and Hardison 1986). Indeed, Grierson's (1945) *Rhetoric and English Composition* turns out to be less of a guide or manual for composition in English than an invocation to turn to literary examples and models to encourage rhetorical dexterity in writing. It is more of a medieval *progymnasmata* (exercises in modeling and copying literary form) than a comprehensive guide to composition, again reinforcing the historical preeminence of the literary over the more broadly linguistic. The tendency to classify rhetorical tropes and forms in minute detail reflects a movement to establish rhetoric as a science, driven by a classificatory and analytical energy; it also happens to create a labyrinth of terms that ultimately has the effect of losing the reader and his or her connection to the starting point of his/her journey: the engagement with and understanding of text and of spoken and multimodal discourse in the world.

However, in examining the encyclopedic traces of one form of a discipline, what can be learnt? What relevance have such manuals for a theory of contemporary rhetoric? *The New Princeton Encyclopedia of Poetry and Poetics* (Preminger, Brogan, and Warnke 1993) and its more selective, more focused *The Princeton Handbook of Poetic Terms* (Preminger et al. 1986) are not only repositories of and toolkits for literary analysis; they are, it is claimed by some writers, essential for composition. First, it is instructive to see how the *Handbook* defines its own relationship with rhetoric in the entry on "rhetoric and poetics." There is a long entry, starting with the Aristotelian definition of rhetoric as the art of persuasion, and of poetics as "the art of making or judging poetry" (1986, 230). In "most general" terms, the *Handbook* defines rhetoric as not only the study of the means of persuasion, but as an "inventory or tropes and figures"; whereas poetics is seen "as precepts for the production of verse or as an account of the qualities of literary creation and the nature of literature" (230). The dialectic between rhetoric and poetics, set up from Aristotelian principles, tends to diminish the power and scope of rhetoric in four ways: by containing rhetoric to the "art of persuasion"; by seeing it as "show" and "artifice" as opposed to substance; by including the category of the literary within poetics, and by erecting the literary above the demotic and everyday (realized in the fiction/non-fiction relationships explored earlier in this chapter); and by seeing rhetoric as a principally historical phenomenon, looking back to its classical antecedents. Looking at rhetoric from a poetics standpoint, and in line with Grierson and his disciples of literary culture, the imperative appears to be that a study of literature and its tropes will equip the student with a refined literary sensibility that will be of use in operation in the world in terms of making fine distinctions and judgments. If "all of human nature" is captured by literature (especially by Shakespeare), then poetics, which dissects and classifies literary production, serves as a model and manual for the arts of discourse in the world.

One of the interesting logical moves in the account of rhetoric in the Princeton *Handbook* is that it sees medieval and renaissance rhetoric as resurrecting the principles of invention and arrangement (*inventio, dispositio*), but then suggests that such re-instatement of these concepts and terms puts rhetoric in a difficult and unsustainable position, referring merely to style and presentation. There appears to be a lacuna in the argument here, as invention and arrangement, dealing as they do with the motivations for composition and the macro-level structural arrangements of discourse, are different from style and delivery. From the point of view of the current reconception of rhetorical theory, it is poetics and literary study—rather than rhetoric—that has confined itself to style (not even to performativity and delivery) by separating itself off from invention and arrangement. While this may appear to be a battle of definition of terms and scope between rhetoric and poetics, it is the clear position of the present book that poetics is a subsection of rhetoric, rather than the other way round, and that the definitional "battle" for rhetoric (fought by Vickers 1989) is with Platonic-derived philosophy, not with poetry, literature, and poetics. Preminger et al. (1986) instead see rhetoric as declining through the seventeenth and eighteenth centuries in the form of "monuments of a discipline reaching its end" (232), culminating in the "revolt . . . [against] codifications of the rhetorical tradition . . . accompanied [by] the rise of *aesthetics*" in the Romantic period and the nineteenth century. We have seen elsewhere in the book that the nineteenth century marked the rise of literary study and its oppositional counterpart, historical and diachronic linguistics, dividing up the territory of rhetoric into two separate (and only tenuously related) disciplines. Despite a number of attempts to provide overarching rhetorical theory to discourses of all kinds, especially in the American twentieth century tradition of rhetoric represented by Burke (1969), the *Handbook* sees rhetoric as confined to *analytical* imperatives rather than to generative and compositional meaning-making. This approach is reinforced by rhetoric and composition courses that look back to classical models for their inspiration.

Nevertheless, let us take some of the conventional poetic tropes and figures and look at them from a contemporary rhetorical perspective. The devices chosen for this purpose are rhyme, metrics, and alliteration. Interestingly, rhyme is defined as "a metrical rhetorical device based on the sound-identities of words" (Preminger et al. 1986, 233) but, like much of poetics, focuses conventionally on the internal systemic properties of rhyme, rather than on its functions and connections to other properties of language and its deployment in particular genres such as poems. Rhyme schemes; the sub-categories of full (phonetic) rhyming, half rhymes, unrhymed verse; and the sonority of rhyme are all seen to be matters for discussion. From a rhetorical perspective, however, rhyme has functions: it is there primarily to reinforce rhythmic shape. Rhythm, in turn has the function of marking the selection of words in time and arranging them in such a way as to engender an aesthetic and feeling response. Rhythm, indeed, might be said to be one of the defining characteristics of a poem. The framing of language in poetic form—whether seen and/or heard—is more to do with its rhythmic identity than with its selection of words (its "diction") or its rhyme. It is identified by the reader or listener *as a poem* because of this rhythmic shape. Rhyme, then, is a secondary device used to point up rhythm. This is where is relates, also, to metrics, in that the regular beat of a meter as opposed to the more jazz-like rhythms of free verse is reinforced by rhyme. Alliteration might therefore be seen as a tertiary analytical level of operation from a rhetoric perspective as it is a form or element of rhyming. In summary, a rhetorical perspective on poetics starts from the wider political shaping of words. They are framed in order to convey something to someone/an audience. The author chooses from a repertoire of language and rhetorical devices in order to make his/her "message" aesthetically pleasing, communicative, and rhythmically effective. The repertoire is as much a resource for the artist as it is for the analytical reader or listener.

It might be said that the thinking set out in this chapter applies more to public verse—for example, the work of neo-classicists like Dryden and Pope—than to the lyric outpourings of the Romantic tradition. And yet the challenge of Romanticism to rhetoric, captured, for example, in the "Preface" to *Lyrical Ballads,* is a challenge to outmoded rules of operation and rhetorical conventions, rather than to rhetoric itself. The argumentational move to establish a new kind of poetic is a rhetorical move and sets up a new kind of rhetoric: one in which (in the case of *Lyrical Ballads*) expressiveness, the individual voice, narrative, and the lyrical spirit infuse the conventional poetic modes. It is interesting that Wordsworth, Coleridge, and many of their contemporaries did not innovate much in the formal sense; they used the ancient forms. What they were arguing for was a different position for the poet in relation to his or her audience and in relation to subject-matter ("nature"). This re-alignment is itself a deeply rhetorical move. That is why the view that Romanticism signaled the "death of rhetoric" must be countered by a view that suggests it merely presaged a *different kind of rhetoric.* Take *The Prelude* for example: as England's first autobiographical/philosophical poem, it marks a new moment in how poetry could act as the vehicle for the delineation of a life-story as well as providing a mode for lyric and philosophical expression. As such, it might be seen as the precursor of the subject English in schools and universities. It is rhetorically significant in these respects, as one of the prime examples of the presentation of self in poetry, is also at the same time a radical repositioning of the self in society.

10

Rhetoric and Theatre

In the Renaissance and into the sixteenth century, rhetoric provided the theoretical basis for acting manuals. With simple staging, the emphasis on acting in public or private spaces was paramount. In a precursor to multimodal theory, the gestures, movements, and choreography of acting were the subject of comprehensive acting guides.

Although such manuals were mocked by Shakespeare and fell into disuse, the fundamental vocabulary of acting has remained. The current chapter looks at rhetoric in relation to these historical precedents, to the "empty space" that is theatre, to contemporary acting and classical training, to drama, and to the voice. All these aspects of acting and theatre emphasize the spatial and gestural dimensions of communication, as well as the production through voice and voices, rather than the linguistic dimension.

The Nature of Theatre

Brook's (1972) "the empty space" provides us with a starting point for exploring the rhetoric of drama and theatre. In effect, any space can be the ground for drama and theatre. A space for dramatic performance can simply be identified, then (crucially) framed by, in effect, saying *that* territory is outside the dramatic space, and *this* is inside it. The space may be framed by an already defined space like a garden or warehouse or porch, but it can equally be created by drawing a line in the sand, demarcating the acting space with a rope or with pieces of wood, or merely by saying "here is the line." What is inside the demarcated space is magical in that it circumscribes the space in which we give attention to the action through a suspension of disbelief: the action can be realistic or surreal or anywhere on that spectrum. Wherever the action sits in relation to the real world, it is defined as a fictional world, a possible world. This separation of the real world from the fictional world is no more distinct than in Japanese Noh theatre, where the fictional world can take on the status of a spiritual world. In a production witnessed in a forest outside Osaka in the 1980s, the raised stage was lit by four fire beacons at each corner of the stage, fueled by logs with which teenage young people kept the fires going. They would crawl in the dark of the area beyond the stage, so as not to be seen by the audience (or, in the suspension of disbelief that occurred, not noticed).

As with all framing, what is inside the space "speaks to" what is outside. The audience is conventionally outside the space and see and hear what is inside as representative, in some way, of their experiences in the real world. The action inside the space can mirror that outside it—directly, or indirectly, in various degrees of abstraction from the real world. Just as with a framed painting, or a poem framed by white space on a page, the theatrical space provides the parameters for action of a different order from that of the real world and invites contemplation, reflection, emotional response, and comparison with the real world.

As with painting and the other arts, trangression of the line between the action and the audience is now common practice. In a production of *The Taming of the Shrew* by the Royal Shakespeare Company at Stratford in the 1970s, Sly appeared from amid the audience at the beginning of the play, with the house lights up, and staggered drunkenly on to the stage. Fighting off stewards and ushers, he proceeded to destroy the set while half-dressed actors, the director, and stage managers tried to stop him. Finally collapsing on the stage, the rest of the set fell on him, the lights went down, and the cry of the hunting horn that presages the hunt who find him, lying drunk in a ditch, signaled the start of the play proper. As the stage lights came up, a new, barer set was revealed, and the hunt entered to find him. In other productions, naked dancers at Sadler's Wells have cavorted through the audience in dance; actors have engaged directly with members of the audience, as in *One Man, Two Guv'nors* (National Theatre production in London and New York, 2011–13); in a production of *The Master and Margarita* by Complicité at the Barbican Centre, London in 2013, one of the actors turned to the audience *as citizens* in a totalitarian state to ask for their vote on a decision in the play. At the Globe Theatre on London's Bankside, characters frequently move through the groundlings who are standing in front of the raised stage. Entrances and exits, in the latter example, are often through the audience, and some of the action takes place amid the audience.

In film, Woody Allen's *The Purple Rose of Cairo* has the main actors moving in and out of the cinema screen into the audience, between the world of film and the real world of the cinema stalls.

Why does the transgression of the line between action and audience cause such surprise and either excitement or shock/outrage? Because the framed space of the fictional action is not only fictional, but sometimes sacrosanct, the crossing of the boundary by either the actors or the audience is seen as crossing more than a functional line. First, it surprises the audience from their state of suspension and the pleasure that ensues from sitting back and watching/listening. Suddenly their physical space is encroached. Second, it suggests that the relationship between the fictional space and the real space is more complicated than had been assumed: indeed, that the membrane between the real and the fictional/possible/ spiritual/"other" is more delicate, more permeable, and more interesting than had been imagined. Third, it raises the possibility that a member or members of the audience might be transported to the "other side," however momentarily. Such transgressions almost always engender laughter: as much from nervousness as to what might ensue as well as from the comic potential of incongruity.

From a director's or actor's point of view, the trangression of the line between the acting space and the audience is simply another device they can use to generate a response, to shape the structure of feeling in the "auditorium," and to map out their designs upon the audience. These possibilities are part of the rhetorical armory of the theatre.

Acting

If we were to attempt to write a contemporary manual of rhetoric for the modern actor, where would we start and what would it contain? First, with the body and gesture, including facial expression. Second, with movement. Third, with the voice. Each of these affordances of the actor—or dimensions of possibility of expression—have further subcategories.

In terms of the arts, the body has its purest form of expression in dance, where the form of the physical shape, both in stillness and in movement and the relations between them, is central. Just as with theatre, dance performance is circumscribed by the stage, as defined by the theatre and/or by the dancers themselves. (In a different context, we could say that formal or free-form dancing to a live band, or in a disco, is rhetorical in the moves that people make, both by themselves and in relation to others—a "conversation" in physical movement.) Formal, staged dance performances are choreographed, using a technical score like that for music or words, but with its own vocabulary. The range of dance moves—from athletic to statuesque, from dramatic to "pure," from classical to modern—indicates the rhetorical range. In addition to these, specialized forms of physical acting such as fighting, period dance, contemporary street dance, dying, and acrobatics are all practiced by those training to act.

Gesture is a specific form of movement, usually using hands and arms but in concert with movement of the whole body, that signifies meaning without resorting to sound or words. This form of rhetoric was specifically the subject of acting manuals of the Renaissance period but is also the subject of anthropological studies; for example, Morris (1979). In theatre, it is foregrounded in dumb shows and plays within plays, such as "The Mousetrap" or "The Murder of Gonzago" in *Hamlet,* where the actors perform a play that is prefaced by a dumb show or mimed reprise of the action. Gesture is also used in acting as one of the devices to convey character, response, and feeling.

Facial expression is another aspect of bodily movement that operates as part of the rhetorical armory of the actor. Whether the expression is fixed, as in Chinese opera or in masked performance; or whether the whole range of expression is used, as in conventional Western theatre, the importance of facial expression is evident—and the audience's perception of its significance is sometimes lost if the play is performed in the round. In film or television, where close-up is possible, facial expression takes on even greater significance as the conveyer of feeling to the audience via the character's expression.

The second major category of physical expression in acting is movement. Within the framed space of the stage, the positioning of the actors, and how they stand or sit or lie (or fly) in relation to each other is as choreographic as in dance. Students of acting are sometimes asked to observe animals and to sustain an animal-like set of movements over a period of time. The concentration involved in such an action requires the whole body to move in a particular way and, if the other actors in the exercise are different creatures, to move in relation to each other. The notion of flying reminds us that the framed space of the stage is vertically defined as well as on a horizontal plane. Not only do the stage and its set have a vertical as well as depth dimension; actors sometimes fly in or descend from the "flies" (and also emerge from underneath the stage). Such verticality in the framed space had moral and religious significance for Shakespeare's theatre and for his predecessors in morality and miracle plays, with heaven above the stage and hell below it. But most relative movement is on a horizontal plane.

Thirdly, the voice is an instrument used by actors to speak lines, to sing, to modulate feeling, to convey thoughts, and to utter sounds that are significant and communicative. Rooting the voice in the stomach, in the lungs, or in the throat and head has different resonances and different effects. Changes in volume, tone, emphasis, pace, rhythm, projection, and other features of the spoken voice all bear upon the rhetorical influence an actor can have upon an audience. In addition, variations in social dialects and accents, regional dialects and accents, national and international dialects, plus the whole range of languages worldwide provide a wide range of possibilities. In 2012, at London's Globe theatre, all 37 of Shakespeare's plays were produced, each in a different language. Although the physical (dance, gesture, choreography) aspects of communication were strongly in evidence, the spoken languages of the plays were foregrounded.

Bringing together the elements of the acting space and the acting itself, actors must learn to fill the space and work with the audience to generate the effects they wish to create. It is a marked difference between a play that is performed, on the one hand, in a space where there is light and where the parameters of the space are hard to define (or are defined loosely); and, on the other, in a space that is more tightly defined and where the light can be controlled in order to separate the acting space from the space in which the audience sits. Without such separation, trangression is more difficult. The differences between rehearsals, rehearsed performances, and fully fledged performances are marked by increasing definition. As has been suggested, the definition of dramatic space can be made by a theatre, or it can be made anywhere where lines are drawn to create a framing of dramatic space.

The rhetorics of such spaces and what goes on within them suggest that multimodality is seen in its fullest and most explicit forms in theatre, opera, and other art forms where all channels of expression are used and where the possibilities of communication between the real and possible worlds is at its most open and vibrant. Rhetoric defines these possibilities and the basic language of the arts of discourse that is employed.

Dramatic Discourse in Relation to Poetics

How is dramatic discourse different from literary discourses and the field of poetics? How does poetics relate to rhetoric?

One aspect of rhetoric is concerned with text, specifically, in what form that text appears: linguistic text, semiotic text, or multimodal text (the categories overlap). We could include in that set of texts other "languages," such as that of mathematics and musical scores. These texts tend to be printable, meaning that they either appear in print (e.g., in book form, on paper) or are on an electronic screen and can be printed if required. The history of printing informs the myriad ways in which text can appear.

Dramatic *script* can appear in printable form, but its full realization, that of music, is in performance. The fact that dramatic and musical performances can be recorded in analog and digital codes is yet another dimension of their realization, but it is not the core of the art of the discourse.

Dramatic discourse is based on speech and action (forming characters and plot) but also on "setting." The setting manifests itself in the stage set, which indicates place; on the costumes of the actors, which indicate the period in which the play is set; and on other physical and temporal features that are designed by the director, the stage designer, and the actors. (The issue of design is one to which we will return later in the present chapter.) Even if the stage set suggests no particular period, or is minimal in its suggestion of place, it is situating itself in relation to place and time. In such a way, the stage set contributes to the rhetoric of the whole and has its own vocabulary, its own syntax. Changes of scene in performed plays are often accompanied by changes in the stage set. These are sometimes undertaken on a darkened stage so that the impression is one of magical transformation; on other occasions, the changes are swiftly undertaken by stage hands dressed in black to distinguish them from actors; and sometimes the actors themselves change the sets by moving furniture, by changing the lighting, and by moving props.

But it is in speech, gesture, facial expression, and physical movement—as described previously in the section on Acting—that the realization of dramatic script takes place. The process of moving from a two-dimensional script on a page to a three-dimensional performative realization or *enactment* is part of rhetorical transformation. The words in the script have to be learnt, tried out, sometimes adapted, sometimes cut or elaborated, and embodied in the voices of the actors. The learning of lines for an actor means not only learning the actual lines assigned to his or her part, but also keying into the cues that the other actors and other parts provide. The rhetoric is deeply dialogic, in principle and in action: the stage is a place where dialogue is exhibited, even when the play is a monologue and where the character is talking to him- or herself (and a further dialogic dimension is always with the audience). In no other art form is the dialogic imagination so explicitly demonstrated. Characters speak to and with each other, and as an audience we observe their interaction. Through such observation, we reflect on the possible world presented before us and how it relates to our own worlds.

If dialogue is one principal form of expression in dramatic discourse, another is narrative. In drama, the stories are told via a combination of the setting on the one hand, and what the characters say and do on the other. As with narratives in short story, novel, or oral form, the principle of *post hoc ergo propter hoc* obtains. But the narrative development is different from that in the printable forms. In dramatic discourse, the setting and what characters say and do take place within the confines of the framed set and within the time frame of the play. Some plays are a single scene and relatively short in duration; others are made up of a number of scenes and can take hours, if not days. As printable forms, a play can be divided into sections, such as acts and scenes. The relationship between these acts and/or scenes, especially their sequence, makes up the narrative flow and argument.

The third element of dramatic discourse is tension. This tension is generated between the characters, often in the form of differences of style (dress, speech, and other social markers) but also through ideology, values, and political positions. The power play between the characters (see chapter 5), especially those main characters whose story is told, is the source of the tension that must be resolved in some way. It is thus that plays in performance manifest argument (the product) and argumentation (the process). Their rhetoric is designed to show how tensions are created and how they are resolved. Indeed, the very intensity of theatre is when the tension is evident, and the audience is fully engaged in feeling it and witnessing how it develops. It is possible to say that the enhanced tensions on stage—as in a sporting arena where contests take place—are a way of understanding and alleviating the tensions in everyday life. They can also serve to bring to the surface tensions that are buried within the audience. In these ways, plays operate by allowing the presentation of problems, often in the form of clashing ideological positions, and showing how these might be resolved, or how an action (which can also take the form of a speech act) can lead to another action, and then another, and so on.

Dramatic discourse is distinctive in these ways and, as has been discussed in the chapter on Moffett, presents in the here and now what *could* happen. The very framing of the action on a stage of whatever nature intensifies the action so that we look at it and experience it, expecting that it will provide us with some insight into our own lives.

The Aesthetic Dimension

Because dramatic discourse is framed, we experience it as we would a painting or a book; it is separated from everyday experience by a frame, however intangible. We often pay to enter the space—a theatre, an art gallery, the purchase of a book—that affords us the time and space to experience the potential intensity of the framing. Once in that space, we tend to slow down and pay more attention to the words, brush strokes, sculptural shapes, sounds, and other expressions than we would if they were unframed in the real world. We are attentive and receptive to the structures of feeling that are presented to us in these framed spaces.

What framing does, in addition to that described previously, is to provide the ground for aesthetic experience. The very drawing of a line and creation of a frame around artistic experience, *in order to define it as artistic experience,* brings a different kind of attention to what is inside the frame. We have already referred to the intensity of action within it and of the attention brought to it. There is also the sense that when looking at what is inside the frame, we are looking at possible worlds and comparing our own worlds to these projected worlds. The sense of causal connection is enhanced so that when we see action on the stage, for example, we expect there to be a higher degree of causal connectivity than in the real world.

In addition to these different states of attention, we will expect a greater sense of order, balance, and harmony than that experienced outside the rhetorical frame. That orderliness is formal, that is, it takes formal shape. Whether the work is a painting or a book, or a play or musical score in performance, the sense of designed order is heightened. Such order can be symmetrical, or it can inhere in the relations between movements in music, between scenes and acts in a play, or between chapters in a novel. In theatre, the aesthetic dimension may not be beautiful in a conventional sense, but it may have a structure and pace and rhythm that is a combination of devices for eliciting and generating an emotional and/or intellectual response. Almost always—and often hidden from view—is the underlying formal structure of the piece that subliminally affects the response. The structure works by putting elements in relation to each other (com-posing) and saying, in effect: these are related to each other. Look at the connections that are offered. There is a design element that is deliberate and orderly. Such order, balance, and harmony operates at an unconscious level, informing the emotional and intellectual response.

When we "return" from such an aesthetic experience in a theatre (or from reading a novel, hearing a concert, or looking at an exhibition), back to the real world, we carry with us a memory of the ordered, intense, enhanced experience. There can be immediate parallels between the highly framed aesthetic world of the play on the one hand, and the less obviously (but still sociologically and politically) framed worlds of our everyday existence. But there can also be delayed responses, where the patterning that has taken place through the dramatic discourse informs future ways in which we might see, hear, and generally experience the real world. The territory of rhetoric is how the highly framed aesthetic worlds relate to the looser frames of the real world; what communities of interest and expectation are formed; what is *learnt*, not only within those different worlds but in the parallels and tensions between them; and what transformations take place in consciousness, and whether these transformations can be described at all, or whether they can be accounted for in degrees of transformation.

In a sensibility informed by the arts of discourse, perception becomes heightened so that patterns in experience are seen more readily. We can thus talk of a rhetorical consciousness and sensibility that is sensitive to the way things are framed, the way people talk, the way actions take place and impact on the world, and the way events unfold in the real world. There is much in the latter case that is beyond the limits of rhetoric; but rhetoric, as a humanistic discipline that maps the arts of discourse both in terms of what happens and what could happen, contributes to the way we deal with those events.

Finally, in considering how dramatic discourse operates, it is helpful to reflect on the institutional framings for theatre: built theatres, ranging from Greek amphitheatres to elaborate Victorian edifices; from converted barns or railway stations to temporarily adapted spaces in school halls, on hillsides, or in naturally occurring framed spaces; from portable theatres to performances in town and village squares . . . all these framed spaces define an outer shell within which the dramatic performance itself takes place within an inner shell. We enter such outer shells with expectations: to be entertained, disturbed, amused, stimulated, transported, or any combination of these. There is no society that lives without such framed dramatic space, whichever cultural form it takes. For example, in the *Arts Directory* of the Arts Council for the Northern Adirondacks for 2012–13, in an area of wilderness with low density of population, as well as 44 gallery listings, there were the Adirondack Theatre Festival, Our Town Theatre Group, modern and classical ballet performances, a Shakespeare-in-the-Park festival, the Depot Theatre (a converted railroad station), a school of music, the Boquet River Theatre Festival, Essex Theatre Company's 20th season, Lake Placid Center for the Arts, a Pendragon Theatre program, The Community Theatre Players Inc., and many more. In amateur, community, and professional groups, it seems that the human need to create a rhetorical space in which the arts are presented fulfils much more than an expressive need; it also creates framed worlds in which social tensions and patterns are played out for consideration, reflection, and perhaps future action.

The Inner Space

Of all the arts, drama and theatre (including opera) are the ones that most fully use the modalities of space, time, and the expressive faculties of voice, movement, the body, and gesture. Film, though a medium in itself, builds on drama. It could be said to derive from drama, though it has carved out special territories of its own. Drama also provides the fullest external and tangible representation of the dualities and tensions of the inner space: thought, reflection, dream, and physical tension. In this sense, the rhetoric of the public art form provides a "mirror" for the inner space; and before we explore this analogy any further, it must first be acknowledged that the process is two-way. As well as the inner operations and states being reflected in drama, dramatic discourse also prefigures and structures inner cogitation and feeling.

Based on the latter premise that the higher orders of thinking and feeling were once "real relations between people" (Vygotsky 1991, as discussed earlier in this book), how does rhetoric serve as a way of understanding and describing the transformation between "real relations" and inner operations? Although we are in the realm of social psychology, the problem of such transformations can be accounted for in rhetorical terms. To take the most obvious example: a debate takes place in a public meeting, or in the letter columns of a newspaper. It rehearses, over several hours or days, the lineaments of an argument, putting the case for and against, say, the siting of a new cell phone tower near a village. The very parameters and lineaments of the argument rehearse what can be replicated in inner thought. Those thoughts might be assisted by notes made after the debate or after reading a sequence of letters in a newspaper, to map out the main points; or they may simply be remembered, adapted, and elaborated upon. Thought may stimulate a new perspective on the problem, just as a voice from a different perspective may do so in public discourse.

Issues of the relation of thought to public discourses, and *vice-versa*, can be evidenced also in the conventional written genres via which thought is represented in academia. For example, the default genre (in the sense of text-type) in the humanities and social sciences is the essay. The structure of the essay derives from classical models of argumentation in any number of parts: a two-part structure (statement and proof); a three-part structure (beginning, middle, and end); and then anything up from there, selecting from the range of identified parts of an argument: *exordium, narratio, disputatio,* arrangement, *refutatio, peroratio,* and other subdivisions and variations. The composer of the essay is free to put the elements in the order that he or she prefers (or that he/she thinks will have maximum persuasive power) and to include as many such elements as he/she thinks are required for the particular argument in question. Such freedom in structural design reflects the freedom in thought and also offers templates and scaffolds that can be followed or broken and adapted to suit particular rhetorical needs.

This psycho-social, or socio-psychological composing process has swung between learning and composing theories that privilege either the social or the psychological. A different approach is to see the process as rhetorical. The principles of such a perspective are that the manifest products of communication are the result of thoughts, feelings, and other imperatives that (ideally) closely match them; that when the match is not close, the rhetorical process allows adjustment and revision; that meaning is conveyed as a social transaction between people, aided by social conventions; and that intention and purpose are shaped by the available resources. These principles are predominantly social and political in nature, as has been emphasized throughout the present book, but they also have a psychological dimension that is more than an "application."

Rhetoric, we could say, maps out the network of possibilities for communication between the inner and the public domains. It provides conduits and channels through which such communication has been and is made, but it is always aware that there might be other possibilities, other connections that *could* be made. The "how to" manuals of medieval and Renaissance rhetoric do not fully account for the possibilities because there is no overarching rationale for the range and extent of the devices that are listed. The current book attempts to chart the larger territory of rhetoric, suggesting that it is unified by an interest in the arts of discourse and communication within a socio-political context.

What *is not* rhetorical helps define what *is*. Beyond rhetoric are areas where human communication does not operate: silent walks in the mountains, the way beams are attached to pillars and joints made in wood, the immovability of objects, much of the material world. Furthermore, higher states of spirituality and religious consciousness are not the domain of rhetoric because they (tend to) inhabit a unified space or state in which there is no dialogue. But wherever these states and phenomena and experiences interface with communication, exegesis, articulation in the human world, there is rhetoric: in the design and execution of a map, in instructions for the making of a joint in carpentry, and in descriptions and categorizations of material phenomena. It so happens that these states are not those commonly explored in drama and theatre, other than via a dialogic route and in brief depictions (e.g., Beckett's *Breath*). Theatre provides not only the physical instantiation of how rhetoric operates in the world, but also a metaphor for how a multidimensional experience can be represented and also provide a template for possible action. We might also say that other art forms imply dramatic and theatrical tension and possibility: in reading a poem on a printed page, we supply the color, imagination, three-dimensional properties, and projection to make the imprint mean more than words on a page. Such transformations are silent but always rhetorical, operating at the interface of the public and private.

Design

If rhetoric is the overarching theoretical concept in the arts of communication, what is the principal process, given that framing is a key aspect of composing and "receiving" communication? Because we have expanded the repertoire of modes and media of communication beyond the verbal, *writing* is no longer either the actual description of the process, nor is it even suitable as a metaphor for the range of communicative possibilities. We have already identified *composition* (chapter 4) as a better way of describing the making and receiving processes, but composition does not necessarily include the aesthetic or dramatic dimensions we have been exploring in the current chapter.

Design is a helpful construct when it comes to describing the part played by the rhetor in dialogic communication. Emerging from the fields associated with drawing and with spatial representation, such as furniture design, stage design, and fashion design, the term brings with it not only making and composition, but *conscious* and *aesthetically driven* creation for a particular real-world purpose. That is why the term is separated, but also often yoked with, "art," such as in Art and Design courses, and sometimes seen as an inferior, less pure field than "fine art." The aesthetics of design carry one more aspect than those they share with fine art: that is the area of functionality. Good design for a kitchen knife or a stage set or a shirt will usually include fitness-for-purpose as well as a pleasing (i.e., harmonious) look. That design derives from the visual-spatial world and is practical as well as beautiful, which makes it suitable for inclusion in a repertoire of subsections of rhetoric. It acts as a counter-point to the more abstract symbolizations of writing.

And yet design and writing are complementary. Design applies to the shape, look, and functionality of an object or creation in its context. Writing applies to the inscription as part of the design, but also to the way the design relates to (is interpreted, is mediated by) its human discoursal context.

Any rhetorical moment is designed. In other words, the need for expression and communication is chosen from a repertoire of possibilities. It is intended to have an impact on the real world—on relations between people—and it has an aesthetic dimension. Indeed, rhetoric is the theory within which aesthetics and functionality are brought together. The better designed communication, the more effective; the more effective, the better designed.

What are the tools of the rhetorical designer? These are best thought of, first, through the metaphor of the director and stage designer in the production of a play. They have a script they are working with, and they have actors at their disposal. They have a space within which they are working, however informal or formal that space is. They may have to define the space. They can certainly redesign it, if required for their purposes. Once the basic elements are in place, they begin by working out what aspects of time and place they wish to convey and how those dimensions fit into their overall conception of the meaning of the playscript. These decisions, in turn, drive the work of the set designer who creates a set to fit the overall intention. Set design involves not only what the overall structure of the set will be, but what props—furniture—and what lighting (in collaboration with the lighting designer) will be needed. The conception of the design of the whole also sets the tone for the costume design.

In concert with the decisions made about setting, the director works with the actors—taking cues from them as well as deliberately directing them to fit in with the overall design—asking them to work in a particular way, using the tools at their disposal (body, facial expression, gesture, movement, voice) and the relations between them (choreographic design) to engage in action that will convey to the audience the overall effect. The actors will come with their parts learned; they often do not read the whole play, but work toward that wider knowledge in rehearsal. The script thus emerges for them into a production, on the whole, like photographic images in an old-fashioned developing tray. Some actors will read the whole play to get a sense of their part in it; and if their reading is a fully engaged one, they may have suggestions to put to the director about the direction in which the play might go. But it is the director whose design of the whole informs the approach the actors will take and the specific tone, modulation, pace, rhythm, and interactive dynamic that is created.

Such close analogy between rhetoric and theatre is not meant to suggest that rhetoric operates in the shadow of the real world, or that it is concerned with illusion. Rather, that the conscious decisions taken by directors and set designers to compose, shape, and design an experience, and to transform words on a page into actions in time and space, are exactly what speakers, writers—rhetors—do on a daily and frequent basis in order to get the day-to-day business of the world transacted and in order to nurture and strengthen human relations. Rhetoric, it is argued, provides the fullest theory that marries the abstract/conceptual and the practical, that enables description and analysis of the aesthetics of communication in social and political contexts, and that is core to democratic processes as well as to human interaction. Drama and theatre, with their inclusive, comprehensive, multimodal, and core properties for a range of media representations, offer both an analogy to the more theoretical conception of rhetoric, and also a tangible insight into possible worlds of action and representation. In that sense, we are all actors in a production. Where that notion takes us is not to "higher" and more ethereal explanations of being, but to issues of power in its relation to design, and to both in relation to the aesthetic, to argumentation, and to moving on in the world.

In the final chapter of this book, we look at the future of the field and how rhetoric might stand in relation to the other major domains of knowledge; but first we will look at rhetoric in relation to multimodality, digitization, and education.

11

Rhetoric and Multimodality

It is one of the significant leaps forward in communication theory that multimodality is increasingly accepted as a norm in thinking about the resources for meaning-making. The work of Kress (e.g., 2003, 2010) has been central to this movement. He positions multimodality as an aspect of the theory of social semiotics. Social semiotics, we could say, has emerged from a combination of sociolinguistics; the turn to the social in studies of cognition, culture, and learning (exemplified, for example, in the work of Vygotsky); and from the natural development of semiotics into *social* semiotics on the assumption that the social is prior, but that the social and sign systems shape and inform each other.

It is the aim of this chapter to argue that a social semiotic view of multimodality is complementary and close to an exploration of the relationship between rhetoric and multimodality and that social semiotics, as a theoretical frame, is not far from rhetoric in its scope and values. Both social semiotics and rhetoric see the prime mover in communication as being the social. Both are interested in how, ontologically and culturally, social patterning affects communicative systems and practices. Both value the individual expression and reception of speech, writing, and other modes, as well as the more social, collective patterns that emerge and change over time. Both see a dynamic interaction between sign systems and functionality.

There are some differences, however, between rhetoric and social semiotics that must be addressed. They could be seen as a matter of emphasis, but I think they are important to define as they help us to see how the two bodies of theory could be related and what application such a relationship could have to the practices of communication in society and education.

The first is that rhetoric is more avowedly political than social semiotics. Unless we coined an approach that might be termed, by analogy with critical literacy and critical thinking, *critical social semiotics,* social semiotics *per se* has a social rather than a political set of parameters. Rhetoric, on the other hand, had its origins in politics and power relations in the pre-Athenian Mediterranean and in Africa. These origins tended to focus on one particular mode of communication: speech, and more specifically as an oral genre, political speeches in public forums. Today, rhetoric continues to be associated with politics, often to its detriment: "political rhetoric" is universally decried as misleading, over-persuasive, low on evidence, and high on party political ideology. At worst, it is seen as the egocentric outpourings of politicians with power but insufficient knowledge in language, dressed up in over-persuasive garb. Social semiotics could apply itself to the analysis of political discourse—and it does—but that is the application of a theory and technique to a particular social practice, not a politically and socially informed theory of communication.

Second, there is a difference in starting points. Rhetoric starts with the politico-social need to communicate. Social semiotics starts with the sign and its social significance. The difference is masked by the fact that both theories are interested in the relationship of the social to signs, but they start at different points in the universe of communication. The differences can be characterized partly by their origins, as suggested previously, and partly by the fact that semiotics is a science of sign *systems*. Any scientific theoretical enterprise becomes concerned with categorization and technical terms—that is partly what distinguished it as a science. Social semiotics is no stranger to classificatory terms and systems: affordance, coherence, cohesion, design, discourse, functional load, genre, materiality, modality, transduction, and so on. Some of these are created to serve the field of social semiotics itself; others are borrowed or emerge from previous theoretical formulations in linguistics, sociolinguistics, critical discourse analysis, pragmatics, and other related fields or disciplines. Rhetoric has tended to classificatory systems and extensive glossaries in phases during its history, particularly during the Renaissance and in rhetoric manuals. But it is at its strongest and most flexible when it finds a balance between a simple set of tools for analysis and sufficient clarity and distinctiveness in its definitional terms to make them useful in theoretical and functional (real world) terms. However, the point remains that rhetoric starts with the socio-political nexus; social semiotics with signs and systems. The *language* of rhetoric is about positioning, contextual factors, social dynamics, and the deployment of particular multimodal combinations for particular purposes. The *language* of social semiotics denotes the available resources and tools for the creation and reception of meaning. Perhaps that is one of the Achilles heels of rhetoric—and has certainly been one of the abiding battles that rhetoric has fought, cast as it was in Greek civilization as counter to philosophy, the science of meaning (see Vickers 1989). This does not mean that rhetoric is agnostic about meaning—far from it—but that meaning is the read-off of social interaction, the generation of a web of conceptual filigree that is continually negotiated by agents in society. It is about *how* something is communicated between, at its most simple, two people, not essentially about *what*.

Third, rhetoric—as hinted in the last paragraph—is more generative than social semiotics, which tends to be reserved for analysis. Rhetoric affords designs for the rhetoric or maker on the one hand, and the receiver, reader, or audience on the other. It is intimately interested in the relationship between the rhetor and the receiver of the message, and plies its trade between these two poles. Social semiotics is more interested in the traces of communication, the actual materiality of communication. Rhetoric, then, can offer the maker the resources and means via which to communicate via the heuristics of framing, multimodality, and agency; it is more akin to the arts of discourse. Social semiotics offers more of a scientific means of analysis, informing multimodality and framing via its rich account of the sign systems available.

The respective histories of rhetoric and social semiotics are very different. Rhetoric as a meta-discipline and theory has its origins in pre-Athenian (African/Mediterranean) emergent democracies, though attained one of its first major consolidations in the work of Aristotle and others in classical Greece. The conventional Western history of rhetoric, however, seeing Athens as the progenitor of the rhetorical tradition and Greek democratic operations as the testing ground for the discipline, needs to be put in a more global context. One of the key analyses in this regard is by Blake (2009), who, in *The African Origins of Rhetoric,* identifies African principles of ethos, morality, and values in the governance of social relations. He goes back to Battiscombe Gunn's (1906) translation of *The Wisdom of the East: The Instruction of Ptah-Hotep and The Instruction of Ke'Gemni* to source the principles of rhetoric in pre-Athenian times (and further back from the pre-Athenian Mediterranean traditions, for example, Corax in the fifth century BC). This move to resurrect the significance of African rhetoric is partly spurred by the need to get beneath the cultural carapace of colonialism. *The Instruction of Ptah-Hotep* was written 3,000 years before Corax, and partly to establish the founding principle of rhetoric on moral grounds. Blake further argues that there is a close connection between the revival of rhetoric studies in Africa with African national development, thus positioning the debate in relation to development studies.

The *moral* dimension to rhetoric is worth considering in relation to an emergent theory of contemporary rhetoric. The ultimate purpose of rhetoric is to service the pursuit of the truth, through an emphasis on integrity, clarity of communication, a belief in the power of discussion and debate to understand and resolve problems, and a drive toward consensus for action for good in the world. In this sense, rhetoric is not a cynical or even skeptical theory of communication: it can expose cynicism, cant, hypocrisy, and the split between meaning and delivery. Its drive is toward transparency of intention and a balanced relationship between intention and action. Its operation within a society is for the common good and to service democratic exchange and representation. It can be deployed to explore the relationship between the discourses of faith, secularism, and action. The emphasis is always on the discourses because its principal interest is in the web of communication that acts as a means to the end: the end being good relations between people, governance of social and political life, charting and appreciation of the inner landscape of spiritual and moral life in relation to the work of the world.

Throughout its long history, it has oscillated between being the foreground of attention and playing a secondary role to philosophy (philosophy being the generation and examination of ideas; rhetoric being the means via which those ideas are communicated). It tends to flourish when there is relativism in a society or civilization, or during a period of rapid change when assumed verities are questioned. It also plays an important role in the discussion of ideas that help societies work toward consensus and action. In other words, it is an essential operational and functional element in democracies: a cornerstone of democratic values, and a means by which difference is understood, tolerated, and resolved in order to "move society on." The high points of rhetoric as a unifying theory of communication, following Athenian and Roman democracies, have been the Renaissance and the late twentieth and early twenty-first centuries. It is no coincidence that there has been a rise in interest in rhetoric during these periods. For a particular moment in the history of rhetoric that is not unrelated to the history of social semiotics, see chapter 3 for an extensive discussion of the split between rhetoric and English studies in the late nineteenth century in England.

Social semiotics, on the other hand, has a history of just more than a hundred years. Saussure's (1983) lectures between 1906 and 1911 at the University of Geneva, published later as *Cours de Linguistique Générale*, are generally agreed to be the starting point for structural linguistics. It would be interesting to read an account on the context in which Saussure generated his theory of synchronic relations and system-internal relations of difference. The assumption can be made that the theory is counter to (but also complementary to) the diachronic approach of historical linguistics in the late nineteenth century, which included lexicology, philology, etymology, studies of language variation in dialects, and the history of the development of languages, as well as developmental studies in the acquisition of language in relation to contemporary advances in cognitive psychology. Saussure's emphasis on synchronic relations (we will not go more deeply into other aspects of Saussurean theory here) paved the way for studies in linguistics and semiotics that took the *sign* (and its division into the *signifier* and *signified*) as its basic unit of classification and analysis. The genesis of *social* semiotics or "semiology" was already there in the work of Saussure, as indicated in the following:

> It is . . . possible to conceive of a science which studies the role of signs as part of social life. It would form part of social psychology,

> and hence of general psychology. We shall call it semiology (from the Greek *semeîon,* 'sign'). It would investigate the nature of signs and the laws governing them. Since it does not yet exist, one cannot say for certain that it will exist. But it has a right to exist, a place ready for it in advance. Linguistics is only one branch of this general science. The laws which semiology will discover will be laws applicable in linguistics, and linguistics will thus be assigned to a clearly defined place in the field of human knowledge. (Chandler 2013)

Fifthly, rhetoric is distinguished from social semiotics in general usage by having pejorative associations of sophistry and distortion. It is hard to determine the beginnings of such a depreciatory sense, but the Oxford English Dictionary has it going as far back as Chaucer. This sense that rhetoric can be used to define artificial or over-elaborate expression—and, by implication, artificial and distorted ideas—goes with the territory. It probably stems from a suspicion of words and other forms of communication to misrepresent ideas and meaning (a suspicion going back to Plato and Aristotle)—a conundrum, as meaning is only expressed through communication. Social semiotics carries none of this baggage. Rather, it comes with associations of a systemic science: one that is cool, objective, and dispassionate. As in the work of Bakhtin (1982) and others, *rhetoric* is used in this book in the more ameliorative sense of the arts of discourse and communication, but often the term needs to be rescued from its too-close association with politicians and cant.

Lastly, rhetoric and social semiotics can be distinguished in terms of their position in relation to what we will call, for the moment, the "outside/in, inside/out" relationship. "Outside/in" perspectives privilege the wider, social, political influences on behavior, discourse, and systems. The notion that "the social is prior" would seem to share this perspective. It would also be behind Vygotskian theories of historical and social relations informing cognition (which is generally thought to take place "inside" the head of the individual). Rhetoric, of the two theories or disciplines (more on this choice later), is the more inclined to address the social and political determinants of individual action and communication because it always sees the participants in any act of communication as being "prior." Social semiotics, despite the "social" qualifier and Saussure's conceptions of "signs as part of social life," has more of an "inside/out" perspective. That is to say, it starts from a premise that the sign systems themselves, in whichever modes or combinations of modes, are interesting and worthy of study. These are informed by the social nexus and context, but are nevertheless examinable as sign systems in their own right. They also, as systems, *determine the parameters of* social interaction in a way that rhetoric rarely conceives.

Breaking down binary formulations such as "outside/in" and "inside/out" helps us to see that rhetoric and social semiotics are more closely related than we might have acknowledged, although the Mu Group, founded in 1967, developed a structural version of rhetorics and visual semiotics.

In order to do so, we would need to move, in Hegelian style, from the thesis of social instigation of communication and its antithesis of psychological or individually generated communication to a synthesis in which the categories of "inside" and "outside" were no longer deemed significant, but where the arts of communication were seen to be inevitably about the link between the two dimensions of experience. To use an analogy: if rhetoric is a plain glass window through which we see inside or outside a house, social semiotics (because of its derivation from linguistics) is more of a stained glass window where we are also interested in the passage of light through the window itself (from either the social side or the semiotic side). A third position—the synthesis—would be to open the window and to admit no impediment between the outside and inside worlds.

Another way of conceiving the relationship between rhetoric and social semiotics is to see the latter as a theory and discipline—a way of looking at a particular aspect of the world and its actions. The former could be conceived as a meta-theory and meta-discipline, operating as a higher level of abstraction and generalizability, and including social semiotics as one of its repertoire of frames through which it sees the world and its actions. From this more hierarchical point of view, rhetoric would re-assume its seat as one of the small number of meta-disciplines that once informed the Renaissance curriculum in schools and universities (the others being grammar and logic). While logic might sit alongside it as the progenitor of mathematics, grammar would be subsumed as one of the operational syntagmatic and paradigmatic subsections of verbal and visual languages. As such, grammar could be replaced by analytic philosophy as one of the meta-disciplines.

Rhetoric and Multimodality

Rhetoric is naturally multimodal. It does not confine itself to verbal language(s). It is eclectic in its relationship to modes and media. It assumes that in the act of communication a number of modes will be at play and that their inter-relationship is crucial to understanding how communication works. The aesthetic dimension of rhetoric is also an aspect of multimodality that is important to consider. The combination of modes is a conscious decision, driven by design. Where it is unconscious (say in a face-to-face conversation), the modes at play in the rhetorical moment can be analyzed.

But rhetoric is not a "dimension" of multimodality, confining itself to political discourse or (more generally) issues of power. Rather, it is the other way round. We have discussed previously the similarities and differences between social semiotics and rhetoric. Multimodality plays a part in both theories and is a matter of the deployment of semiotic resources for a particular communicative purpose. If we accept the definition of rhetoric as the "arts of discourse," then multimodality contributes to those arts.

As Kress points out (2010, 26–7), the rhetor's interests in any act of communication need to be fully acknowledged. He or she stands in relation to a world of resources (print, image, sound, physical movement, and gesture) wishing to communicate to a particular audience about something. For example, the father of a bride at a conventional European wedding takes center stage for part of the reception. Conventionally, he makes the first speech at the wedding reception. Although there are conventions shaping and framing the occasion (e.g., welcoming the guests, saying nice things about the daughter, giving "advice" to the groom), there are other constraints to be borne in mind: don't go on for too long, and don't cover the ground that the best man might cover (e.g., amusing stories about the groom).

Such a speech can take some time in gestation. It has to be "right"; in other words, it must not offend, it must continue the joyous momentum of the wedding, and it should not bore the guests. It is a semi-public performance, designed not so much to persuade as to mark a ritual. It is given, then disappears, as is the case in many speech genres. Although it is often prepared as a script, it is done so in a way that makes space for improvisation and for "natural" spoken delivery. It is delivered at an appropriate part of the reception meal, while dessert is on the table and just after the cake has been ceremonially cut by the bride and groom (allowing the cake to be taken away for cutting up so that guests could have a piece later). The guests know that speeches will follow at some point; they are suitably primed. We could say on this occasion, and many similar ones like it, that the audience is ready to listen and to be amused, moved, and informed.

The actual delivery often involves stepping up on to a small stage so that guests can see the "rhetor." The pace is slow enough to be able to articulate clearly. In multimodal terms, there is the combination of speech, gesture, dress (formal wedding attire), the setting (wedding reception in formal room), and the expectation that this speech will be followed by at least two more—the best man, the groom, and possibly the bride—thus providing a string of after-dinner entertainment, each speech having a different function, a different speaker. In essence, a written script becomes a delivered oral speech in a highly visual setting.

Although the genre of the wedding speech runs along fairly well-grooved tracks in a particular culture, there is an element of remaking and consideration of fitness-for-purpose that cannot be underestimated. There is no off-the-shelf package that would fit the bill. The speech has to be personal, for the particular occasion, and of the moment. When the tracks are less well-defined, in situations that are unstable or unpredictable, the rhetor's work is harder in that he/she has to construct the frame for delivery and interpretation. Such framing (as an active verb) becomes more conscious, more essential, and more pressing if communication is to be "successful."

Return to Framing

As expressed in *Re-Framing Literacy* (Andrews 2011) and in chapter 7, framing is a key act in composition, particularly in an age where uncertainties about the audience or about the social conventions that bind the rhetor to the audience are not clear or conventional. Framing, like multimodality, is one of the resources available to the rhetor as he/she makes choices about the act of discourse. It is not always a matter of adopting existing frames from the repertoire of social communication. Rather, it is sometimes a matter of constructing and/or adapting frames that can provide the parameters of communication.

Framing is a creative and necessary act. It operates in space and time, mostly invisibly, to define the parameters of a social situation and the communication that will take place within it. First, space. A situation can be framed by a room in which an encounter takes place. Let us take a coffee shop as an example. It is an established space for drinking and social engagement. Chairs—perhaps sofas—are laid out so that customers can drink and socialize at the same time. They might seem like customers to the business that is running the coffee shop, but the participants themselves see this as a space in which they can relax, talk, and refresh themselves. The actual orientation of the seating is crucial to the nature of the communicative encounter. It partly defines the encounter (sitting alongside is different from sitting opposite each other; sitting at a angle to each other is different again; and three people sitting sets up a different dynamic; and so on).[1] Second, time. Even an encounter in a coffee shop is time-limited. But more formally time-limited are classes in school or university, appointments with doctors, assignations at the school-gates, or the catching of trains, buses, and planes, where the timetable determines the encounter. Time, like space, is elastic so that tightly defined framed time slots, as described previously, are at one end of a spectrum. At the other end are "moments" and longer periods of time that are not measured by the clock, but by other means (days, weeks, months, years, etc.; time as measured by the experience, rather than quantified, for example, Shakespeare's seven stages of development, or the duration of a love affair).

It can be seen, then, that framing plays a central part in social life. It defines the parameters of a social and communicative encounter. But frames can also be transgressed and broken, according to need. A production in a theatre that breaks down the border between the actors and the audience by placing actors in the audience, or taking a member of the audience on stage—or any such transgression of convention—is playing with the notion of framing.

Framing is an important tool for rhetoric in that it helps to define the parameters of the communicative experience. In most encounters, it is taken for granted because it is accepted by both parties in the communicative act. But it becomes a more conscious construct when the analysis as to why communication has not happened well is explored. One person might come to an encounter with a particular set of expectations in mind; another might have another set. Let us take the example of a five-minute presentation that is required before an interview (itself a tightly framed social schema). Unless the presentation has been specified tightly, one interviewee may provide a written statement that he/she reads out to the interviewing panel. Another might provide a Powerpoint presentation. Yet another might simply speak to the panel without notes. These communicative choices are rhetorical choices. They can set the right tone, if the rhetorical moves are well-judged and meet the expectations of the panel; they can also get the interview off on the wrong foot if the rhetorical choices made are inappropriate, like standing up in a round table, informal-style interview, or lolling back in a chair in a more formal set-up.

In many cases where schemata are clear and conventional—in other words, where the frames are clearly defined and have become the expected norms—we do not think about the frames. We simply operate within them. But as social conventions blur at the edges, the act of framing rather than the frames themselves become more important. Framing is thus seen as a critical, creative act that aids communication; it is an operation that both rhetor and audience can play a part in. Frame-breaking is also an important possibility, not only in theatre and the arts, but in social situations where convention has become stultifying.

The Issue of "Reception"

Much of the history of rhetoric has been concerned with Kinneavy's more recently expressed notion of rhetor, audience, and subject matter. That is to say, the assumption has been that the speaker/writer/composer "sends" the substance of the message, via different modes and media, to a listener/reader/audience who "interprets" it—either perfectly or imperfectly. Rhetoric, from this perspective, is seen as the arts of how best to convey that message and its intentions.

Recent studies in multimodality, however, have begun to question the nature of the relationship between rhetor and audience and, as a consequence, the nature of the "sending" and "receiving" model of communication. The compression of the communicative act is further brought about by digitization. Jewitt (2011), in an article on "Technology and Reception as Multimodal Remaking," challenges the communication orthodoxy and argues for a more considered view of the receptive end of the process, preferring to call it "remaking" and suggesting a more dynamic creation of meaning than is the case in the conventional model. Rejecting communication models that operate on the stimulus-response and linear, verbal-only basis as being biased toward the author, she argues that such a model does not "acknowledge the situated, social and agentive work of communication" (99). A sense of the inadequacy of the linear model is also shared by reader response theory (e.g., Iser 1980), Bakhtinian dialogic theory (e.g., Bakhtin 1982, 1987), and other aspects of reception theory that privilege, or at least recognize, the work of the "receiver" in making meaning. In other words, such theories, including social semiotic theory, do not see the meaning inhering in the message or text but in the overall social construction of meaning between all parties concerned.

A contemporary theory of rhetoric sits well in relation to these more balanced theories of meaning-making. First, rhetoric does not assume that communication inheres or is fully embodied in the text. Rather, it sees the "text" as a means to an end, and once the moment of communication is enacted, as a trace or repository of the meaning that was transacted. Second, rhetoric is grounded not only in social relations, but in power relations, too. It charts the framework for the operation of meaning and communication in any social situation. Third, and more philosophically, it does not conflate "meaning" and "communication." *Meaning* is seen to be the accrued and shared social capital that is generated by communication; *communication* is the means by which that social capital is built up. Fourth, and more pertinent to our discussion of the relationship of multimodality to rhetoric, meaning is constantly *remade* in the act of social communication (and, we could add, in the act of learning).

A propos this last point: a constant remaking of meaning, implied by multimodal theory and enacted by rhetorical principles, suggests a restless and provisional world in which meanings are not fixed, and consensus is constantly negotiated before action takes place, often via argumentational processes (Habermas 1984). Such a world privileges rhetoric in a positive sense because economic uncertainty, social fluidity, and migratory cultural practices require constant renegotiation through a range of multimodal discourses in order to fabricate consensus for action. However, there are risks in such a world, as rhetoric without evidence or a grounding in backing and warrants (Toulmin's [2003] terms) becomes deracinated and "beyond proof," thus making itself subject to ideology and assertion. In such a world, claims cannot be connected to evidence, nor can the means by which such connections are made (the "warrant" for the argument) be made transparent and therefore be critiqued. Rhetoric, if it is associated with such unsatisfactory modes of communication, becomes a pejorative phenomenon.

Jewitt's argument is that digital technologies compress the relationship between rhetor and audience, thus further exposing the limitation of theories that privilege the author. For example, the creation of an interactive website, a cloud-based shared document, or a blog, by very nature, invites the reader to become a writer/composer, both practically and in the generation of received meaning. We are thus moving to a position in which it is becoming increasingly unhelpful to distinguish between the rhetoric and his/her audience. Rather, we see the rhetor/reader (the terms are being deliberately interchanged for variation, but also to signify the range of roles) communicating with other rhetors/readers through the media and modes offered by the semiotic resource bank.

Let us illustrate this with discussion of a project that involved a number of composers/editors (to use a different configuration of author/audience). A number of writers and editors were gathered to bring about a third edition of a series of Shakespeare plays, designed for school use. The first two editions, in the 1990s and 2000s, were created by single or joint authors working independently, then submitting their manuscript to the publisher where editors worked on it to produce the final text for publication. In the 2010s, the third edition involves "authors" and "editors" working much more closely together on what could be described as a palimpsest rather than a text. Their collective energies and input are used to create a refreshed and updated third edition—also redesigned—that will "speak to" a new generation of school students. The printed edition is accompanied by an e-book, applications ("apps") that allow access to the texts via cell phone, and a website that keeps teachers and students up to date with ancillary material, changing exam board specifications, current performances of Shakespeare, international developments that pertain to the "reading" of the plays, and other resources. Not only is the distinction between writer and editor blurred by such a process, but also the readers of the new editions are invited to "lift the script from the page," enact it, and transform it multimodally into action, voice, gesture, moving image, and so on. As Jewitt (2011, 109) points out, layering and hyperlinks are other ways in which the stabilized author-reader relationship is disturbed; and "mashing" and "remixing" are evidence of the new interactive relationship between the rhetor, his/her audience, and existing material. Finally, the fact that the third edition of the series is being considered for translation into a bilingual English/Chinese version suggests again (chapter 8) that multilingual rhetorical theory is required to make sense of the initiative.

Conclusion

In summary, we could say that the social semiotic and rhetorical traditions have run alongside each other, both gaining prominence in the period from 1990 onwards as linguistics faded into niche inward-looking interests in specific *systems* of language production and form. Social semiotics and rhetoric start from somewhere else: *signs*, the *social*, the *political*. They also embrace the range of modes of communication in a world where these have become more evident as digitization, and digital media, have brought about a communication revolution. They share an interest in how *action* is brought about in the world as a result of the deployment of semiotic *resources* and how that *social action*—including speech acts and other modal *acts*—in turn affects future communicational acts. Internally, they see the social and political construction of identities as informed by social, historical, and political influences.

Their differences are to do with their starting points: social semiotics is most closely identified with social relations, social network theory, and the disciplines of sociology; blending that trajectory with the semiotic tradition. Rhetoric is more closely associated with social *and* political relations; it assumes a close relationship between social and political developments (and thus historical ones) in relations to the formation of identities and selves. Its emphasis on the political associates it with governance issues, with public discourses, and with the framing of individual communicative acts. It is thus less scientific than social semiotics in that it does not—in its contemporary forms, at least—associate itself so closely with systems, categorization, and classification. On the other hand, it is more inclined to the *arts* of discourse as manifested by social and political relations. Whereas social semiotics might define itself in relation to (and in opposition to) linguistics, rhetoric defines itself in relation to philosophy.

12

Rhetoric and the Digital Age

In a seminar held at the London Knowledge Lab at the Institute of Education in December 2011, titled "New Media, New Literacies, New Learning," a number of position papers were given, largely of a theoretical nature. Although the term *rhetoric* was not mentioned, the gradual emergence of *textual practices* as the principal focus for the communication dimension for the digital age was evident. This term emerged from a dissatisfaction with notions of the appendage "literacy" and/or "literacies" to denote areas of communicative practice in the digital world.

Literacy and its pluralistic version *literacies* are terms that have carried a great deal of weight, particularly from Hoggart's *The Uses of Literacy* (1957) through the work of Street (1984, 1993, 1995, 2001; Street and Lefstein 2008), Barton (2008), and the UK's National Literacy Strategy (see, for an overview, Andrews 2008b). What characterizes the conceptions of literacy in these academic studies is the social embeddedness of reading and writing in a range of situations; in comparative terms, an ethnographic dimension that links reading and writing to ecologies of practice and an embracing of the diversity of literacy forms in various contexts. Such generosity of range was countered in the UK's National Literacy Strategy (circa 1996–2007) by a common (and narrower) model of literacy, distilled (reduced) to a pedagogical device at its most narrow as "the literacy hour" in which teacher presentation of some aspect of reading and writing was followed by group and individual work, and then completed by whole-class convening by the teacher.

Such tensions in the field of literacy/literacies (from here on, the term *literacy* is used to suggest both) are productive, and a result of differences between narrow conceptions of literacy—"the ability to read and write"—and wider conceptions that embrace social literacies, diversity in literacy practices, multilingualism, and "digital literacy."

However, the terms *digital literacy* or *digital literacies* seem now anachronistic, largely because of the stretch between the two terms in the compound phrase. On the one hand, the "digital" and all that it suggests, from the instantiation of information in digital form to the potential transformation of that information across modes and media, represents one dimension of signification. On the other, "literacy" in all *its* forms and situations represents another, embedded in the actualities of communicative form. We know *vaguely* what digital literacy might mean, but its very vagueness does not help conceptual clarity, thinking, or communication with others. "Literacy" in this sense—as with "computer literacy," "media literacy," "emotional literacy," or "physical literacy"—means little more than capability or competence. *Literacy* is too closely associated with the reading and writing of verbal text to be a useful or clear term to denote what is going on in terms of contemporary communication.

Before we abandon the term *literacy* for the contemporary, multimodal, and digital age of communication, what might we lose? "Literacy" has been used, not only to broaden and deepen the conception of what it means to read and write, but to explore the operation of power in communication. In particular, it has helped to highlight inequalities in society: between the genders, between societies, and between power groups and the oppressed within societies. The term *critical literacy,* like *critical discourse analysis,* has been coined to ensure that the power dimension is not forgotten when literacy practices are examined. But the "critical" dimension can be retained without terming it as such and without yoking it together with "literacy."

In fact, "critical literacy," or "critical discourse analysis," or "critical thinking," or "critical media studies" all indicate what rhetoric provides: the political dimension to communication and clarity of thought/purpose/intention. As terms, they are fusions, compounds that bring together two elements in a dynamic relationship. Once that relationship is understood and embedded in consciousness, the term becomes redundant and actually begins to blur the meanings that can be generated or associated with it. Rhetoric, on the other hand, provides a high-level umbrella term under which mode-specific, or multimodal, or media-specific, or multimedia devices can position themselves; under which framing as a critical and creative act by the rhetor or receiver of the message can operate; and under which "textual practices" can provide a more accurate, representative, and powerful way of making sense of communication.

Another good reason for using terms such as *framing, textual practices,* and *rhetoric* is that, despite the association of text with tangible forms of communication (written texts, images, bricolages, etc.), the less obviously tangible forms of communication such as speaking and listening, or the less explicit forms of communication such as "body language" (and more explicit versions like gesture) can be embraced within the notion of framing, text, and rhetoric.

Textual practices cover a wide range of social communication. The emphasis on "practices" suggests that the text created is inextricably woven into its social context. The power relations that obtain or are challenged, the linguistic nuances that are represented, and the agency of the actors that take part in the communication—all these are part of the relationship between text and social practice. Because the actors in the communication have agency, they are involved in an act of framing. As suggested elsewhere in this book (chapter 7), the framing may use or adapt existing frames ("genres") but need not be bound by them: the act may require hybrid genres, new genres, or the subversion of existing genres.

The emphasis on "text" is the one that has been explored for some time in the work of Kress and van Leeuwen (2001), and others: the notion of text as always being multimodal, even if it appears to be mono-modal; examples of bricolage; and the bringing together of speaking, listening, image-making, writing, reading, and other modes of communication into a framework that is aware of the affordances of each, and of the particular dynamics that occur when they are brought together.

Rhetoric and Digitization

In order to explore the relevance of rhetoric in the digital age, let us approach the problem via the notion of framing and textual practices: two of the means and lenses via which rhetoric operates. First, however, we need to define briefly what is meant by "digital." Digitization functions via the arrangement of binary signs that encapsulate "information." Its principal affordance is that it allows the transfer of such information from one device to another, and sometimes from one mode to another. So, for example, a conversation or interview can be recorded digitally on a small voice recorder. The data can then be transferred to a computer where it can be transcribed. From there it can be translated into another language via digital recognition of the letters/characters. What is going on is at least three key operations: the move from one medium (device) to another, the move from one mode (speech to writing) to another, and the move from one language to another. Such fluent transition from one medium, one mode, and one language to another would have been unimaginable in the pre-digital world.

One could generate a simple formula from the affordances of the digital and suggest that "the digital is social." It is also political. The connection with rhetoric begins to become clearer: digitization, which is the coding of information into binary format so that it can be transferred and transformed from one mode, medium, and language to another, involves communication. It does not necessarily infer the *arts* of communication and discourse, nor does it necessarily suggest that *learning* takes place in such transfers and transformations. The simple formula—the digital is social—therefore needs some explication.

It would be more accurate to say that digital processes have been adopted by the social (and political) to develop further social engagement and action. One only needs to walk along a street in the developed world to see (currently, in 2013) people communicating with each other and accessing information digitally on their cell phones. The widened accessibility to each other, the increased communicative action, and the (near) ubiquity of such communication is now taken for granted (see Andrews, Fransman, and Haythornthwaite, forthcoming, for an update on the affordances and inequities of digital access and use worldwide). Communication is generally *briefer*—texts, twitter messages, cell phone calls—and not only ubiquitous but undertaken *on the move*. The communities within which people operate are extended so that not only are families, clubs, schools, universities, and workplaces the learning communities (cf. Rogoff 1992) in which people operate, but also electronic/digital communities, such as distribution lists and networks, social networks, interest groups, "crowds," and subscription networks. The digital and non-digital communities overlap, and it is in the engagement at the interfaces of these different communities that learning also takes place, as suggested elsewhere in the present book. In general, we could say that the digital has both increased the opportunities for individualization (and indeed personalization—see discussion on information networks later in this chapter), but also, at the same time, increased the range and interplay of social communities within which individuals operate. Because the social is an effect of the economic and political, and shaped by the distribution of resource globally and within nation states, the wider picture that informs the simple acts of communication between people needs to be borne in mind—and brings us back to the fact that such increased (not necessarily enhanced) communication is rhetorical.

Now let us explore the notion of social digitization in more detail, via the notions of framing and textual practices.

Framing allows us to see that the initial conversation takes place between two people, and there is a degree of formality about it. It is an interview. There are roles to play: those of interviewer and interviewee. There are power relations in that the interviewer sets the questions and frames the overall social encounter of the interview genre: when it begins and ends, how many questions there are, and whether there are probes and prompts. Even if the interviewee is a more powerful person (e.g., the head of an organization) and will help to frame the occasion by, perhaps, making available a slot in his or her diary for the meeting, introducing and welcoming the interviewer to his/her office, and ending the meeting because of a further appointment, the interviewer still has control over the core part of the encounter: the interview itself. The framing of the interview will depend on these contextual or situational influences, but the generic nature of the interview (whether it is formal, semi-structured, or unstructured) will determine the shape of the conversation. Recording such an interview adds another dimension: both parties are aware that what is said "may be used as evidence." Such a presence adds a degree of formality and usually has the effect of making the interviewee consider what they are saying more carefully.

What sort of textual practice follows from this encounter? First, we have speech: the words that are uttered during the interview (typically the preliminaries and post-liminaries are not recorded). We must recognize that speech of this kind does not happen in a vacuum and that gesture, facial expression, reference to papers on the desk, or books and reports in the interview room are not represented in the digital recording. The words are recorded digitally and can be retrieved via a numbering system on the recorder (a different kind of digitization). They can then be transferred directly into a computer, or via a USB/memory stick, and stored for future use and reference. The digital recorded voice file now appears as a file on the computer alongside numerical, written, graphic, and other files. Like any oral text, it can be edited, rearranged, quoted from, and repurposed.

Via voice recognition technology, it can be transposed into written language. The written version of the text is itself editable and subject to rearrangement, quotation, and repurposing. It can also be translated into a number of different languages. The reasons that "textual practices" is a useful way of thinking about communication is that it recognizes the multimodal, is open to what digitization can do, and keeps a strong concentration on the text itself.

In rhetorical terms, framing and textual practice allow a multiplicity of perspectives and possibilities for communication. Existing patterns of framing (genres) and textual practice (the tendency to see texts as monomodal, even though they are almost always multimodal) can be used, but a rhetorical framework allows for deployment of and creation of texts as appropriate to the social and communicative situation. Furthermore, the media via which messages are transmitted play a part by embodying the framing and textual practice within specific forms of hardware: from cell phones to computers, from physical bodies to sound, and from paper to voice (and indeed, these media provide further frames within and between which communication takes place). The aspect of physicality, and especially of the integration of the human into the technological, is explored by Gourlay (2011) under the compound term *cyborg literacies*.

Rhetoric, therefore, provides an overarching framework for thinking about digitization and textual practices, framing, and social communicative acts. Such a framework allows the social and political to be seen to inform such communication. But it also allows an exploration of mode and multimodality, of the media used to make the communication, and the relations between these various dimensions. Although that conception appears to be theoretically heavy, such a framework actually makes possible the lightweight creation and interpretation of messages based on the principle of choice. Digitization increases the choices available to a rhetor and audience; and the increase in choice, once the framing of the encounter is made clear to all concerned, ought to maximize the communicative quality of the interaction. The reasons for this emphasis on quality is that rhetoric operates in the digital world and elsewhere alongside the idea of the economics of attention (Lanham 2006). Choices made are for the best form of communication in any given context, for maximum communicative potential and effect, and for concentration of the quality of attention. That is why rhetoric provides a powerful theory for interaction and communication: it enables the clear distinction of art from not-art; it is sensitive to context and nuance; it embraces the plethora of possibilities of transduction, transformation, and translation that is offered by digitization; and it is grounded in every social occasion and encounter in the real world.

Rhetoric and Social Media

We have so far suggested that rhetoric is informed (and informs) social and political dimensions of experience; that it provides a range of modes and media, which, in combination, can be selected to make successful communication between people; furthermore, that there is an "art" to this range of possible discourses. "Social media" fully reflect this range and function, and rhetoric therefore provides a sound theory for explaining what takes place via these media.

In 2013, social media are in a second generation state of development. They began in well-documented networks of students, using Web 2.0 technology to allow the exchange of user-generated messaging. They are now used for background checks for employment, by companies and institutions as an alternative to intranets, for marketing purposes, and by groups of individuals for social organizing and exchange. Kaplan and Haenlein (2010) created a classification scheme that covered blogs and microblogs, content communities, collaborative projects, social networking sites, virtual social worlds, and gaming worlds.

The dimensions of interest as far as rhetoric is concerned are several. First, the use of internet-based applications for communication is *social*. Like any form of social engagement, there is exchange of communication—sometimes more from one party than the other, but in the wake of Web 2.0 always with the possibility of dialogic exchange. Second, the *digital* dimension allows for anytime, anywhere, and asynchronous communication. Of these subdimensions, the "anywhere" factor is the most limiting, dependent on the degree and quality of wireless connectivity. Thirdly, the competence of the user is a dimension that is often not addressed in communication theory. It may be that access is possible to the internet, but the degree to which the user is capable of using the technology must be taken into account. Many people choose not to use social media; some who do use it are primitive, minimal users—largely receivers of messages rather than senders; some simply are not competent in digital media use. At the start of the present chapter, we critiqued the use of the terms *literacy* and *literacies* to denote competence in communication in the twenty-first century. The advent of social media redefines what is means to be "literate." No longer is basic literacy in being able to decode print for the simplest, functional purposes the benchmark for being classified as "literate"; rather, to be "literate" now means not only being able to *read digitally*, but being able to *compose digitally* in a range of genres, in a range of modes, and via a range of media.

Like any form of social networking, *trust* is a key ingredient in the exercise of communication via social media. As such, trust is linked to the ethical dimension of communication that the classical rhetoricians understood as necessary to the persuasion of an audience. Trust is generated by the moral standing of the message-sender, who "gatekeeps" their circle of friends and contacts with the help of the social network site. In academic and business fields, trust and reputation are essential to the credibility of the message.

It follows from the ubiquity and increasing use of social networking sites that *digital strategy* is important, both for individuals, groups, and institutions, and that protocols of use, the management of information, security, maximum value in communication, etiquette, and other issues come into play (see Wellman 2012).

Finally—though the picture is changing fast—it is noticeable that political action (the *primum mobile* of rhetoric) is often coordinated through social media. The uprisings in Egypt in 2011 and 2013), for example, were coordinated via social network sites. When used by governments to monitor the communication of individuals, the abuse of social media becomes evident – a far cry from the liberating and clarifying functions of rhetoric in democracies. Although such impact and cause-and-effect can be exaggerated, there is indubitably a degree of influence taking place through the rhetoric of digital media.

Mobility

It is now a truism to say that the prevalence and ubiquity of social media, and the creation of smartphones and other small, portable devices (mini iPads and even iPads and other tablets) allow for engagement with social media *on the move*. No longer is it common to see workers carrying laptops on trains, buses, and planes; now they tend to operate on tablets and on phones. Attributes that mobile devices have, in the latest generation of such technologies, include location sensitivity, allowing location-relevant data to be accessed. For example, you are in a meeting in a city you don't know, and you want to know the nearest available Japanese restaurant, along with reviews of that restaurant; you also want to know what time it is in a city around the world so that you can make a call at an appropriate moment. Businesses use the personalization of data to develop relationships with customers through loyalty programs, which enable the creation and consolidation of markets, and through discounts, vouchers, and other inducements.

Again, enhanced digital mobility reinforces the increased emphasis on the individual and his/her information networks. We are not far off the scene in *Minority Report* where Tom Cruise enters a clothing store that recognizes, via camera, his retina "signature" and triggers messages to him to head toward clothing of his size and his preferred colors and styles. As far as rhetoric goes, mobility and individually tailored information and communication systems engender a different kind of communication world: one in which the individual sits at the center of a range of different networks, in which communication is (currently) via touch-screen application or the written word (completed forms, texts, Twitter, etc.), and which, we can speculate, might become even more isolating and silent as access to information and action becomes more mediated by such devices.

One further aspect of mobility is that time-delay or asynchronicity in the sending and receiving of messages and information can be said to reinforce individualization. While these are not necessarily linked only to mobility, they do suggest that anytime-anywhere access to television and radio programs (e.g., BBC iPlayer), email, and social media status updates.

Digitization, Rhetoric, and Research

Access to knowledge and information is changing. Looking at this changing picture from the perspective of students in higher education is illuminating, as their excursions into knowledge creation, especially at Masters and doctoral levels, are changing the way learning is taking place. Students still, in 2013, routinely use printed works—books, journal articles, reports—in libraries to access knowledge and information. The printed work may have been written, composed, edited, and produced with digital operations, but its format as text on a printed page still provides an excellent medium for investigation. Textbooks are still used widely in many countries, mainly for revision and for understanding difficult topics, and mainly at school, college, and undergraduate levels rather than at Masters or doctoral levels, where independent reading is required. Printed works still give the aura of authority (though increasingly less so), but also have the advantage of being able to be laid out on a desk in a spatial arrangement that is different from that of a digital display, which is usually limited by the screen on which it appears. In terms of getting the whole picture of information or of a problem, such expansive display is often helpful.

But the availability of online and digital resources is increasingly determining purchasing practices. Indeed, freely available resources mean that books and e-books are not necessarily purchased any more. In some cases, they may be rented. As the number of devices owned by students increases, and as the integration and transfer of information between those devices becomes more and more possible, print becomes a matter of choice rather than the preferred medium for reading. It is also the case that the preferred economy of media for individual students more closely matches their kinesthetic disposition as learners; if they are spatially and visually driven, they are more likely to favor the screen. If they are verbally and textually driven, they are more likely to favor the printed word as their primary source of information and knowledge. Publishers are adapting to the changing nature of access patterns in relation to information by publishing across platforms. It is now common to have key works available in printed book, e-book, interactive e-books, application and website formats, video, and audio, as well as providing links via social and information networks. Learning becomes a cross-platform experience, using the preferred medium and range of modes not only according to individual learning preference, but also in relation to actual physical location (home, including kitchen or anywhere in the room, apartment, or house; college or university, including libraries; and in between the two). Some aspects of this are offered without charge; other aspects are charged. The availability of experts in the field is also becoming prevalent, with Twitter, blogs, YouTube, and Facebook presence, as well as even personal email contact, being made available to students. The communities for learning are, as expressed previously, becoming more individualized, more accessible to those who have digital access and can use it, and, in parts, more freely available.

Linked to individualization of learning is the public drive toward open access to knowledge, made possible by the internet, by financial pressure on library budgets, and by ideological commitments to making knowledge freely and openly accessible. This movement is particularly strong in the sciences, mathematics, and technology disciplines and less so in the humanities, arts, and social sciences. Nevertheless, movements like Creative Commons with their commitment to developing, supporting, and stewarding "legal and technical infrastructure that maximizes digital creativity, sharing, and innovation" via the provision of "licenses" (see creativecommons.org), which enable different degrees of publishing and knowledge distribution, are changing the landscape of access. Another resource that is becoming increasingly available for research is access to archive collections, not only through the major libraries, but also through smaller libraries and organizations that hold such archives. An example of such an archive is the emerging National Archive of Children's Compositions, housed at the Institute of Education Library, University of London. This embryonic archive, once it has framed the parameters of its collecting policy, will be available to researchers and to students to trace writing and compositional development in children—whether the compositions are initially in writing and drawing (and then digitized) or digitally conceived and executed.

The individualization of research and learning is being accelerated through web-based applications such as ORCID, which "provides a persistent digital identifier that distinguishes you from every other researcher and, through integration in key research workflows such as manuscript and grant submission, supports automated linkages between you and your professional activities ensuring that your work is recognized" (see about.orcid.org). Such applications enable researchers and scholars to bring together various aspects of their work and manage them: version control, information management, personal research notes, publications, citations, blogs, and other aspects of scholarly work are integrated. In rhetorical terms, such a resource puts the author at the center of a potential network of interested parties who "visit" and who engage in receptive and interactive ways with the author. The personalization of work and academic interest in this way can be seen to be an exercise in vanity publishing, unrestricted as it is by peer review. Instead, what is driving interest is the presence and success (or otherwise) of such enterprise in a freer market for scholarly activity. We could say, rhetorically, that self-profiling and self-promotion like this reduces the discourses of exchange in the academy, foregrounding entrepreneurial individuals who use digital means for their own egotistical ends. But part of the impetus is to encourage exchange and to release knowledge and learning from the institutional framework of the academy. The same could be said for Massively Open Online Courses (MOOCs), also prevalent in the early years of the second decade of the century, but at that point unable to loosen the grip of institutions on accreditation and degree-awarding powers. Such cultural shifts in academic practice are not confined to the organization and dissemination of knowledge, but are also changing the genres as well as the media via which knowledge is shared. The academic monograph—for so long a staple form for the humanities—and academic peer-reviewed articles (playing a similar function in the social sciences) appearing in print-based journals are being replaced by web-based publication in smaller chunks. Granularization of knowledge, and the discourses that attend it, now sit alongside longer publications and extended colloquia.

The Digital Dissertation

One aspect of practice for students in higher education that offer challenges—rhetorical and now digital—is the dissertation. This requirement tends to dominate the last year of undergraduate education, as well as being the *sine qua non* of Masters programs (sometimes in shorter forms like the report) and being at the heart of the doctorate, especially in the humanities and social sciences. In conventional, predigital format, there was not much interest in the form rhetorically. Like many fixed genres, it provided a firm template with little variation: an introduction, literature review, context chapter, methodology, results, discussion, and conclusion. In this sense, it was like an academic article scaled up to dissertation length. It was always presented in bound and printed form, with two copies submitted—at least one of which would gather dust on a library or supervisor's shelves. We could say its function was more of a *rite de passage* than a contribution to knowledge; its destiny more like the abandoned carapace of learning than learning itself. Much of the vestigial character remains in the genre, but the digital revolution has brought something else to the dissertation, with profound rhetorical implications.

Whereas for the conventional dissertation digitization meant the inclusion of sound or film or textual files on a CDRom or DVD appended at the back of the submitted work, social science and humanities students—borrowing practice from arts departments where installations, artworks, and other creative forms had been included as part of an overall submission—the advent of digitization has meant that the appendix could be brought into the main body of the work. If, as well as still images, a dissertation could contain film, other forms of moving image, sound, and other digitally instantiated material, then not only the nature of the dissertation itself would change, but also the linearity that characterizes word-based documents, with all the attendant notions of logic, argumentation, the linking of theory and evidence, and possibly also a driving narrative.

Instead, the dissertation could take the form of a website, software, or an artifact of some kind—sometimes with accompanying words, but in extreme cases, without. In non-linear forms like websites, the lines of argumentation are not defined by the writer. The reader has more responsibility for identifying and creating an argument, which may be partially supplied or not at all. From some points of view, such creations are not dissertations at all, and universities have taken different positions on a spectrum that embraces the conventional submission at one end, to non-linear, non-narrative presentations on the other. Often a half-way house is the submission of a "creative" element with a "critical" element attached to it, making the whole submission more assessable. Examples of such digitally innovative dissertations are described and justified in chapters by Yamada-Rice, Domingo, and Milsom in Andrews et al. (2012).

The rhetorical implications of the digital dissertation are several. At inception, researchers who wish to explore the digital nature of communication can do so, designing their research questions, literature reviews, methodologies, and methods according to the nature of their exploration. A starting point for a contemporary research student would be to devise a search strategy, including the definition of keywords, the selection of key digitally accessible sources of information, and criteria for inclusion and exclusion. Given the increasing range of research information, plus portals and packages for accessing and managing such information, research students will increasingly need to make explicit the parameters of their searches. In methodological terms, new means of investigation will be developed that are fit for purpose. Supervisors will need to be up-to-speed on the supervisee's intentions and interests, though in due course, research students at doctoral level always exceed the knowledge of their supervisors in the specific field in which they are working. Regulations at universities will need to be adapted so that the spectrum of possibility in terms of submitting a final dissertation can be extended and can reflect contemporary demands. It is a safe prediction to say that all universities will require a digital submission, with the possibility of a printed version as optional (according to need), rather than the other way round. Examiners will need to be schooled to read such submissions, understanding that not only will the formats be different from what they are used to, but the argumentational structure of the dissertation may also be different (as suggested previously). More specifically in relation to rhetoric, the role and position of the examiner(s) changes if they are asked to construct an argument themselves from a non-linear presentation, or one in which the argument is implied rather than explicit (in, for example, artworks without commentary, or web-based submissions that allow multiple points of entry to the material). Finally, in terms of archiving, storage, and accessibility, dissertations are now more freely and readily available to other students and researchers to read, as and when they need to (and on any appropriate digital devices). In short, the relationship between the student, the supervisor, the examiners, and the university regulations is changing. One implication is that dissertations are likely to be accompanied not only by 300-word abstracts, but by summaries in distilled (say, 20 pages) and highly distilled (say 2 pages) form. Not only the interactional rhetorical demands of the relationships between students and gatekeepers (supervisor, examiner, university) are changing, then, but the actual compositional, technical, and presentational demands upon the student him- or herself.

Conclusion

Digitization is seen to be social in its implications. It has enabled a reinforcement of existing social and rhetorical patterns, running along lines (technically, "ties," "links," or "connections") as defined in social network theory in which nodes—both organizations but also, as has been noted in the previous discussion, individuals—act as points at which transfer of communication takes place. The mapping of social network theory on to rhetoric, and vice-versa, is crucial to this analysis. Nodes are individual agents within networks, and ties are the relationships between these agents. Every act of communication along these ties is a rhetorical act, taking into account the power relations between the agents, the nature of the information to be communicated, aspects of intention, framing, and the modes and media via which such communication takes place.

As has been suggested about rhetoric in the course of the present book, it works at many levels: from the personal and familial to the local-political, the institutional and work-based, to the national and international. So, too, social networks work on these levels, *making things happen,* resolving or at least understanding disputes and problems, conveying information, enabling trade, and encouraging intercultural exchange. Each act, from the most (seemingly) minor and personal, to grand international treaties, is politically as well as socially informed. Rhetoric would see no major difference in shaping communication between the political and social, given its democratic/neo-Marxist nature.

In relation to social network theory, rhetoric is particularly interested in whole or complete networks that attempt to specify all the ties in a defined population (say, for example, a school or a business company) on the one hand, and personal networks on the other. In the discussion so far in this chapter, emphasis has been on individualization and the affordances of the digital to enhance the possibilities for individual and personal centrality in communication and information/network management. But institutional nodes also play a significant part in everyday life, communication, and networking. The relative strength of large corporate organizations at the international level, governments at the national level, and regional and subregional entities such as local authorities, states (e.g., California, New South Wales), and other mediating agencies is crucial to the balancing of rhetorical power and consequent direction and speed of flow along the social network ties or lines of communication. Hybrid networks, where relatively large corporations interact with personal nodes and ties, are further manifestations of how rhetoric operates—often with the individual or subcontractor exercising less and less power, sometimes manifested in contractual arrangements but almost always in (largely) one-way communicational dynamics. However, individuals can exercise political and rhetorical power by bridging social networks that hitherto had operated separately. It thus benefits the individual to be a member of a number of social networks so that the possibilities of connection can be perceived and realized.

At the core of the argument in this chapter has been the notion that digitization not only oils the grooves of existing social networks—and by implication, the rhetorical connections that are made between individuals, institutions, and larger corporations—but that it also creates new possibilities that are grafted on to existing practice. Among these are increased mobility in communication; the affordance of anytime-anywhere communication; brevity of messaging; a fusing of the personal, work-based, and political; possibilities in information management and access; personalization of one's communicational preferences; and, as is noted in relation to the field of research and knowledge creation, new forms of relationship between the actors in the process of undergraduate,

Masters, and doctoral study. Key concepts in social network theory include "betweenness" (the positioning of a node between other nodes), cohesion (the strength of communicational bonds between participants in a node), flow (the degree and fluidity of communicational movement between actors in a social network), prestige (the status accorded to a node), and reach (not only the extent to which actors in a node can reach others in that node, but the extent to which collectively they can reach out to other nodes of influence). All these analogies between rhetorical positioning and flow can be made, and strengthen the socio-political nature of rhetoric as a means of accounting for communication in the contemporary world.

13

Rhetoric and Education

Discussion about learning to communicate on the one hand, and education on the other, is often constrained by existing curricula, national interests, assessment regimes, and vested interests. Mid-level theories and models are used to justify the design of such curricula, interest, and regimes. These are based on predilections for particular aspects of communication studies, such as literature, media, language, and/or literacy, or on sets of values and ideologies, such as "personal growth," "life skills," "cultural development," or "heritage." The relationship between rhetoric and English studies in general is explored in chapter 3. "English" has a strong hold on the curricular imagination, at least in the UK and English-speaking world. In many ways, its presence as a school subject, a university discipline, a national language, an international language, and a particular country's culture has not only blurred the debate about what counts in communication, but also prevented such discussion from taking place at all. In the present chapter, we revisit the question of rhetoric and education, but we do so with a broader theme in mind and from a fresh perspective: communication.

Communication is a *sine qua non* of life in the everyday world and in almost every dimension of it. Even a Trappist or Buddhist monk, dedicated to a life of silent and asocial meditation, is engaged in communication; communication is also essential for those who have lost the means or power of communication (e.g., Judt 2010). Most communication fulfils a social need; much of its is functional, efferent, expressive, aesthetic, and/or necessary for the maintenance of consciousness and identity. Communication is conveyed by many different kinds of media—cell phone, computer, face to face, in print, via film and social media, and so on—and in combinations of modes—speech, physical engagement, writing, gesture, still and moving images. It is also subject to differences between languages—English, Mandarin, Spanish, Arabic—and differences within languages—dialects, registers, and accents.

Given the ubiquity, needs, and varieties of communication, how is education to position itself to help people to induct themselves into the world? What forms and aspects of communication do people need to know about as well as to practice? Are the needs of children and young adults different from those of mature adults? Is the apparent depoliticization of schools in fact a way of politicizing what is taught and learnt, for national ends?

Rhetoric and the Curriculum

Every country has to work out for its education system the selection of knowledge that it wishes to "promote." This selection, usually tiered from preschool stages through schooling to employment and further or higher education, is the curriculum—the course to be followed.

At one of rhetoric's previous high points, in the European Renaissance, rhetoric had a central place in the university curriculum as one of the three strands of the *trivium*, along with grammar and logic. In effect, this trio of disciplines is comparable to a first-year induction program in higher level thinking. Rhetoric, within this curriculum, signified the art of communicating from one mind to another and the adaptation of language to circumstance. It contributed to a core higher education curriculum that emphasized the "languages" of discourse and thinking (logico-mathematical, linguistic, and textual) at a time when the burgeoning availability and attractions of print required scholars to focus on *text* and *textuality* to an extent not experienced previously. This early interest in the relationship of speech to written text, of printed multiple copies in relation to original and copied manuscripts, and of image to text in illuminated manuscripts provided the ground for rhetoric to flourish. Troyan (2004) notes that the history of medieval rhetoric has hardly been investigated, nor the relationship between grammar and rhetoric. He points out, also, that the scholarly practice of glossing and commentary on canonical texts is central to the practice of rhetoric at the time. This meta-textual practice prefigures contemporary hyper-textual practices via the computer screen (e.g., Milsom 2012). Clearly, what medieval rhetoric and contemporary rhetoric have in common is an interest in textual practices. Troyan (2004) suggests that "Rhetoricians were concerned not only with saying something, but also with re-positioning it. By re-positioning itself, rhetoric came to say something new. It also came to suggest different ways of interpreting" (223). In other words, the transformation of speech into writing and vice-versa, the ways in which interpretation could be effected, and, implicitly, early considerations of multimodality were all matters of concern during the Renaissance. Rhetoric itself expanded its reach as the communication landscape widened.

Argument in School Education

What, in addition to what Vygotsky and Habermas have already suggested (see chapter 6), has the foregoing discussion of argument and rhetoric's place in social discourse and cognitive development got to do with education? First, in classic Toulminian rebuttal (or counterpoint) terms—and based on fact, not just rhetorical positioning—is argument fostered in educational settings? The answer, in too many cases, is no. The English educational system has moved, over a period of 20 years or so, to one in which an increasingly prescriptive and narrow curriculum has been increasingly assessed. To put it another way, the commodification of learning into assessable packages, in a model that derives from the failed 1980s American business discourse of targets, products, and learning outcomes, has led to a situation where rarely in the 5–16 curriculum are pupils and students asked to articulate at length, either in speech or writing; where the regurgitation of information takes up more time than thinking about that information; where the celebration of a single voice through narration, again, in the 1980s-informed, late-Romantic tradition, is still prevalent.

There are systemic changes for the good, like the broadening of the range of types of writing that are required in the 2000 version of the National Curriculum in England. There are "green shoots" of good theory and practice, such as Alexander's notion of dialogic teaching (2008); philosophy in primary schools (Lipman 1976); and the work of the critical thinking movement (though critical thinking is not the same as argumentation).

Three examples, from different stages in the education process in England, will suffice to demonstrate the importance of argument and rhetoric in education. The first is a discussion between four children from a Year 1 class of 5–6 year olds, recorded in the 1990s. This extract was first analyzed in *Teaching and Learning Argument* (Andrews 1995) but is here reviewed in the light of a rhetorical perspective. The pupils' brief was to record a discussion on a topic that was important to them, and to do so independently of the class teacher, in a corner of the school, and equipped with a recorder:

RICHARD: What do you think about playtimes, Carly?

CARLY: I think they are quite good because you can play and my best friend is Anna . . .

RICHARD: James? Emma?

EMMA: Well I think playtimes are good because sometimes people want to play with you and they are kind to you when you fall over.

RICHARD: James?

JAMES: Sometimes you can meet people, play with people.

RICHARD: What I think is playtimes are pretty bad but I like them. They are pretty nice things.

CARLY: Look outside now. It's quite sunny. That's part of the good things.

RICHARD: And sometimes when it's sunny we're allowed to have our coats off.

CARLY: Yes. That's the best thing really.

JAMES: We can go on the grass.

RICHARD: Yes, that's a good part.

EMMA: I think the bad thing is when a bully pushes you over. I don't think it's fair when nobody helps you.
RICHARD: It's awful when you fall over and people laugh.
JAMES: It's really awful. You've got to go and tell Miss, don't you?
CARLY: Emma, I thought you said a minute ago that you like playtimes.
EMMA: Well it doesn't mean actually playtimes are nice. It's bad and good.
CARLY: Yes. I think it's a mix, isn't it?
EMMA: Yes, it's a mix, a mix, a mix.

Putting aside Richard's chairing skills, what can be identified as argument here? Carly and Emma each start with a statement and proof informed by logical or quasi-logical connection ("I think playtimes are good because. . .") though you could say that Carly's proof ("because you can play") is quickly followed by what my teachers used to write all over my essays: a *non-sequitur* ("and my best friend is Anna"). It could be the case, however, that this is no *non-sequitur* for Carly; and that the "and" in her utterance signifies a causal or relational connection of a kind. The first third of the extract establishes some propositions and some supporting "evidence," simply to give the propositions some ballast. Richard's position is typical of that of a chair: ("I think playtimes are pretty bad but I like them. They are pretty nice things"). The important thing is that he introduces the notion that playtimes can be bad as well as good.

The second third moves to finding more evidence, more proof for the two propositions that are now established. The discussion is largely consensual, moving the argument along together with supporting points and a desire to ensure the coherence of the group itself: a pattern that can be seen in many school small group conversations. In such discussions, the idea of argumentation can be threatening; it can disrupt or destabilize the cohesion of the group; it can be "taken personally." This is why many such groups prefer the term *discussion* to the term *argument*. Argument looks like "discussion with *too much* edge."

But "edge" is exactly what starts the third part of the earlier extract: "Emma, I thought you said a minute ago that you like playtimes." The ploy is a devastating one, and one with which we are familiar from parliament: "The right honourable member contradicts precisely what he/she said last week, and what is said in the policy statement. . . ." But Emma moves on to the position that perhaps Richard was stumbling toward earlier in the discussion: "It's bad and good" or the succinct outlet that Carly offers her: "it's a mix." The collective understanding that at least three of the participants have come to—that "it's a mix, a mix, a mix"—is an important one for 5–6 year olds to have come to through their own deliberations: that the question of whether playtimes are good or bad is a complex one; that there is evidence that can be brought to bear on propositions; that people can disagree without falling out with each other; that thesis and antithesis can lead to a new synthesis; that if pupils and students argue about topics that they care about, they don't seem to have a problem in bringing complex abstraction and interaction to bear. This last point leads on to the practice in some schools of schools councils, where, if there is genuine consideration of pupils' views leading to action in the community of the school and/or the wider community, then young people will feel "franchised," that what they say matters and that they can make a difference in the world. The "nesting" of the discussion between four 5–6 year olds within a separate space where they could discuss and record, within a classroom and school, within a curricular framework, and within national priorities regarding the development of speech and thought is a rhetorical contextualization. The fact that school councils and the forging of consensus through argument are taking place is indicative of rhetoric at work in democracy, albeit within the protected space of the classroom. Rhetorically, these 5–6 year olds are assuming agency in their discussion; they have been afforded such power by the teacher, who has given them the freedom and responsibility to try argument together in a relatively safe space.

The school curriculum, since the birth of state schooling in the mid- to late-nineteenth century in England, has moved away from rhetoric as a founding discipline, even though the arts of discourse are central to educational training and development. "English" as a school subject derives from English literature as a university discipline and has a history of about 100 years. Its central ethos is one of a humanizing subject at the core of the curriculum, replacing Classics, and based on literary appreciation and criticism. That emphasis on literariness, in the early part of the twentieth century, was developed further by a remaking of English as a school subject in the 1940s and 1950s with an exploration of speech, a valuing of the everyday experiences and accounts by young people of their ordinary and extraordinary lives, and a consequent rebalancing of the English curriculum (see Hardcastle, Medway, Brewis and Crook, in press). Despite successive governments' attempts to send the English curriculum back to a national heritage model based on a narrow selection of literature and a narrowing focus on to "phonics" and grammar teaching, contemporary curriculum theory has to embrace the demands of real world communication and to adapt to the relationship of in-school and out-of-school modes and media of communication. This means reconceiving curricula in relation to the broad sweep of communication needs, rather than narrowing it down to a directive, functional, and/or elitist conception of "what needs to be taught."

Argument in Undergraduate Education

The second example is from close to the other end of the spectrum: from the work of a third year undergraduate student in English Literature. The course is "Shakespeare on Film," and the essay question to be answered is

" 'I believe that Shakespeare was a feminist, and all the plays I direct analyse . . . the roles of women from that ideological point of view' (Michael Bogdanov). Discuss this view of the presentation of women in one or more Shakespeare films." The essay has the virtue of diving in at the deep end—though the angle of the dive is very carefully judged, both rhetorically and substantially, to make a point right from the start:

> Ostensibly the role of women in Shakespeare's writing seems a negligible one—they can be seen as purely wives, sisters, daughters, mistresses or servants of the male protagonists, functioning only as subservient confidants or messengers. Yet . . .

What is interesting and impressive in argumentational terms about that opening is that it is contrapuntal: to move the metaphor away from pools and diving, it starts on the offbeat. Immediately, an argumentational voice is established, and the main beat is hit at the beginning of the second sentence with one of the main propositions in the essay, *viz* that despite the seeming deference of women in Shakespeare (and it can only be the case in some of the roles), they are foregrounded in performance and on film—though this foregrounding in itself may not be ideologically sound:

> In film these feminine narratives are constructed technically, in the way the director "photographs women, in close-up, in mid- or long-shot, in tracking shots; by turns intensifying concentration on a face, an eye, a foot or impassively observing, or drawing back, marooning women in compositions that register isolations and them as objects" (Rutter 2007) [and so] their roles are exposed in different ways according to the director's intention.

The essay continues with a critique of Trevor Nunn's film adaptation of *Twelfth Night,* then comes back at the end, more generally, to readdress the question. The contrapuntal start is something many undergraduate students find difficult, in reading argument as well as composing it: they cannot distinguish the main points from the subsidiary ones, and according to research with first year Psychology students in a midwestern university in the USA (Larson, Britt, and Larson 2004), they may often misconstrue an argument because they do not know that an argument can start on the counterpoint. Such tangential writing is typical of arguments in Literature and perhaps other humanities subjects. Such elliptical angles are not the case in Engineering.

The third example, then, is from a Masters level final dissertation project in Engineering—where the argument manifests itself differently. There are words in this 60-page dissertation, but they sit alongside diagrams, mathematical calculations, and computer programming. The argument is embodied in the whole multimodal work:

> The objective of the project was to develop a piece of software for use with gear design. It would act both as a learning aid for students studying engineering . . . and as a research tool to aid the stress analysis of gear teeth.
>
> The produced software was tested, first with students to measure its usability, then against example calculations from gear handbooks to assess the accuracy of the software's built-in calculations.

The dissertation progresses from an introduction, which sets out the background to the problem and reviews existing gear software, through gear transmission theory to an account of the software development. It then discusses the software capabilities; tests the software, gauging its effectiveness as a learning aid and research tool; and finally discusses and concludes. The argument is basically, "there is a need for new software in this field. I created it, tested it, and conclude that it makes an effective contribution to the field. Here is the tested product." Behind that ostensibly simple argument is a wealth of data that provides evidence for the claims and the process.

The main point is that argument manifests itself in different subjects and disciplines in different ways, and these ways have to be learnt as the pupil or student makes his or her way through schooling to university. Differentiation increases as subjects turn into disciplines. Often the criteria for success in argumentation are hidden or not made explicit, and yet they remain one of the most important criteria for success.

To return to the main theme, however, certain elements of argument and argumentation remain constantly important throughout education. These are: the formulation of propositions or claims; supporting and/or testing those propositions with evidence; being clear about how the links are made between propositions and claims (what Toulmin calls the "warrant"); using rebuttal to challenge the proposition, the evidence and/or the link between the two; and understanding the sets of values, ideologies, or disciplinary practices and *mores* that provide further contextual validation for the argument.

It was noted that the engineering dissertation used a range of modes to build its argument. The chapter now turns to consider whether, and if so in what ways and to what degree, an argument can be carried by visual images alone.

Rhetoric and the Representation of Research Knowledge

At the advanced and cutting edge of learning—the production of dissertations at undergraduate, Masters, or doctoral levels—learning and knowledge take conventional forms. The convention is that a dissertation or thesis is presented for examination. It is usually bound, taking its model as the monograph or published book. In the arts, humanities, and social sciences at least, but spilling over into other meta-disciplines and fields of enquiry, the thesis or dissertation is seen as the summation of a phase of education and the gateway to an award. At a symposium at the Royal College of Art in London in 2012 (RCA 2012), four contributors from the *Handbook of Digital Dissertations and Theses* (Andrews et al. 2012) and a visiting professor of Design Theory and History gathered to present and discuss issues of the representation of research knowledge. The event, situated within a series on research methods, raised issues that were deeply rhetorical (see Boyd Davis 2012; Andrews 2012; Dogantan-Dack 2012; Milsom 2012; and Hohl 2012). In turn, the topics addressed were a defense of the *power of words* in the thesis or dissertation, *non-verbal argument* and argumentation, capturing musical *rehearsal and performance,* representing *ethnographic "thickness"* in the dissertation by using a multimodal approach to translation, and consideration of *grounded theory* in relation to the evaluation of an immersive art work.

Let's take two of these in more depth (full accounts of all except Hohl are to be found in Andrews et al. 2012): Dogantan-Dack on performance research and Milsom on multimodal presentation of translation research. Performance studies have grown in response to the idea that—in musical performance, for example—the actual rehearsal and performance of musical works is under-researched and somehow taken for granted. Musicology has explored scores, notations, the history of styles, social history of music, and the languages of music, but not the performances. The paper explored the differences between rehearsal and public performance and the particular "magic" that ideally is generated by the performance of musical works to an audience. That "magic" is a result, first, of hard work in practicing and rehearsal; the confidence that a musician brings to a piece, having practiced it on his or her own before coming together in a chamber group or orchestra to rehearse it; and his or her knowledge of the instrument. But it is also a result of the interaction between the musicians as they rehearse together, their prior knowledge of each other and each other's styles, and their exploration of the piece as it lifts from the score and becomes realized in sound.

The core performance moment, then, is the production of the piece in sound before an audience. Social conventions frame the occasion: people buy tickets, they dress accordingly for a lunchtime or evening concert, and they arrive in time for the concert, perhaps buying and reading a program (words, images) about the history of the piece, of the chamber group or orchestra that is performing, and of the composer. Lights may or may not illuminate the stage; the performers emerge through a door on to stage; the audience is aware that this movement signals the beginning of the concert. Some tuning up takes place. Then the piece begins, and—save for coughing between movements—proceeds to its conclusion and appreciation from the audience (applause). The concert may be made up of a number of such pieces and an encore or two. What comes together in such a performance is a rich complex of context, engagement, and activity that makes for the communicative experience: the historical moment, the presence of the audience, the preparedness of the musicians, the nature of the piece. Such is a rhetorical occasion because of the multifaceted communication in sound, sight, word, and image. The sound is different from that of a recording because of its physical resonance and multidimensional spatial character. The dynamics of the performers add to the experience. Ultimately, if the technique is impressive, the interpretation is fresh and insightful, the degree of concentration and energy is high, and the audience is attentive, the occasion will generate the quality of attention and experience that is characterized by the somewhat mysterious term *magic*.

Researching such phenomena is difficult. Like all research, it is a question of pattern-seeking. Methods and data are almost always tangential to or partial to the core experience. They provide traces of the actual performance, or recordings of it (in video, sound, transcription) that attempt to capture the essence of the experience via framed approaches in order to understand it better. In the light of our broader theme of the relations of the communication arts and rhetoric to learning and education, it can be said that there is no substitute for engagement with actual moments of performance, for both performers and audience; but that the vestigial traces of the experience can be used to "capture" the essence of the experience, to "frame" it. No (apparently) single mode of communication—like the notation of a score, the conversation prior to a rehearsal, or the listening to a recording of the performance in the dark, on a CD—can do justice to the full nature of the performed experience. And yet education often reduces aspects of full experience to coded two-dimensional takes on it in order to rationalize and "bring order and system" to it. Research often requires the distillation of the experience into written form, following the conventions of academic journal or book-production.

In the case of the translation of the narratives and sketches of Lydia Cabrera (Milsom 2012), the rhetorical and multimodal affordances are explored differently. The original core of the activity that is captured consists of the oral stories of Afro-Cuban heritage, as told to Cabrera and transcribed by her in field notes. These transcriptions, many of them in original note form but some worked up into fully fledged written stories, are stored in archives in Miami. In investigating these archives, Milsom has not only fulfilled the requirements of the written convention of the traditional thesis or dissertation, but also provided a CDRom, the "front page" of which is a representation of her desk, complete with computer, folders of stories, post-it notes, "how to navigate" guidance, a CDRom, and a brown envelope of instructions. The written thesis is accessed through the computer screen and is there in its entirety. The whole submission, then, is a combination of the conventional written thesis and the material available by exploring on the accompanying CDRom. It is multidimensional, multilayered (in terms of showing the different types and stages in the production of text), multimodal (it contains readings of the stories as well as images and written texts of different kinds), and multimedia (printed thesis/CDRom).

Rhetorically, the completed artwork and thesis provide a rich insight into the research question: how to represent the life and works of Lydia Cabrera. Unlike moments of performance, the thesis and its CDRom can be accessed at any time. It becomes live in the moment of reading and interpretation. The same could not be said of a "pure" presentation of the thesis as a printed and bound volume: one format that hidebounds many researchers who are working with multimodality and/or multimedia. The reason is that much is lost in the transduction into a single mode and medium: the sense of tactile exploration of folders of short stories; the visual exploration of the desktop on which the work was completed; insights into the processes of research. Indeed, the very topic of *transcription* (see Kress 2010, 96–102) is revealed as a fascinating aspect of research when the drafts and processes are made evident, related as it is to *translation* from Spanish to English in this particular project.

In education terms, from the point of view of production, the CDRom allows different points of entry, different stages of the process, and different types of research product to be represented. From the point of view of the reader or audience, there is no single sequence in which the material must be read, no single argument that is represented (though the main one is in the text of the thesis itself), and a closer engagement with the original material than is possible in conventional formats. Such *engagement* is crucial to the learning potential of the work. This is a work to visit and revisit, not only for its intellectual perspectives on the stories of Lydia Cabrera and the problems of translation, but also for the pleasure of exploring the archives via routes that the researcher has created.

These two examples indicate the complexity and the possibilities in the representation of research at advanced levels in education. They move the practice of education beyond abstract considerations of ideas in single modes of expression and beyond the framing of knowledge and knowledge systems in single modes. Rather, they invite the audience and reader to engage in *live* interaction with the performance or archive, getting closer to the core of cultural experience in all its sensory and intellectual dimensions. One could argue that the closer one gets to the core of such experience, the harder it becomes to capture or distill the messages that are at play. But the distance that has been created between everyday lived experience and culturally framed experiences on the one hand, and academic and educational mediation of those experiences on the other, has become too attenuated. Rhetoric and education can thus operate more closely together if the modes and media of the engagement are reflected upon and a proximity to the core experience is attempted. For example, conventional practice in interviewing for research is to undertake audio-recorded interviews, and then to transcribe them laboriously. A rhetorical approach to this activity would be to ask, how many of these interviews do you need to transcribe in order to see the pattern that is emerging from the data? Despite the fact that a written transcription and analysis of an interview may enable the researcher to see patterns that would not have been observable otherwise, the main bulk of the recorded data might just as well be retained in its "original," in digital audio files that can be copied to CDRom or, indeed, accessed via a website that is indicated by a url address or live link in the thesis.

On Education, Learning, and Assessment

We have seen in this chapter, and in previous ones, that a key element of a rhetorical view of communication is multimodality. For medieval textual practices in relation to learning in universities, the multimodal nature of texts was unwritten and unacknowledged in explicit terms (as far as we know). Now that multimodality has been given new prominence in thinking about the social semiotics of communication, there is a need to address questions of learning and assessment from both a multimodal and rhetorical perspective.

Kress (2009, 38) comments on the relationship of multimodality and learning to assessment:

> Multimodality by itself is not a theory of learning, though it does focus on the need to attend to all the modes through which meaning is made and learning happens. Adequate forms of assessment need to address these givens. In systems of assessment that have hitherto focused on the pre-eminence of the linguistic modes of speech and writing as the secure route to understanding of meaning and learning (or of specific canonical modes in other disciplines—numbers, chemical formulae, etc.), this demands a conscious attempt at recognition of meaning-making and learning in all modes involved, in which signs of learning are evident. A theory of learning that aims to be adequate to contemporary forms of communication and engagement with the world, with contemporary views of power and authority by those who are (seen as) learners, and in fact, that wants to be adequate to the facts of human communication, needs to pay close attention to the actions of learners in all environments of learning. These are prerequisites for any serious attempt at assessment of learning. Only what is recognised and accorded full recognition as means and modes

for learning can be assessed. What is not recognised will not and cannot be assessed. That leads to severe misrecognition of learners' capacities and actions.

The challenge to curriculum designers and to educationalists, to teachers and policy makers is clear: what would a curriculum predicated on a multimodal and rhetorical view of learning look like?

First, it would accept that communication goes on, not only within the classroom and the school, but beyond it. Indeed, communication before and outside school prefigures communication within the confines of the school, the classroom, and the curriculum. This apparent truism has been the focus of research and practice since at least the 1950s, viz. that what the child brings to school in terms of their language and communication is the foundation of what can be achieved and built upon in school. But thinking about what the child brings to school has, to date, been largely in terms of speech and prewriting. The child also brings exposure to family discourses, television and other media, and engagement with the world beyond the family home. He or she also brings production: drawings, made objects, scribblings, early attempts at writing, and all the accrued speech acts that he or she has been engaged in. Following Vygotsky, a rhetorical perspective on early childhood would suggest that the young learner is rhetorical in his or her actions from the start: a cry, initial engagement with the mother's breast, reciprocated looks, giving and taking—all of these early acts of communication use the multimodal tools of rhetorical engagement. But these acts develop as the child develops as a social being. Such development, as well as the modes accounted for previously, includes physical positioning and dynamics through movement, touching, and feeling: aggressive as well as consensual acts. The child who enters the classroom at age 4, 5, or 6 has a repertoire of learned communicative moves that are already part of his/her rhetorical world. How to build on this in the school curriculum?

The conventional stripping down of the modes into teachable and seemingly discrete "languages" or codes—writing, reading, and so on—can be countered by a more inclusive approach to communication. So, second, there would need to be a "communications arts" curriculum in which there were not only clear accounts of progress in the individual modes of communication, but the facility for exploration and commerce between the modes. This proposal has more behind it than a mere "crossover," organic, or "whole language" approach. The very act of transduction between modes (e.g., the repurposing of a told story as a written one, the creation of a painting to represent what is seen out of the window, and all receptive acts of interpretation) is a learning act in itself. Learning is instantiated in such transductions.

Third, a curriculum founded on rhetorical principles would engage beyond the classroom to audiences and contexts in the "real world." At primary or elementary school level, these audiences could include parents and family as well as figures from the local community (police, traffic wardens, shopkeepers, artists) who could provide real audiences for produced work, as well as come into the school and classroom to bring their own expertise and experience, thus inspiring children to engage socially and politically in communication with them. Such community engagement can be taken into the secondary or middle/high school level, too, and widen its scope to include regional, national, and international engagement.

Fourth, assessment of such activity cannot be undertaken in examinations or even by coursework or portfolio assessment. Evidence of social engagement via communication can be recorded, and the presentations of such engagement can take a number of formats: written-up reports, displays, audio-recordings, films, showcased plays, and other performances. Even the most inclusive of assessment methods—the 100% portfolio—has limitations in that work must be transformed into something that can be stored or presented in a portfolio. This act of presentation for assessment could be a worthwhile act in itself in learning terms, in that it does involve transduction and transformation from one or more modes into another. But there is another dimension in a rhetorical approach to learning and assessment that must be taken into account.

The fifth aspect of curriculum and assessment design is fitness-for-purpose in a world in which the economics of attention are at a premium (Lanham 2006). If it is the case that the economics of attention are crucial to understanding the nature of and capacity for learning, then time spent on producing material for assessment must also be subject to economics of this kind. How valuable is it to re-present work for assessment when a better use of time would be to put the findings of a small research project, say, into action, or to use the constructed stories of 9 year olds, composed over weeks with oral and written dimensions, in retelling them to 5 year olds? The notion behind such application of knowledge in communities of learning that will in itself, improve the quality of human life and/or generate further positive responses has to be weighed against the needs of assessment systems, which partly have a diagnostic function but which primarily are used to grade performance in preparation for entry to further academic or vocational study and ultimately to the world of employment. Politically, in a period of history in which young people graduating from education systems have much less prospect of employment than previously, the endgame of assessment in education is exposed for what it is really is: a means of ordering, controlling, and defining (not always accurately) the nature of individual human potential.

Kress's (2009) notion that "what is not recognised will not and cannot be assessed," which "leads to severe misrecognition of learners' capacities and actions" (38), challenges us to think about the way in which assessment systems not only aim to define what the outcomes of learning are, but often miss what these outcomes are. The problem of the mismatch between what is taught, what is learnt, and what is assessed is acute. But it is compounded further by the fact that such assessments often have little bearing on the nature of communication in the real world—a world that includes schools and classrooms. A rhetorical view of learning, curricula, and assessment suggests that what we need to do, at the very least, is provide more engagement between schools and the real world, value what young people bring to school in the whole range of its multimodal nature, see the school as a reflection of its communities, generate possibilities for action and thought, and design assessment systems that enable us to review individual and collective achievement and progress. Computerized versions of drill or multiple-choice schemes do not get close to the range of communicational possibilities that are envisaged in such an approach.

14

The Future of Rhetoric

The rhetoric proposed in the current book is different from Aristotle's rhetoric, as framed in the *Rhetoric* and the *Poetics*.

There are a number of ways in which Aristotle's conception of rhetoric as the art of persuasion, or as a general theory of the persuasive, is different from the conception set out here. The *Rhetoric* takes the form of three books: two on thought, one on style. Although the two major elements are related, the division indicates that the bulk of the work focuses on thought, taking into account philosophical and emotive considerations and grounding issues of style in a more general theory of the responsibilities and powers of the speaker in relation to his or her audience. The *Rhetoric* also builds its theory of persuasion on syllogistic mechanisms or micro-logical arguments like the enthymeme. These deductive approaches, deriving as they do from philosophy or logic, are not central to the theory of contemporary rhetoric outlined in the present book, largely because the scaling up from the enthymeme to dialectic encounters in everyday life does not work.

Persuasion, although it is a central concern of Aristotle's work, is only one dimension of interest in the present book. Argument, for example, is seen to be persuasive here; but it also has other functions, as discussed in chapter 6, such as clarification, resolution, defense, and entertainment. That is to say, *persuasion* per se is not the focus of a theory of contemporary rhetoric. Because, in contemporary terms, rhetoric covers the arts of discourse in public *and* private settings, the persuasion of an audience by an orator or an actor is not the main focus of the present theory. To explore this central tenet of Aristotelian rhetoric in more depth, persuasion is concomitant with one-way discourse: A tries to persuade B of something. The persuasion *may* be two-way, but in each case, A is trying to persuade B, and B is trying to persuade A. We can see how such dualistic persuasive encounters can be conceived of as argument, but suggest that such two-way encounters are not essentially dialogic or dialectical.

Indeed, there is a fusion in Aristotelian thinking between persuasion and dialectic, which may well lead to the confusion about the parameters and nature of the field of classical rhetoric. For the purposes of the present book, it is useful to separate persuasion (one of several functions of argument) from dialectic (the private, public, and/or academic practice of making an argument).

Rather than persuasion, it is dialectic that classical and contemporary rhetoric have in common. There is a close affinity between the two in Aristotle's *Rhetoric,* and an equally close but somewhat different affinity between dialectic and contemporary rhetoric. In classical rhetoric, dialectic—the practice of making an argument—has as a subcategory the deployment of the enthymeme as a device to secure deductive proof. Elsewhere, we have suggested that the micro-logical nature of the enthymeme (itself a type of syllogism) is not scaleable to everyday discourse, nor indeed to public discourse. Such an approach to dialectic is driven by logic and logical proof. In contemporary rhetoric, dialectic is a two-way operation or practice of making an argument, drawing on deductive and inductive reasoning to make its points. In other words, it is more dialogic, more interactive. It can be seen as a subcategory of argumentational rhetoric.

Although there is close affinity between dialectic and rhetoric in such a contemporary theory, it is also important to note that, whereas for Aristotle dialectic was the practice of making arguments in private and academic fields and rhetoric was the domain of public practice in persuading (including defending, or accusing), the case is different in contemporary rhetoric. Dialectic and rhetoric are not seen as operating in different fields or domains. Rather, rhetoric can operate in private, public, and academic fields; dialectic serves rhetoric in providing an operational means whereby arguments can be conducted in a civilized, rigorous, and mutually beneficial way.

Finally, with regard to the *Rhetoric,* the separation of thought from style in Aristotle prefigures the fissure that periodically leads to the decline of rhetoric. It is as if such a conception of classical rhetoric has a fault-line. Earlier in the present book, we referred to Grierson's (1945) work on rhetoric as a form of literary stylistics. But any reduction of rhetoric to a stylistic addendum to thought diminishes and relegates it. In the present book, thought and the manifestation of thought in action and/or in its representation in one or a number of modes makes thought and expression integral.

We now turn to poetics, where there is ostensibly a closer connection between classical and contemporary thinking about rhetoric; not because they have a common interest in stylistics, but because the deliberations about the relationship between the rhetor and his/her audience, and with the subject matter to be exchanged, are central to the *Poetics* and to contemporary poetics and rhetoric.

The *Poetics* is ostensibly about the art of poetry, covering the genres of epic poetry, tragedy, comedy, "dithyrambic poetry" (lyric poetry performed by a chorus), and music for the pipe or lyre. Much of the *Poetics* is concerned with the differences between tragedy, in all its aspects, and epic—clearly the issue of the time for Aristotle, as the oral epic tradition transformed into a period in which drama was prevalent.

What is notable about comparisons between contemporary rhetorics and the rhetoric/poetics of Aristotle is that the terms of reference are changed. We can no longer undertake a direct comparison between classical and contemporary rhetoric on the basis of these terms. First and foremost, the scope of the *Poetics* is more limited than any such poetics today; furthermore, as has been established in the present book, rhetoric subsumes poetics.

Take, for example, the three respects in which types of imitation (*mimesis*) can be differentiated from each other in Aristotelian poetics. Aristotle discusses the three ways in respect "of their different *media* of imitation, or different *objects,* or a different *mode* (i.e., a different manner)" (1996, 3). Whereas for Aristotle, *medium* means what we would now called *mode,* for example, the spoken voice, still images, or "rhythm, language and melody" (3); for the contemporary rhetorician, "mode" is reserved for the code in which the message is transported (spoken voice, the written word, gesture, etc.), and rhythm, language, and melody would be category errors: rhythm and melody being a feature of musical sound that could also apply to the other arts, and *language* being a term of such generality, using the basic meaning of verbal language to apply metaphorically to a range of languages, including musical language, mathematical language, and choreographic language.

The category of *object* is one reserved by Aristotle for the moral nature of the subject of the composition and is closely connected to the concept and practice of imitation. The notion that comedy "aims to imitate people worse than our contemporaries, and [tragedy] better" (op.cit, 5) is not one that is used in contemporary rhetoric because the value judgments that applied for Aristotle are not applicable now. Furthermore, contemporary rhetoric is more amoral than classical rhetoric.

Mode is used by Aristotle to mean the "way" in which imitation takes place, meaning, for example, whether the message is narrated, and/or is a monologue "or else with all the imitators as agents and engaged in activity" (5). In contemporary terms, we could characterize this Aristotelian category as concerned with genre, meta-genre (narrative, argument, description), and voice. But as part of the terminology of contemporary rhetoric, *modes* are best deployed as they are in multimodal theory, *viz.* as the principal codes or "languages" via which communication takes place.

Another difference between Aristotelian and contemporary rhetoric is that, for Aristotle, narrative is seen as the *sine qua non* of epic, but as one element of the evolution of tragedy as a genre. Aristotle traces the origin of plot-construction to Sicily (the home of pre-Athenian rhetoric) and identified plot as the main element of tragedy. In his study of the emergence of tragedy as a major art form, Aristotle is keen to see it as "better" than epic in that it contains all the elements that epic contained, and more. It also contained the elements of character, diction, reasoning, spectacle, and lyric poetry. In an interesting section of the *Poetics* as far as the present book is concerned, the elements of tragedy are ranked in importance: first, plot, or an arrangement of events; second, character, as the agents who instigate plot.

> Third is reasoning. This is the ability to say what is implicit in a situation and appropriate to it, which in prose is the function of the arts of statesmanship and of rhetoric. (12)

Fourth is diction or verbal expression; the rest are song ("The most important of the sources of pleasure" (13) and spectacle. Interestingly, *à propos* our discussion of theatre in chapter 10, "the effect of tragedy is not [merely] dependent on performance and actors [because] the art of the property manager has more relevance to the production of visual effects than does that of poets" (12).

The distinction between the domain of the *Poetics* and that of the *Rhetoric* is clear in the previous listing. Rhetoric is seen as doing the work of the world in prose; poetics is seen as the world of drama, theatre, tragedy, comedy, and the arts. In contemporary terms, however, poetics covers prose as well as poetry and drama (including drama in prose). It is still limited in twentieth-century terms to literary production. But as argued in the present book, in twenty-first-century terms, poetics is an increasingly defunct category because rhetoric is the more powerful, comprehensive theory via which to make sense of literary production as well as of the operation of the other arts and of communication in the real world. The key in making this leap to a higher level of theoretical application is via framing, specifically the liberation of the act of framing from its reification in genres and other text-types, and via multimodal theory.

What is also notable about the significant place of reasoning in the Aristotelian theory of tragedy is the fact that reasoning is seen as the "ability to say what is implicit in a situation and appropriate to it." We could see this as manifested in the speeches of the Chorus in Greek tragedy, providing commentary on the actions of the tragic heroes and heroines. Such commentary is an abstraction from the main action; a place of reflection between that of the main actors and the audience; explication and exegesis of the action; the beginnings of literary criticism, in terms of interpretation and commentary; and a suggestion that the public recognition of the import of the action is part of the main aim of the dramatic performance itself.

Practice Driving Theory

The present book has not started with a comparison between classical and contemporary rhetoric, partly because it has wished to build the case for a new rhetoric from practice rather than in counterpoint to existing theory; and to undertake a full comparison between the *Rhetoric,* the *Poetics,* and other manuals and theories from the classical period (and their derivatives in medieval, Renaissance, and twentieth-century, as well as in multilingual and intercultural rhetorics) would necessitate a multi-volume work in itself. The process of working from practice toward theory has another purpose: to indicate that a contemporary rhetoric must be lightweight, fit-for purpose and transportable, like scaffolding to put up a building.

Theory, and its diagrammatic representation in modeling, is an imagined art. It takes the form, metaphorically, of a canopy or umbrella under which a range of practices have commonality as well as differences, and in which they make sense. Most importantly, it "explains" specific phenomena and occurrences by providing an over-arching rationale for them. Necessarily, it has an ethereal quality and can be easily discounted as irrelevant, over-abstract, or self-referential. However, good theory is connected to each and every practice or event that it purports to explain. It is "practical" in the sense that it provides an explanation of how practice works and of what the key informing variables are. It should not dictate, but instead provide a framework for positive and successful action in the world.

It needs to be lightweight in order to fulfil its framework-like function, but also so that the attention is not so much on the theory but what it allows to happen and the connections between phenomena that it reveals. If the framework it provides becomes a constraint, or if it is no longer fit-for-purpose, the theory becomes outdated and redundant. That is why I believe the manuals of Renaissance rhetoric were like carapaces of real action. They attempted to classify, in some detail and exhaustively, the possibilities of gesture and action, instead of seeing that the possibilities were endless within an appropriate framework. This category error of attempting to reify, in a comprehensive categorical system, the range of possibilities afforded by a theory, is easily made. But such reification, at the same time as classifying, also fossilizes practice, making it rule-bound and instilling notions of correctness into a wide-ranging set of practices.

The other danger of an over-classificatory approach to rhetoric is that once the finite set of devices is defined and described, it becomes tempting to see the catalog as a template for teaching. The notion that this finite set can be taught and learnt and that this, the science or art or craft—the *technē*—of rhetoric provides a comprehensive guide to success in the field, is a flawed one. Pedagogically, learning is not as simple as that. It is more a matter of practice, guidance within a template of possibilities, finessing of technique, and the bringing together of intention, feeling, intellect, judgment, and the consideration of audience.

In these senses, practice drives theory. Theory must remake itself to adapt to changes in practice and be generous enough to accommodate new practices. It must be able to make links between existing and new practices across a wide range of possibility. The inductive inclination of rhetoric places it in relation to humanities and arts disciplines—and, to an extent, social sciences—where analysis begins from the actualities of the field. Texts in literary and communicational fields; events, people, motivation, and patterns or trends in history; the particularities of languages and contexts in linguistics; making in the arts; social schemata and practices in sociology and social work; the organizational and pedagogic demands of teaching practice—all these disciplinary and practice fields are concerned with interpretation and action on the ground and derive their own disciplinary and practice cultures from problem solving that is inductively driven. That is not to say that they are not also informed by theories; nor that science, medicine, philosophy, and logic operate purely deductively. What we can say, however, is that "the scientific method" takes a deductive approach to investigation and problem solving and that it, too, depends on an interaction of the deductive and the inductive to reach hypotheses and conclusions.

Rhetoric and the Curriculum

There is rhetoric for academic study, for example, "the discourses of the Norwegian North Sea oil and gas industry," that may have real world application; and there is "pure" rhetorical scholarship, which I have suggested in this book should be reserved for reconfiguration of theory rather than the proliferation of manuals, as was the case in the Renaissance (and which led, ultimately, to the demise of rhetoric). There is also the place of rhetoric in the school and university curriculum. As fits the tenor of the present theory as a whole, there is no argument here for a return to the medieval Trivium—Rhetoric, Grammar, and Logic—but, rather, a different suggestion that can be interpreted by designers of school, college, or university curricula to suit their particular ends and purposes. In the previous chapter, we have considered some aspects of curriculum and assessment. Here we sketch the outlines of a new curricular design that takes into account rhetorical principles and a range of modal expression on one axis, and a range of epistemological categories on the other.

Because the modes and media of communication are essential to accessing the range of substantial subjects, and also because they are essential to an education in how to operate in the world, the proposal is to array the rhetorical fields and disciplines along one axis, and the "substantial" subjects—subjects that are "about" something—on the other (see Table 14.1).

Table 14.1 A Curriculum Matrix Based on Rhetoric and Multimodality

Rhetorical field/ Examples of subjects-disciplines	*Geographical knowledge*	*Historical knowledge*	*Scientific knowledge*	*Social and political knowledge*	*Etc. >>>*
Linguistic (including more than one language)					
Visual (including still and moving images)					
Physical (including gesture, movement, dance, drama)					
Spatial (including architectural and sculptural form)					
Mathematical (including logic and all other symbol systems)					
Sound (including music)					

All curricular designs are limited by time and resource. Curricula are a selection of what is teachable from an unlimited world of knowledge. Nevertheless, we can bring some theory to curricular design by the combination of the vertical axis and the horizontal axis in a grid, as in Table 14.1. The vertical axis arrays the range of modes we have been discussing in the present book, all coming under the broad heading of rhetorical approaches to communication and the arts of discourse. The horizontal axis shows a selection of the possible bodies of knowledge—a selection that could be extended along the horizontal axis as new subject areas are deemed worthy of inclusion (computer science, for example), or that might be added as components or subcategories of the main "subjects" (in the way that engineering might be seen as a subcategory of science, or geology of geographical knowledge).

How would such a curricular grid work in practice? The rhetorical subjects could be taught generically, meaning that the characteristics of each of the subjects could be taught, including the modes of operation, the systems, and the core principles and features. In each of the boxes on the grid (take, for example, the visual/scientific nexus), the particular applications and rhetorics of the use of the visual in science would be taught. Work on the visual presentation of data could form part of such an education; the use of photography in science, with everything from Landsat to microscopic photography, could be employed; the observation of the visual properties of phenomena form part of the curricular approach. In each of the "substantial" subjects, the emphasis on the communicative means of representing the knowledge would be brought out, thus providing not only a mechanism as to how the subject can be understood and taken forward, but also insight into how the particular discoursal mode operates in a specific subject, thus providing the possibility of a critical dimension to study in that subject.

Balancing the subject-based rhetorical fields across the subjects is a way of ensuring broad-based communicative understanding, but also reducing overload. For example, it could be in science that the visual is given prominence; and it could be in history that the linguistic is privileged. This arrangement does not mean to say that the study of history would be without images (photographs, maps), moving image (documentary film), movement (drama), or sound (recording of oral history)—all these would be available as the rhetorical curriculum would ensure that history teachers and students knew the range of communicative possibilities. But it does mean that in history, the depth of access and analysis would be through linguistic texts, thus enhancing both the study of history and of linguistic texts themselves.

The advantages of such a principled matrix for curriculum design are many. Any school, college, or university (and university department) can map their particular focus on the broader template, thus making clear how their work stood in relation to other areas and means of knowledge and knowledge creation. The range of subjects on the horizontal axis can be limited or extended as necessary. There would no longer be misconception between, say, those who teach sport and those who teach language, as both would find their place on the rhetorical spectrum—and both would see that their expertise and teaching was part of a modal spectrum that can be applied in the study of particular "subjects."

Rhetoric or Rhetorics?

In the mid-1990s, proponents of socially situated literacies used the plural form of literacy to indicate that there was no single "literacy" that was suitable to describe or proscribe for all situations and purposes. Indeed, that the universal notion of literacy was inappropriate in that standards differed from country to country, and from place to place. "Literacy," it was argued, had, through its generation of its antithesis, illiteracy, hindered more than it had helped. The social turn in literacy studies thus differentiated and distinguished between different types of literacy by its very nature as an aspect of social study.

A similar problem faces rhetoric. It can be argued that a single rhetorical system is insensitive to local subtleties; that it appears to create a hegemony (e.g., male-driven, corporate rhetoric) that is "imposed" on others; that it carries the pejorative associations of cant and sophistry; and that it ties contemporary references to rhetoric too closely to classical precedents. *Rhetorics* seems attractive as a term for the field because it avoids all of these problems: it is sensitive and representative of differences in social and political positions; it is more broadly democratic and can admit new voices and new perspectives; it carries fewer of the pejorative associations; and it does not seem so closely linked to classical "Rhetoric," especially in its capital letter form.

The present book argues for the singular form, qualified by the adjective "contemporary." First, there is a need for a unifying theory for a number of reasons. One of these is that without such a unifying theory, there can be no integration or full understanding of the field of communication as a whole. Such a theory, like any theory, allows for a number of disparate elements and phenomena and practices to be placed in relation to each other and for their *common* elements to be acknowledged so that their different and *distinctive* elements can be highlighted more sharply. Communication itself, of all kinds, is understood more fully, and there is less likelihood of misunderstanding (which, at the extreme, can be catastrophic). The function of theory is to play the role of unifying agent among a number of different phenomena and practices and for clarification of the various parts that make up the whole. Its function is also to link practice to theory. The adage that "there is nothing so practical as a good theory" indicates that theory must explain the operation and relations of its constituent parts.

Second, as has been argued earlier in this chapter, the theory must be singular but lightweight. It must be fit for purpose, which is to shed light on a wide range of phenomena and practices. It must not become an end in itself, nor the subject of endless reference. It works best in the background, out of sight; but at the same time, an understanding of its workings is essential for the maintenance of the system—the commerce of meaning and expression. Its goal and purpose is effective communication.

The qualifier "contemporary" is deliberate and is meant to indicate that rhetoric can and must be renewed at every turn to ensure that it is fit for purpose. The adjective is *not* intended to suggest that what is contemporary in 2010 will be the same kind of contemporariness in 2020; but rather that a set of principles and questions will be as current at the moment you read this as at the time of composition.

Lastly, the capital letter can be dropped to suggest that rhetoric is a modest and economical theory about the processes of communication, not a theoretical edifice that has its own *raison d'être*. It can and should be reconfigured. Part of the problem with some twentieth-century rhetorics was that they adopted the classical template and applied this to problems of the time, rather than remaking rhetoric to fit the needs of the present. Inevitably there are scholars who wish to explore the minutiae of rhetorical and/or argumentative theory through classificatory systems that have outlived their social and political usefulness. There is historical justification for such study, but in terms of application for real-world purposes, including that of helping students to learn academic rhetorics, the use of classical or other outmoded rhetorics as a guide to write well, for example, is itself misguided. Over-classification, the over-use of "rules" for a good essay, a general approach that suggests there is a technique to be learnt—all these approaches mistake the system for the solution.

The Future of Rhetoric

Rhetoric suffered a fracture in the late nineteenth century in England, leading to a separation of language/linguistic studies on the one hand, and literary studies on the other. In Scotland and the United States, for different reasons and in different ways, it has survived: as an ancient and unbroken tradition in the former, and a field of academic interest; and in the United States, despite various attempts at remaking in the twentieth century, as a theoretical partner to composition in introductory undergraduate programs, drawing on classical rhetoric and grafting upon it new understandings about writing process. With continued use of the term *rhetoric* in a pejorative sense in the media, what hope is there for the future of rhetoric?

There are a number of trends that offer such hope. One is the growing recognition that communication is multimodal. The dominance of the verbal in education has been reinforced for the last 600 years by the invention of the printing press, making the printed word a source of authority and dissemination. That picture is now changing with understanding that other modes of communication—speech, still and moving images, sound, gesture, movement—play a significant part in communication. Not only is each mode important in its own right, but the norm is for them to work in combination. This multimodal and hybrid nature of communication is not only critical to reading and interpretation, but also to "writing" and composition. Rhetoric offers a theoretical perspective that allows consideration of the various modes and their combination in relation to the intention of the rhetor and his or her audience, and within a wider context of social and political imperatives.

Secondly, there is a need for stronger links between home, work, and academia. It is now no longer tenable to assume all learning takes place in school, college, or university. Learning is an effect of the inter-relationship of communities and the way the learner is primed to make connections between these communities—including electronic communities. Rhetoric provides a means of describing the communicational dynamics of each of these communities, of the way power operates within them, and of the social nature of each of these communities, bound as they are by their own conventions and practices for social engagement. Rhetoric thus draws on the sociology of the new work order, the changing nature (and wide range, globally) of family and community life, and the changing demands of education in its mediation between family and work.

There is also, thirdly, a "push" factor in that current models of language education are unable to account for the richness of contemporary communication or the need for an adequate theory to inform practice—both in their actual manifestation in social life or in curricular and assessment design in education. As this book goes to press, the coalition government in the UK is proposing a narrower curriculum for English in schools, as if to retreat, "assured of certain certainties," to a particular conception of heritage that they think will form the foundation for communicational needs in the early twenty-first century. To build such a curriculum on a narrow foundation of literature and grammar (there is no research to show that the teaching of formal grammar in decontextualized exercises is helpful in improving the quality of children's writing) is badly informed and retrogressive, symptomatic of a narrowing of the curricular aperture in the face of a widening and more complex dynamic of communication. Consequently, the curriculum will move further from the actualities of cultural experience and need, schooling will become less relevant to everyday life and work, and disaffection will spread.

Fourthly, there is a renewed need for a theory to bring together first and second (or additional) language acquisition and development. The different theoretical bases for the two fields has been partly the reason for a different set of pedagogical practices that have characterized teaching. First, language acquisition has been driven by cognitive theories of development and a desire to widen and refine the range of spoken and written genres that define the scope of being highly literate in one's own native language; as well as by the connection between language, culture, and identities. Second and additional language acquisition has been predicated more on linguistic descriptions of the languages in question and has operated on a spectrum of approaches from immersive theory at one end to the so-called grammar-translation approach at the other, where the lineaments of the *system* of the target language are taught and learnt. What rhetoric offers these two worlds is a theory of the arts of communication that embraces both approaches, that sees language development and acquisition as part of a social and political nexus, and that offers a range of pedagogical approaches that can be used for first or additional language learning.

Related to this last point about first and additional language learning is a final and significant advantage of rhetorical theory for the future of language education. Rhetoric is not attached to any one language. It can see that the emergence of four main global languages in the twenty-first century (English, Mandarin Chinese, Spanish, and Arabic) is a result of economic and political power. Rhetoric allows comparative studies between these languages as well as an overview of how languages operate in relation to each other. It also protects the space for post-colonial, national, and regional languages (e.g., French, Polish, Portuguese, Thai, Swahili) to flourish in a wider economy of languages, while foregrounding the need for one or more global languages to be taught within curricular frameworks of each national educational jurisdiction. Language policy, therefore, can be informed by rhetoric, in that the needs of the citizens of a particular country as it finds its place in the global community can be met by a judicious selection of what can be taught (increasingly, from the age of 7) in the school curriculum. The advantage for rhetoric of not being attached to any one language is that it can provide a non-partisan basis for communicational need; at more advanced academic levels, it can provide the basis for comparative study of the particular characteristics of different languages.

It is hard to imagine a future without the affordances that rhetoric offers. In educational terms, such an absence would mean an uncritical acceptance of how communication takes place; in many situations, it would mean no communication. We would be living in a world where decisions were made outside our own powers, and we would be unable to question them. It would be hard to reach consensus for action because there would be no conception of disagreement or difference. Language and communication would become meaningless and without point, other than in the most clichéd maintenance of the status quo. Furthermore, the emphasis on the arts of discourse in the present book has been deliberate, in that there is an aesthetic dimension to communication. Without this dimension, communication would become functional in the most reductive sense. There would be no framing of experience with principles of design and unity at play; no sense of beginning or end in discourse; no pleasure in the act of communication.

Beyond Rhetoric

Ultimately, rhetoric is not important. It is a high-level theory for understanding the relations between communication, intention, and action; it helps in linking communicational first and second order systems to operation in the real world; through its subcategorical fields, such as argumentation, it serves democratic processes; it provides a perspective on the spectrum of resources (modes) and delivery mechanisms (media) via which communication takes place and meaning is made. It acts as a mediating resource at key and ritual moments of life and death: birth, social practices of union between people, moments of celebration, death. But it is a mediating phenomenon, enabling consensus to be reached so that action can take place; providing the means by which ritual events can take place; providing a human dimension to experience and incorporating the abstract and ethereal within the materiality of everyday life.

The limitations of rhetoric have been pointed out *passim*. In summary, these are that rhetoric deals with the arts of communication and discourse. It does not purport to cover areas of philosophical or religio-spiritual experience that "cannot be named," though the expression of these fields in discourse (for example, hermeneutics) does entail rhetorical consideration. It has little application in fields that are intensely practical: horticulture, forestry, physics, for example, though again each of these is subject to rhetorical consideration in *how* and via which modes aspects of the field are classified and communicated. In real world hardship that occurs in poverty, war, or famine, it helps little, other in being able to analyze how messages about these disasters are communicated, and with what effect, to the rest of the world. Nor does it help you in navigating across Mongolia without a map; in the supply of water and aid to torment-stricken places; in how to build a fire for survival in a wilderness. There are few areas of experience and places in the world, however, where rhetoric does not play some part. The book ends with a look beyond the confines and influence of rhetoric—all the more important to consider, as they help to define what is inside the field of rhetoric, and its significance for human communication and relations. Ironically, this poem—almost inevitably—is framed in words.

Postlude

Midway between Dial and Bear Den Mountains
in the deep wilderness of the Adirondacks
there is no rhetoric. My cellphone is out of range.
The trail markers—all signs—have disappeared.
Afternoon sun shines down through the leaf canopies.
The ministry of insects, animals and birds
are busy tidying and rearranging the forest.
Moss and lichen, the first colonizers,
creep over rocks and tree stumps.
There is no sound of water.
An occasional crackle as a branch falls.
Wind is the only accompaniment
in the limbo state between the roads and the rivers below
and the clouds writing their signatures
on blue parchment, out of sight.

Notes

2 Why Rhetoric?

1. There is much more to Prior et al.'s (2013) argument that is not discussed here, particularly in regard to socialization processes and the Platonic conception of rhetoric as "the leading or formation of people's *souls* through discourse" (15). Readers are recommended to look at Prior et al.'s piece in its entirety.

3 Rhetoric and English Studies

1. Harold Rosen was a radical English teacher and teacher educator at the Institute of Education, London, notable for his championing of the diversity, depth, and range of everyday language in the curriculum, and, latterly, for his celebration of narrative.

7 Rhetoric and Framing

1. David Kirkland—see acknowledgements and Kirkland (2012).
2. LSO, conducted by Valery Gergiev, 15 May 2012, London Barbican Arts Centre: *Rite of Spring* and *Oedipus Rex*.
3. See also Matisse, *Open Window,* Collioure, Autumn 1914; Matisse, *Interior with Egyptian Curtain*; Matisse, *The Inhabited Silence of Houses,* 1947; Matisse, *Letter to George Besson*, 30 March 1918; Bonnard, *Still Life with Lemons,* circa 1917–18; Bonnard, *The Window,* 1925; and Camoin, *Lola on the Terrace of the Hotel Bellevue in Toulon,* 1920.
4. Henry Moore, *Late Large Forms,* Gagosian Gallery, Britannia Street, London, May 31–August 18, 2012.

11 Rhetoric and Multimodality

1. But see the narrative with which the present book begins. The café as a site for social schemata is only part of the picture. A wider frame would take into account the street and the immediate environs of the café, especially where there are tables on the street.

References and Further Reading

Abrahamson, R.F. 1977. *The Effects of Formal Grammar Instruction vs the Effects of Sentence Combining Instruction on Student Writing: A Collection of Evaluative Abstracts of Pertinent Research Documents*. Houston, TX: University of Houston.

Alexander, R.J. 2008. *Towards Dialogic Teaching: Rethinking Classroom Talk*. 4th ed. Thirsk: Dialogos.

Andrews, R., ed. 1989. *Narrative and Argument*. Buckingham: Open University Press.

Andrews, R. 1992. "An Exploration of Narrative and Argumentative Structures in Writing, with Particular Reference to the Work of Students in Year 8." PhD thesis, University of Hull, July 1992.

Andrews, R. 1995. *Teaching and Learning Argument*. London: Cassell.

Andrews, R. 2003. *Research Questions*. London: Continuum.

Andrews, R. 2007. "Argument, Critical Thinking and the Postgraduate Dissertation. *Educational Review* 59 (1): 1–18.

Andrews, R. 2008a. *The Case for a National Writing Project for Teachers*. Reading: Centre for British Teachers (CfBT) Educational Trust.

Andrews, R. 2008b. "Ten Years of Strategies." *Changing English: Studies in Culture and Education* 15 (1): 77–85.

Andrews, R. 2009. "The Importance of Argument in Education." Inaugural Professorial Lecture delivered at the Institute of Education, University of London, May 12, 2009.

Andrews, R. 2010. *Argumentation in Higher Education: Improving Practice through Theory and Research*. New York: Routledge.

Andrews, R. 2011. *Re-Framing Literacy*. New York: Routledge.

Andrews, R., ed. 2012. *Rebirth of Rhetoric: Essays in Language, Culture and Education*. Abingdon: Routledge.

Andrews, R. 2012. "Non-Verbal Argument." Presentation at symposium, *Representing Research Knowledge*, London, Royal College of Art Research Methods Course, February 2012.

Andrews, R., E. Borg, S. Boyd Davis, M. Domingo, and J. England., eds. 2012. *The SAGE Handbook of Digital Dissertations and Theses*. London: Sage.

Andrews, R., and C. Haythornthwaite, eds. 2007. *The SAGE Handbook of E-learning Research*. London: Sage.

Andrews, R., and C. Haythornthwaite, eds. Forthcoming. *The SAGE Handbook of E-learning Research*. 2nd ed. London: Sage.

Andrews, R., C. Torgerson, S. Beverton, A. Freeman, T. Locke, G. Low, et al. 2004. "The Effect of Grammar Teaching (Sentence Combining) in English on 5 to 16 Year Olds' Accuracy and Quality in Written Composition." In *Evidence Library*. London: EPPI-Centre, Social Science Research Unit, Institute of Education. Available at: http://eppi.ioe.ac.uk/cms/Default.aspx?tabid=62.

Andrews, R., C. Torgerson, S. Beverton, T. Locke, G. Low, A. Robinson, et al. 2004. "The Effect of Grammar Teaching (Syntax) in English on 5 to 16 Year Olds' Accuracy and Quality in Written Composition." In *Evidence Library*. London: EPPI-Centre, Social Science Research Unit, Institute of Education. Available at: http://eppi.ioe.ac.uk/cms/Default.aspx?tabid=62.

Aristotle. 1996. *Poetics,* translated by Malcolm Heath. London: Penguin Books.

Bain, A. 1871. *English Composition and Rhetoric*. Facsimile ed., 1996, Scholars' Facsimiles & Reprints. ISBN 9780820114972.

Bakhtin, M.M. 1982. *The Dialogic Imagination: Four Essays*. Austin: University of Texas Press.

Bakhtin, M.M. 1987. *Speech Genres and Other Late Essays*. Austin: University of Texas Press.

Ballif, M., D.D. Davis, and R. Mountford. 2008. *Women's Ways of Making it in Rhetoric and Composition*. New York: Routledge.

Banks, A.J. 2006. *Race, Rhetoric, and Technology: Searching for Higher Ground*. Mahwah, NJ: Lawrence Erlbaum.

Barthes, R. 1988. L'ancienne rhétorique: aide-mémoire (December 1970). *Communications* 16: 172–229. (Reprinted in Barthes, R. 1988. *The Semiotic Challenge*. Oxford: Basil Blackwell, 11–94.)

Barton, D. 2008. *Literacy: An Introduction to the Ecology of Written Language*. Oxford: Wiley/Blackwell.

Bazerman, C. 1988. *Shaping Written Knowledge: The Genre and Activity of the Experimental Article in Science*. Madison: The University of Wisconsin Press.

BBC. 2012. "Record Numbers of International Students." *British Broadcasting Corporation*. Available at: http://www.bbc.co.uk/news/business-12671198.

BBC. 2013. "President Obama Praises US 'Fiscal Cliff' Deal." *British Broadcasting Corporation*. Available at: http://www.bbc.co.uk/news/world-us-canada-20886182.

Bergonzi, B. 1990. *Exploding English: Criticism, Theory, Culture*. Oxford: Clarendon Press.

Black, P., and S. Muecke. 1992. "A Moment in Fashion." In *Rebirth of Rhetoric: Essays in Language, Culture and Education,* ed. R. Andrews, 212–27. London: Routledge.

Blake, C. 2009. *The African Origins of Rhetoric*. New York: Routledge.

Block, D. 2009. "Second Language Identities." *Journal of Sociolinguistics* 13(1): 118–22.

Booth, W.C. 1961. *A Rhetoric of Fiction*. Chicago: Chicago University Press.

Booth, W.C. 2004. *The Rhetoric of Rhetoric: The Quest for Effective Communication*. Oxford: Blackwell.

Boyd Davis, S. 2012. "Defending the Thesis: The Power of Words." Presentation at *Representing Research Knowledge* symposium, London, Royal College of Art Research Methods Course, February 2012.

Bradbury, R. 1952. "A Sound of Thunder." First published in Collier's Magazine and subsequently in *The Golden Apples of the Sun*. New York: Doubleday, 1953.

Brook, P. 1972. *The Empty Space*. Harmondsworth, UK: Pelican Books.

Brutt-Griffler, J. 2002. *World English: A Study of Its Development*. Clevedon: Multilingual Matters.

Burke, K. 1969. *A Rhetoric of Motives*. Berkeley CA: University of California Press.

Burke, K. 1966. *Language as Symbolic Action: Essays on Life, Literature and Method*. Berkeley: University of California Press.

Chandler, D. 2013. *Semiotics for Beginners*. Available at: http://www.aber.ac.uk/media/Documents/S4B/semiotic.html.

Combs, W. E. 1976. "Further Effects of Sentence-Combining Practice on Writing Ability." *Research in the Teaching of English* 10: 137–49.

Combs, W. E. 1977. "Sentence-Combining Practice: Do Gains in Judgments of Writing 'quality' persist?" *Journal of Educational Research* 70: 318–21.

Corbett, E. J. 1998. *Classical Rhetoric for the Modern Student*. 4th ed. New York: Oxford University Press.

Cremin, T., and D. Myhill. 2012. *Writing Voices: Creating Communities of Writers*. Abingdon: Routledge.

Cummins, J. 1996. *Negotiating Identities: Education for Empowerment in a Diverse Society.* California Association for Bilingual Education. Corina, CA.

de Saussure, F. 1983. *Course in General Linguistics*, edited by Charles Bally and Albert Sechehaye, translated by Roy Harris. La Salle, IL: Open Court.

Dixon, J. 1991. *A Schooling in English: Critical Episodes in the Struggle to Shape Literary and Cultural Studies*. Milton Keynes: Open University Press.

Dogantan-Dack, M. 2012. "Capturing Musical Rehearsal and Performance." Presentation at *Representing Research Knowledge* symposium, London, Royal College of Art Research Methods Course, February 2012.

Duncan, S. 2012. *Reading Circles: Novels and Adult Reading Development*. London: Continuum.

Eagleton, T. 1976. *Marxism and Literary Criticism*. Berkeley: University of California Press.

Eagleton, T. 1983. *Literary Theory: An Introduction*. Oxford: Blackwell.

Eagleton, T. 2004. *After Theory*. London: Penguin.

Enos, T., ed. 2009. *Encyclopedia of Rhetoric and Composition: Communication from Ancient Times to the Information Age*. New York: Routledge.

Fransman, J., and R. Andrews, eds. 2012. *Learning, Media and Technology* 37(2). Special issue on Rhetoric and the Politics of Representation and Communication in the Digital Age.

Gee, J., G. Hull, and C. Lankshear. 1996. *The New Work Order: Behind the Language of the New Capitalism*. Boulder, CO: Westview Press.

Goffman, E. 1986. *Frame Analysis: An Essay on the Organization of Experience*. New edition. Hanover NH: Northeastern University Press.

Goldsworthy, A. 2004. *Passage*. London: Thames and Hudson.

Gourlay, L. 2011. "Cyborg Literacies." Paper given at New Media, New Literacies, New Learning seminar at the London Knowledge Lab, Institute of Education, December 15, 2011.

Green, B. 2006. "English, Literacy, Rhetoric: Changing the Project?" *English in Education* 40 (1): 7–19.

Grierson, H.J.C. 1945. *Rhetoric and English Composition.* 2nd ed., rev. Edinburgh: Oliver and Boyd.

Gunn, B.G. 1906. *The Wisdom of the East: The Instruction of Ptah-Hotep and The Instruction of Ke'Gemni: The Oldest Books in the World—Translated from the Egyptian with an Introduction and Appendix.* London: John Murray.

Habermas, J. 1984. *The Theory of Communicative Action: Vol 1 Reason and the Rationalization of Society*, translated by Thomas McCarthy. Boston MA: Beacon Press and London: Heinemann. (Originally published in 1981 by Suhrkamp Verlag, Frankfurt.)

Hardcastle, J., P. Medway, G. Brewis and D. Crook. In press. *Re-Making English for the Post-War World.* Basingstoke: Palgrave Macmillan.

Haythornthwaite, C. 2007. "Digital Divide and E-learning." In *The SAGE Handbook of E-learning Research*, ed. R. Andrews and C. Hasythornthwaite, 97–118. London: Sage.

Hoggart, R. 1957. *The Uses of Literacy.* London: Chatto and Windus.

Hohl, M. 2012. "Grounded Theory in the Evaluation of an Immersive Art Work." Presentation at *Representing Research Knowledge* symposium, London, Royal College of Art Research Methods Course, February 2012.

Hunter, I. 1997. "After English: Towards a Less Critical Literacy." In *Constructing Critical Literacies: Teaching and Learning Textual Practice*, ed. S. Muspratt, A. Luke, and P. Freebody, 315–34. Cresskill, NJ: Hampton Press.

Iser, W. 1980. *The Act of Reading: A Theory of Aesthetic Response.* Baltimore, MD: Johns Hopkins University Press.

Jewitt, C. 2011. "Technology and Reception as Multimodal Remaking." In *Multimodality in Practice: Investigating Theory-in-Practice-through-Methodology*, edited by Sigrid Norris, 98–112. London: Routledge.

Joseph, M. 2002. *The Trivium: Logic, Grammar and Rhetoric—Understanding the Nature and Function of Language.* Philadelphia: Paul Dry Books.

Judt, T. 2010. *The Memory Chalet.* London: William Heinemann/Vintage.

Kahane, H., and N. Cavender. 1997. *Logic and Contemporary Rhetoric: The Use of Reason in Everyday Life.* Florence, KY: Wadsworth.

Kaplan, A.M., and M. Haenlein. 2010. "Users of the World Unite! The Challenges and Opportunities of Social Media." *Business Horizons* 53 (1): 61.

Kaufman, M. 2001. *The Laramie Project.* New York: Vintage Books.

Kinneavy, T. 1971. *A Theory of Discourse.* Englewood Cliffs, NJ: Prentice-Hall.

Kirkland, D. 2012. "Rhythms of Justice: Hip Hop in the Development of Literacy." Public lecture, Faculty of Children and Learning, Institute of Education, University of London, May 2012.

Kress, G. 2003. *Literacy in the New Media Age.* London: Routledge.

Kress, G. 2005. Communication Now and in the Future. *English 21.* Available at: http:www.qca.org.uk/i2292.html.

Kress, G. 2009. "Assessment in the Perspective of a Social Semiotic Theory of Multimodal Teaching and Learning." In *Educational Assessment in the 21st Century*, ed. C.M. Wyatt-Smith and J.J. Cumming, 19–42. Dordrecht: Springer.

Kress, G. 2010. *Multimodality: A Social Semiotic Approach to Contemporary Communication*. Abingdon: Routledge.

Kress, G., and T. van Leeuwen. 2001. *Multimodal Discourse: The Modes and Media of Contemporary Communication*. London: Edward Arnold.

Lanchester, J. 2013. "Let's Call It Failure." *London Review of Books* 35 (1, January 3): 3–6.

Lanham, R. 1993. *The Electronic Word: Democracy, Technology and the Arts*. Chicago: Chicago University Press.

Lanham, R. 2006. *The Economics of Attention: Style and Substance in the Age of Information*. Chicago: University of Chicago Press.

Larson, M., M.A. Britt, and A. Larson. 2004. "Disfluencies in Comprehending Argumentative Texts." *Reading Psychology* 25 (3): 205–24.

Lawlor, J. 1980. *Improving Student Writing through Sentence Combining: A Literature Review. Technical Note*. Los Alamitos, CA: Southwest Regional Laboratory for Educational Research and Development. ERIC document number ED 192356.

Link, P. 2009. "China's Charter 08." *New York Review of Books* (January 15): 54–56.

Lipman, M. 1976. *Philosophy for Children*. Oxford: Basil Blackwell.

McEwan, I. 2012. *Sweet Tooth*. London: Jonathan Cape.

Miller, C.R. 1984. "Genre as Social Action." *Quarterly Journal of Speech* 70: 151–67.

Milsom, A-M. 2012. "Representing 'Thick' Translation." Presentation at *Representing Research Knowledge* symposium, London, Royal College of Art Research Methods Course, February.

Mitchell, W.J.T. 1986. *Iconology*. Chicago: Chicago University Press.

Moffett, J. 1983. *Teaching the Universe of Discourse*. Boston: Houghton Mifflin Company (1983 re-issue).

Moffett, J., and B.J. Wagner. 1991. *A Student-Centered Language Arts Curriculum Grades K-12: A Handbook for Teachers*. Portsmouth NH: Boynton-Cook.

Morgan, E. 1973. *From Glasgow to Saturn*. Cheadle: Carcanet Press.

Morris, D. 1979. *Gestures: Their Origin and Significance*. New York: Stein and Day.

Navas, I. de 2012. "Boannard and Matisse: Windows with a View." In *Bonnard among Friends: Matisse, Monet, Vuillard*, ed. V. Serrano, 93-101. Cannet: Musée Bonnard and Silvana Editoriale.

Ney, J.W. 1980. "A Short History of Sentence Combining: Its Limitations and Use." *English Education* 11: 169–77.

On, Lee Wing. 1996. "The Cultural Context for Chinese Learners: Conceptions of Learning in the Confucian Tradition. In *The Chinese Learner: Cultural, Psychological and Contextual Influences*, ed. D. Watkins and J. Biggs, 25–41. Hong Kong: University of Hong Kong, Comparative Education Research Centre.

Orwell, G. 1949. *Nineteen Eighty-Four*. New York: Harcourt, Brace & World.

Pavel, T. 1986. *Fictional Worlds*. Cambridge, MA: Harvard University Press.

Perelman, C. 1982. *The Realm of Rhetoric.* Notre Dame, IN: University of Notre Dame Press.

Pinter, H. 1988. *Mountain Language.* London: The Times Literary Supplement, October 7–13.

Porrovecchio, M., ed. 2010. *Reengaging the Prospects of Rhetoric: Current Conversations and Contemporary Challenges.* New York: Routledge.

Preminger, A., T. Brogan, and F.J. Warnke. 1993. *The New Princeton Encyclopedia of Poetry and Poetics.* Princeton: Princeton University Press.

Preminger, A., F.J. Warnke, and O.B. Hardison. 1986. *The Princeton Handbook of Poetic Terms.* Princeton: Princeton University Press.

Prior. P., J. Solberg, P. Berry, H. Bellwoar, B. Chewning, K.J. Lunsford, et al. 2013. "Remediating the Canons in *Kairos* 11.3." Available at: http://kairos.technorhetoric.net/11.3/binder.html?topoi/prior-et-al/index.html.

Ratcliffe, K. 2012. *Critical Literacies.* London: Longman.

RCA. 2012. Symposium on Representing Research Knowledge, Royal College of Art, London, February.

Rogoff, B. 1992. *Apprenticeship in Thinking.* New York: Oxford University Press.

Said, E. 1978. *Orientalism.* New York: Vintage.

Stewart, M.F. 1979. "Sentence-Combining: Its Past, Present and Future." *English Quarterly* 12: 21–36.

Stotsky, S.L. 1975. "Sentence-Combining as a Curricular Activity: Its Effect on Written Language Development and Reading Comprehension." *Research in the Teaching of English* 9: 30–71.

Street, B. 1984. *Literacy in Theory and Practice.* Cambridge: Cambridge University Press.

Street, B., ed. 1993. *Cross-Cultural Approaches to Literacy.* Cambridge: Cambridge University Press.

Street, B. 1995. *Social Literacies.* Harlow: Longman.

Street, B. 2001. *Literacy and Development.* London: RoutledgeFalmer.

Street, B., and A. Lefstein. 2008. *Literacy.* Abingdon: Routledge.

Strickland, S. 2008. *Engladesh.* Final Masters presentation, London, City University. Available at: http://www.engladesh.com and www.samstrickland.com.

Tannen, D., ed. 1993. *Framing in Discourse.* New York: Oxford University Press.

Tindale, C. 2004. *Rhetorical Argumentation: Principles of Theory and Practice.* Thousands Oaks, CA: Sage.

Toulmin, S. 2003. *The Uses of Argument.* Cambridge: Cambridge University Press.

Troyan, S.D. 2004. "Unwritten Between the Lines: The Unspoken History of Rhetoric." In *Medieval Rhetoric: A Casebook,* ed. S.D. Troyan, 217–45. New York: Routledge.

Tufte, E. 1997. *Visual Explanations: Images and Quantities, Evidence and Narrative.* Cheshire, CT: Graphics Press.

Vickers, B. 1989. *In Defence of Rhetoric.* Oxford: Clarendon Press.

Vygotsky, L. 1991. "Genesis of the Higher Mental Functions." In *Learning to think,* ed. P. Light et al., 32–41. London: Routledge. Originally appearing 1930–1931 as "Development of the Higher Mental Functions.

Watkins, D., and J. Biggs., eds. 1996. *The Chinese Learner: Cultural, Psychological and Contextual Influences*. Hong Kong: University of Hong Kong, Comparative Education Research Centre.

Wellman, B. 2012. *Networked: The New Social Operating System*. Cambridge, MA: MIT Press.

White, R. S., and H. Karl. 1980. "Reading, Writing and Sentence Combining: The Track Record." *Reading Improvement* 17: 226–32.

Wikipedia. 2013. "Paul Cézanne." Available at: http://en.wikipedia.org/wiki/Paul_C%C3%A9zanne.

Williams, R. 1977. *Marxism and Literature*. Oxford: Oxford University Press.

Zhu, W. 2012. *Confucian Themes and China's High School Language and Literature Textbooks in the Reform Era*. PhD thesis, Institute of Education, University of London.

Index

Page numbers in *italics* indicate tables